DETOUR

THE TRUTH ABOUT THE INFORMATION SUPERHIGHWAY

Michael Sullivan-Trainor

An International Data Group Company
San Mateo, California • Indianapolis, Indiana • Boston, Massachusetts

Detour: The Truth About the Information Superhighway
Published by
IDG Books Worldwide, Inc.
An International Data Group Company
155 Bovet Road, Suite 310
San Mateo, CA 94402

Printed in the United States of America
First Printing, October, 1994
10 9 8 7 6 5 4 3 2 1

Distributed in the United States by IDG Books Worldwide, Inc.

ISBN 1-56884-307-0

Published in the United States

Dedication

This work is dedicated to Maureen, whose love and energy made this journey possible.

Acknowledgements

s I sit here writing the final lines of this book in the late hours of another long night, I marvel at the tremendous assistance I received in making it happen. My wife, Maureen, and my children, Adam, Christopher, and Kathryn deserve the greatest thanks. I am very grateful for their constant support and patience while I have been absorbed in this project.

Other friends and supports deserve special recognition, especially Tricia Sullivan for ongoing support and proofreading; Colleen Moriarty, for her feedback; and Dennis and Maryanne Spillane for the use of office space, proofreading, and encouragement.

Diane Lorenz and Terry Chadha were a great help in sharing their energy and spirit.

I'd like to thank my parents, Paul and Margaret Trainor, for the solid upbringing and love of books I received. Special thanks to Regina Dewey who was one of the first ones to believe in my ability to write a book.

I would also like to thank the many sources who guided me along the path, especially Tony Rutkowski and Michael Heim. Also, the many government sources who guided me to the National Information Infrastructure documents and the assistance of the Electronic Frontier Foundation are appreciated.

I'd also like to thank my colleagues at Computerworld, including Editor Bill Laberis and my many fellow staffers for the opportunities and assistance they have given me to challenge myself to find deeper levels of creativity and self-expression.

Finally, I would like to especially thank the folks at IDG Books; Trudy Neuhaus, who gave me the "real world" view of the book publishing process; Amy Pederson for her marketing ideas; Karen Goeller, for her patient edits and encouragement; and Elizabeth Rogalin for her unflappable nature and persistence.

Table Of Contents

Introduction

Our journey as a society is taking us toward a greater sense of community and understanding. The vehicle for this journey is the computer technology that will provide an unimaginable array of services and bring us in closer contact with our neighbors and our fellow communities in distant countries.

Technology today is taking the form of the information superhighway, a concept with the goal of exchanging ideas, information, and commerce. The vision of this technology is no less than easy access for anyone, anywhere. Nearly unlimited business opportunities will be opened for the average person. A global library will be created for the cataloging and sharing of the world's knowledge. Because of the superhighway, these and many more services will be part of life in the 21st century.

I wrote this book with the goal of making the coming technology changes clear to everyone. If you are familiar with the technology, or have barely touched a personal computer, you will find the concept of the information superhighway and the forces behind its development explained in simple, direct detail. The services that will become available on the superhighway are described with special attention to entertainment, education, and medical applications.

The characters of this story are many, but fall into three main arenas:

- technical aficionados who have nurtured and mastered aspects of the Internet, the global interconnection of more than 44,000 networks.

- government policymakers who are rewriting telecommunications regulations and fostering a vision of a National Information Infrastructure.

- cable television and telecommunications companies who are making regional information superhighway services come alive in education, entertainment, and research.

You will meet these characters in person through the exclusive interviews and extensive writing and speech-making they have done — through excerpts featured here in this book. From the Internet arena, Tony Rutkowski, the Internet Society's Executive Director, describes the growing capability of the Internet to handle more powerful applications and offer easier to use access. Technologists Roger Samuelson, of the Massachusetts Institute of Technology, and Michael Heim, author and philosopher on the subject of virtual reality are also featured.

The government view is reflected in quotes from speeches by Vice President Al Gore, Commerce Secretary Ron Brown, and Assistant Secretary Larry Irving. The white papers of the National Information Infrastructure task forces reveal the full detail of the government's vision and the underlying conflicts with its goals.

Reports on the research and development efforts of AT&T, Sprint, and U S WEST stake out the view of telecommunications and cable executives. Their visions of the superhighway are far different than those of the Internet clan. Each company wants to build its own version of the superhighway and provide services unique to them. The focus of these companies is wide ranging, from cooperating in government test beds to launching their own partnerships to provide entertainment services.

Any one of these groups can detour the super-highway down a route of its own choosing. Internet culture and services, the fastest growing arena, could become dominant because it will be so pervasive. The government's vision could come to pass because of the legislative and regulatory power it possesses. Or the telecommunications and cable companies could dominate — their services are aimed at the needs of the average person and they already hold loyalty among consumers and businesses in discrete regions.

Besides the different views, there are major technological obstacles to be overcome. How do we guarantee privacy and security of transactions? How do we make the technology easy and open? How do we design networks and computer systems with enough intelligence and capacity to manage the billions of interchanges the superhighway services will foster? This book outlines work underway to address all of these issues.

In later chapters, you will find insights from technological events from the past that shed light on the possible outcome of these many different directions. The early days of radio and television were also filled with competing visions and the struggles of government regulators to address future needs. The implications were not well understood by those who first experienced these new technologies. But the services became so widely distributed and integral to daily life that the conflicts faded in the face of mass acceptance and usage of the mediums.

Ultimately, your chance to experience the information superhighway is a short time away. Entertainment services, such as movies-on-demand, will be available within the next couple of years, while Internet services are available today. Within 5 to 10 years, the superhighway will be pervasive.

Opportunities, adventure, and knowledge await us if we make use of the many available computer networking services. There is no reason to postpone our date with the future. The journey begins here and now.

Worldwide Information Exchange

Today, the Internet, on-line services, and company networks that span the globe provide instant access to information. Shortly, the information superhighway will take us beyond these interconnections. We will have easy access to a wide array of new services, many of which we can't even conceive of now. However, while exchanging information and services worldwide will enrich society, it will also pose new challenges.

Six billion people

will be able to obtain and exchange information from any place in the world when the information superhighway is fully deployed.

Within minutes of the crash of comet Shoemaker-Levy 9's fragments into Jupiter in July of 1994, scientists and amateur astronomers worldwide exchanged photographs and shared data. This instant gratification for millions of space-watchers was possible because of advanced computer networks that span the globe.

Such instant communication is no longer reserved for special events, however. Today 20 million people in 60 countries exchange information electronically over the Internet. Six million Americans alone use on-line services that they access via telephone lines. And employees of large and small corporations communicate every day with each other — whether they're in the next office, the next building, or halfway around the world — through electronic mail and other networking solutions.

And with the current growth rate of information services such as the Internet (nearly 10% per year or 2 million new users), there's every reason to believe access to computer networks will become even more widespread. In fact, when fully deployed, the information superhighway will allow six billion people to obtain and exchange information from anywhere in the world.

This information will be different than what we know today. It will not be limited to a single corporation's data flow, electronic mail messaging, and file transfer, or controlled discussion groups and information feeds like that of the on-line service providers. All types of information will be available in a variety of forms: written, numeric, sound, voice, and video.

Access to this information will be available at a regulated price, much like telephone or cable television bills are structured today. Consumers will be charged for the services they use and the amount they use them.

Consumers of information services will be able not only to access information — they will also be able to buy each other's goods, discuss issues of common interest, and receive entertainment, educational, and product offerings from private and public sector organizations around the world.

Most important, the information superhighway will let anyone access this wide range of information and services easily.

Currently, access to electronic networks requires knowledge of personal computers and an understanding of how to navigate in the network. In the case of corporations, knowledge of the access application built by the company's computer technicians is often required as well.

The Internet, for example, is primarily accessible to the technically gifted. Programmers, researchers, engineers, and scientists compose the majority of its power users. In addition to personal computer knowledge, these users understand networks and the Internet's own unusual categorizations of information types.

By contrast the superhighway will allow voice, touchscreen, or keypad access through navigation systems that will manage the technical work for the user.

Even those who have mastered the technical maze must contend with the Internet's limitations. The information system is designed much like an electronic post office. You need to know the address of the recipient or the location of the information and how it's organized to make use of it. For example, to send electronic mail to President Clinton, you have to know his electronic address (president@whitehouse.gov). In addition, you have to have an electronic mail program (PINE.EXE, for example) and you have to learn unique commands for that program (Ctrl-X to send a message, for instance).

Volume is also a problem. As the Internet grows, demand for its services increases. With more than 20 million users, popular services can easily get bogged down. This creates traffic jams which lock users out of obtaining information due to the number of simultaneous requests. Information databases and programs operate on a first-come, first-served basis. No matter how large the computer, systems only handle a finite number of requests.

The Internet Activities Board, which provisionally governs (but does not control) the Internet, and other individuals and organizations are working on solutions to these and other capacity and ease-of-access problems. Their efforts, such as the development of software that will navigate the Internet for users, will more readily allow the Internet to become a part of the information superhighway as it develops.

On-line services like CompuServe are easier to access. However, the cost of access is much higher than that of Internet usage, and familiarity with a personal computer is still important. In addition, these services only provide access to a limited selection of financial, business, and consumer information. Most are beginning to provide gateways to the Internet to broaden the scope of their offerings, and intuitive software to navigate the Internet, such as Mosaic, is beginning to be released.

These existing information networks are not the information superhighway. The existing networks will likely be connected to it and will feed information into the main artery of the superhighway. Corporations, for example, will use their internal worldwide networks to generate and deliver products, services, and product information to superhighway users. Government agencies, universities, and research organizations will use their Internet connections to make information available to the superhighway traveler. On-line services will also adapt their offerings, prices, and designs to match the superhighway's requirements.

The superhighway will be the combination of advanced versions of these networks. It will provide interconnections between research, commercial, and entertainment networks to support multimedia services. It will be easily accessible and allow users to navigate automatically around the world.

Besides its sheer size, the superhighway will be distinguished from today's network services by its ease of use. Though it will share computer-based networking technology and digital programs with today's on-line services, the superhighway will more closely resemble the models of universal service we think of today for our telephone and television access.

The telephone is a generic, simple, hand-held access device. It allows us to contact anyone whenever we wish by using a consistent, memorizable number. It is also two-way, allowing a fullness of communication that meets many social and information needs.

But imagine being able to touch a screen or issue a verbal command to contact someone visually. The telephone's chief drawbacks are that it is voice-only (unless a personal computer and modem or a video-phone are also used) and the number of the party being contacted must be available. While ensuring a measure of privacy, the need for a number makes intuitive access to information difficult and requires some research or knowledge on the user's part. Printed and CD-based directory services ("the phone books") are a great asset, as is dial-up directory assistance, but both interfere with immediate, direct access.

Television makes access to information and entertainment even simpler, but one advantage of the telephone as compared to television is its interactivity. Push a button on any remote control or TV and you have instant access. Color TV systems can be found in 95% of American homes. The television's strength is generic, simple access, but its drawback is its one-way nature. Before the advent of cable television services, channel reception was limited by the strength and position of a broadcast signal relative to the strength and position of the television; programs were generally limited to major network offerings. With cable, where programs are transmitted though a coaxial cable directly to the subscriber's home from a central service point, signal quality has improved dramatically and program choice has increased greatly, but it is still not possible to choose to watch a specific programming choice at a specific time of the user's choice. Although 62% of American homes have cable, television still lacks the customized selection of a phone call.

> *As evidenced by the popularity of video rentals, the desire to choose specific information or entertainment is very strong among consumers.*

As evidenced by the popularity of video rentals, the desire to choose specific information or entertainment is very strong among consumers. Video-cassette recorders (VCRs), which are in 86% of U.S. households, have helped make television and other forms of visual entertainment easier to manage from a content and scheduling stand-point, but have complicated its ease of use. Products have only recently become available that allow users to program their VCR intuitively, by using voice recognition devices or simplified commands.

Even with simple content control, television still lacks the interactive nature of telephone or on-line network conversations. The information is static and inaccessible for the viewer. Program quality and value are completely controlled by the provider rather than by the user. For this reason and others, television is a poor information medium. Its producers must homogenize the information content to make it appealing to a mass market.

But these models of the telephone, television, and personal-computer-based information networks all have attributes of the information superhighway. The goal of the superhighway is a simple, intuitive access method, like the phone and television. It should be interactive, like telephone and personal computer network conversations. It should have freedom of choice, like VCR and cable television programming. And it should allow customized information delivery and entertainment, like personal computer networks.

In addition, the superhighway will offer the advantage of multimedia. Video, data, photographs, images, text, graphics, and voice will all be available over the same cable and console linking the neighborhood, the country, and the world through a diversity of communications methods.

Already, multimedia programming is widely available in the home. Video game consoles from Sega and Nintendo are the devices of choice for the entertainment of many of America's younger consumers. This video game system is a useful model. Programs are readily available through both purchase and rental. Video game systems are intuitive and interactive. In addition, the purchase price is affordable for most consumers, and rentals are available on a day-by-day basis for a few dollars.

Like the video game, the superhighway's access point will be a console capable of running multiple screens containing different types of media, much as experimental television and personal computer screens do now. It will also have speakers for incoming voice programs or conversations and a microphone for voice transmission.

At the heart of this tool will be a computer that can manage and process the various kinds of incoming information and send outgoing material across the network in the appropriate manner. It will be connected to a network with sufficient capacity for all types of media. The network cable will be part of a nationwide system extending from every home and business to regional or local switches that connect to other national and international control points, much like the telephone system does now.

There will likely be a number of providers of the systems (hardware and software), networks, and services that will comprise the information superhighway. Most will develop from today's communications, computer, and entertainment providers. But common standards for system design, program quality, and price will make the mixture of providers a non-issue for consumers. Government attempts to ensure open access and high-quality service will also provide consumers with equal and safe access to services.

There will be numerous services available on the superhighway, many of which will be beyond what we can predict. They will reflect new ways of interacting that will naturally evolve due to the accessible, global nature of the system. But there are a number of applications we can foresee for the superhighway. Many of them exist in fledgling form today on the Internet or online services. Others are in experimental stages at laboratories or test beds across the world. They fall into the following general categories:

- The buying and selling of products and services worldwide by consumers and corporations.

- Interactive educational experiences for students at all levels through major research organizations and international school systems and corporate training programs.

- Customized entertainment provided by commercial and non-commercial organizations.

- Information sharing for social, political, and life-enabling purposes.

- Medical needs — such as publication of hospital needs for donors of blood or organs for transplants or the ability to have medical experts located anywhere view x-rays and CAT scans from remote locations.

While the benefits of the information superhighway might seem intriguing because of its promise of the ability to go beyond local sources to gain access to information, the local value of the superhighway should not be overlooked. Right now, other than the telephone and occasional social encounters, individuals have little regular interactive contact with their neighbors or fellow community members. Before discussing the global village, we need to first investigate the backyard network.

Imagine that you've just moved into a new community. You have many needs and questions. In the past, this community might have embraced you through a "welcome wagon," or newcomers' club. Or, you might be lucky enough to have moved near family or friends who know the area. But with today's scattered families and decreased cooperation among neighbors, chances are good that the first thing you will experience in your new community is a sense of isolation.

The information superhighway can make a difference. You might, for example, immediately send out greetings addressed to recipients within the neighborhood or town. These greetings might contain a little information about your interests and background. Neighbors, who may have already been exchanging information about you over their local chat channel, might respond with brief information about themselves and some welcoming words and/or images. They might already have a primer about the community (a frequently asked questions list or "FAQ") and local notices of interest. You can search this primer on-line to find out crucial information like when trash is collected, who to call in an emergency, and where the best Italian restaurant is located.

A universally accessible network in which anyone could post anything would facilitate this capability. Enterprising community members would quickly recognize this as a way to get to know their neighbors and help new arrivals feel welcome. With information superhighway access as pervasive as televisions, but more interactive and customizable than telephones, a new channel for building relationships would be open.

Of course, politicians seeking votes, telemarketers seeking business leads, and activists seeking supporters would also find their way to your superhighway address. The annoyances of communications today would be transferred to the new medium. But by choosing to not read or respond to inquiries, superhighway users will have the same ability to virtually "close the door" on unwanted solicitations.

Beyond this virtual substitute for the small town — everybody knows everybody — socialization of the past, the superhighway links the neighborhood with the larger community, surrounding communities, and the world at large. The value of this includes the ability to discover better ways to live.

For example, neighborhood wisdom may have it that there is a certain time to plant different flowers, vegetables, or grass using certain time-honored tools or methods. But contact with someone in another part of town or another region on the planet with a similar climate might alert the local group to the value of a new cycle, different fertilizer, or superior kinds of plants to use.

Similarly, the locality might be suffering from an infestation of mosquitoes, too much crime, or too little water. Methods to address these problems tried elsewhere — across the country or across the world — might lend insight to the local citizenry and leaders as they try to solve the problems.

Unlike today's methods, the superhighway achieves direct, one-to-one communication simultaneously with shared community knowledge and user-customizable information access. The methods used today by individuals to gather information — reading a variety of publications, researching a problem at the library, or

Access to worldwide information sources makes the superhighway intriguing, but its local value should not be overlooked.

calling their acquaintances — foreshadow the future, but fall far short of the reach, speed of access, and comprehensiveness of the knowledge that could be gained via the superhighway.

For example, the Internet already acts as a forum for virtual support groups, where people with common interests — like parents of young children, sports enthusiasts, or technical pros — share information and advice.

This level of interactive connection also allows social contact to be enhanced. When you move into your new home, you might still want to stay in touch with your former community. Even though no longer living there, you can still participate in the conversations and developments of your old neighborhood by keeping in touch with its channel and, through e-mail, with those old friends. Unlike the telephone, the information superhighway would allow a more steady interactive participation, almost as if you never left.

Another value of interactive communication is the ability to share information in the event of a dramatic happening. Whether a natural disaster, military or political turmoil, or financial shift, the average person could instantly tune in to talk with others at the scene and find out what is really happening. News could be passed back and forth about common acquaintances or loved ones. Users would be less dependent on generic programming or telephone lines to obtain information. They would be able to quickly discern the damage to a local home or business from a fire or the impact of a tornado or flood in a distant region or country.

Recent examples of this capability were the use of the Internet and other on-line services to allow news and information to travel rapidly during the breakup of the Soviet Union and the Los Angeles earthquake. Information was able to move faster over the Internet than it would have via traditional means.

The ability to instantly connect and stay in touch with people of common interests is also the basis for political organizing. The information superhighway could bring forth a new level of political activity. National parties in this country are already using on-line services and the Internet, as well as radio and television, to disseminate their views to as many like-minded souls as they can find. Having a single conduit for political discussions would increase the affiliation individuals feel for their party. The Republican National Committee, Ross Perot's presidential campaign, and, more recently, liberal organizations such as The National Gay and Lesbian Task Force are already using the available on-line tools to gain feedback and provide information to their constituents.

Massachusetts Senator Edward Kennedy uses the Internet and a local bulletin board to provide immediate reaction to current events, such as President Clinton's State of the Union address. Constituents can use their personal computers to obtain the latest legislation, read the senator's press releases, or to make a comment for his attention. This two-way electronic link foreshadows the more immediate and tangible contact constituents can have with their representatives using the superhighway.

The superhighway would provide ample opportunity for forming opinions on issues and seeking appropriate candidates to run for office. Polling and surveys could be delivered over the superhighway to gather a sense of consensus or political trends.

This political power could become influential not just nationally in the election of Congress and the president, but it could also become a factor in local competitions for school board, mayor, or governor. A worldwide political movement, such as an environmental preservation group, could keep its members informed and involved through constant communication over the information superhighway.

Campaigns of this sort have already been effective. The National Gay and Lesbian Task Force used their America Online forum to ask members to get a national bank to change its policy on anti-discrimination. The effort caused the bank to receive so much feedback that it altered its policy.

On a global scale, millions of people could be mobilized to act against or in favor of a policy or an organization. For example, there could be tremendous power from a worldwide campaign against human rights abuses or in favor of environmental clean-up.

What would the American reaction be if we learned about the suffering from the war in Bosnia, not from a third-party objective newscaster, but from thousands of emotionally involved Bosnians we could contact over the superhighway? The effect on government policy might be tantamount to the public outcry that was raised when Americans saw the violence of the war in Vietnam on the nightly news in the Sixties.

The political value of the information superhighway will not be a wholly new phenomenon, but it will cause political communication and action to happen much faster and on a much wider scale.

The political, social, and informational applications of the information superhighway are already taking shape in test beds in the United States, France, and other countries where the Internet, on-line services or video-text projects have been deployed.

While laboratories in major corporations seek to enhance network capacity (sometimes known as "bandwidth") and create accessible consoles, one community has built its own precursor to the information superhighway: Telluride, Colorado. Three hundred miles or more away from the nearest population center, Telluride's mountainous surroundings breed isolation. The Telluride Institute, a local research organization, created something called the InfoZone — a computer-based network that allows community members with personal computers to connect electronically with each other and with the worldwide services of the Internet.

The network allows residents to stay in touch with the outside world and to foster businesses that can work through remote channels. The creators have plans to build voice, data, and video connections for the network for local schools, libraries, and museums.

The state of Hawaii is likewise learning how the concepts of the superhighway work through real-world implementation. Hawaii FYI is a statewide dial-in

> *Political communication and action will happen much faster and on a much wider scale once the information superhighway is in place.*

system offered by Hawaii Inc., the Hawaii Information Network Corporation. Created by the state legislature, Hawaii Inc. is charged with promoting development and growth in the state and regional information industry. Connected to the Internet, Hawaii FYI provides access to worldwide networks, but also focuses attention on special services at the state level.

"Without moving from your chair, you decide what you want to do and where you want to 'travel.' Direct answers to your questions can be at your fingertips," states the marketing brochure for Hawaii FYI. "You can 'meet' new people and become friends with people who have jobs like yours, or the same hobbies and interests as you do. Together you and other Hawaii FYI users can share experiences and opinions, solve problems and create new ideas."

Services include access to the Hawaii State Library's databases of books and periodicals; the State Legislature's bills, reports, and hearings; lists of registered corporations; state tourism and business information; a Hawaii Data Book; Software Service Center; and a restaurant guide provided by Honolulu Magazine. The University of Hawaii Libraries and those of other educational institutions nationwide are also accessible.

But perhaps the most amazing thing about Hawaii FYI is that, at the time of this writing, nearly all of its services are free. Services that carry a charge are posted in the system's menu providing users with fair warning before they use them.

Unfortunately, the requirements for access are a personal computer, communications software, a modem, and phone line. Communications parameters must be set and system commands, like those on the Internet, must be learned. The services are directly in line with what the superhighway will offer, but access is still a bumpy technical road for the average consumer.

Another model that brings reality to the concept of the information superhighway is the French Minitel system. Telephone users in France may choose to install a computer terminal as part of their service. These terminals, which are in more than 3 million French homes, provide directory assistance at the touch of a few keys. The system also automatically dials the number.

In addition to directory services, Minitel's more than 12,000 service providers offer banking, insurance, and order-processing transactions as well as bulletin board services including sports results and dating services.

Based on videotext technology, Minitel is similar to services that have been tried (unsuccessfully) in the United States. Both the technology itself and the lack of solid applications that appealed to consumers made the service less popular in this country. Though the access technology may not be attractive to consumers here, the services provided in France are on the same order as those that will be found on the superhighway.

Another country trying to ramp up the super-highway before the superpowers do is Singapore, which also has a videotext system, called Teleview. Like Minitel, Teleview requires special terminals, which are capable of receiving high-quality photographic images. Personal computer users can get their systems to mimic the terminals via a cumbersome set of add-on gear, including circuit boards and a modem. Teleview services include traditional directory services, financial information, news services, travel information, real estate listings, and other consumer goods services.

In addition, Singapore has invested in ISDN (Integrated Services Digital Networks), the integrated voice and data network standard that is one of the paths the superhighway might take toward multimedia delivery of information. Claiming to be the first country to have nationwide ISDN capability, Singapore has had little success in persuading businesses to switch to the service. But its initial investment makes it one of the best-positioned nations to take advantage of the global information highway in the years ahead.

While many of the social, political, and information-sharing applications of the information super-highway are already being modeled on the Internet, commercial applications require a different set of platforms, both technically and culturally, than those offered by the Net today.

Funded by governments (the U.S. National Science Foundation, which runs NSFNET — a main pathway for research and education — once prohibited commercial data traffic) and maintained as an undisciplined search and retrieval system, the Internet lacks the certainty, access, and economic channels required by buyers and sellers of products. This is not to say that the Internet is not adding commercial applications at a rapid rate. It is. In fact, three-quarters of the Internet's recent growth has been fueled by commercial networks like America Online and other service providers signing on. These applications are simply initial learning experiences for companies and individuals who want to participate in making the superhighway a primary vehicle of commerce. Direct advertising by these (or any other) companies is still frowned upon by most mainstream Internet users.

The multimedia nature of commercial applications and the need to make them available to multiple users simultaneously create a problem with the Internet's limited address space — there will be more users of Internet services than there are computer-readable addresses to accommodate them. These applications are further limited by the average user's continued reliance on traditional telephone and personal computer technology. New tools are being created to enhance the Internet's capability to support commercial services. In time these tools will migrate to the superhighway, which will offer superior capacity and access to the marketplace.

CommerceNet is a good example of this. Its consumer services will include multimedia catalogs that offer drawings, videos, and text descriptions of products offered by CommerceNet's more than 50 sponsors. These Silicon Valley companies set out to create an electronic marketplace. While the commercial implications of the effort are important, more significant for the future is the fact that this collection of telephone and computer companies have agreed to use this network as a way to solve both technical and non-technical problems they may encounter in developing information superhighway applications. Based on the Internet and dial-in bulletin board links among the companies' many networks and systems, CommerceNet will offer a wide variety of information and products.

Hyperlinking software, which allows the system to automatically combine any type of information from multiple places on the network, will allow consumers to browse through CommerceNet's contents quickly and easily without worrying about on which computer or at what address a file or information is located. Intelligent agents and customized programs armed with the buyer's demographics will search CommerceNet and find offers of potential interest.

Computer simulations will allow users of CommerceNet to test drive products and services before they purchase them. Companies may even use this "virtual test drive" as an opportunity to try out new business concepts before bringing them to market.

The privacy issue will be addressed through cryptographic software that makes contracts and money exchanges secure. The planned security measures are of sufficient strength to sign up Citicorp and Bank of America as supporters of CommerceNet.

The initial application for CommerceNet will be a virtual computer store in which 20,000 computer products will be offered at below-mail-order prices.

A similar effort is being undertaken by International Data Group (IDG), which is creating Electronic Marketplace Systems in a joint venture with Connect, Inc. This personal-computer-based application will allow corporate buyers to make purchases of goods and services directly from manufacturers.

First, the buyer will read text-based product descriptions and related information provided by IDG's publications. Then the user will send a request for certain products to the network's central computer. The request will automatically be distributed to appropriate suppliers, who will send their bids back to the buyer. Ultimately, the buyer will place an order with the chosen supplier.

These forays into the electronic marketplace are not limited to large companies. The Internet and the Prodigy on-line service are the seed-bed for new businesses that did not exist before. The Corner Store and Indelible Blue, for example, sell computer software that traditional retailers don't stock in volume.

Unable to advertise their services on-line because Internet users discourage on-line advertising, the stores placed ads in trade publications for IBM's OS/2 and Microsoft Corp.'s Windows NT operating system software. They were overwhelmed by the response.

Electronic distribution of software, much of it free, and electronic newsletters and publications are the primary semi-commercial uses of the Internet. Prodigy goes one step further by displaying advertising from consumer products manufacturers as part of its delivery of information services and entertainment.

Direct marketing to consumers is frowned upon by Internet users. Companies that have experimented with direct on-line mail campaigns garner response rates beyond their wildest dreams. Unfortunately, most of them are negative reprimands. As a result, some firms have chosen subtler methods to reach customers, proactively browsing Internet discussions to offer unsolicited, yet helpful, advice or answers to questions. Other corporations make their product and company information available on servers, large computers that users can dial into and browse at their convenience.

Other business applications are being tried on the Internet's World-Wide Web (WWW), an easy-access interface to the Net. These applications vary widely, and include discussion groups as well as marketing and sales efforts. For example, Digital Equipment Corp. allows potential customers to test drive their latest Alpha computers by running their own software via the Internet. More than 2,500 users have taken advantage of the offer, netting $5 million in sales for DEC.

The solution to the problem of business advertising on the Internet is: passive services that allow consumers to browse at their will and use the system menus to get more details about products or services.

While all these services have potential, they still fall short of the more open electronic marketplace of the information superhighway. It is the difference between a research and information platform, with some added commercial content — the Internet — and an open two-way platform for the exchange of products, services, and entertainment — the superhighway. Government and research primarily created and support the former. Businesses and consumers will largely fund and support the latter.

Rather than passive advertising, two-way con-sumerism will be the predominant economic style of the superhighway. Everyone has something to sell: a unique skill, service, or product. The information superhighway will allow every user to advertise in a global market.

Products and services will be available to enable individuals and small businesses to build multimedia advertisements that they will make available to targeted users on the superhighway. Their markets will be worldwide.

Plumbers, electricians, and builders will present services available in the local market. People who have unique home-designed products, knowledge-bases, or special services will be able to buy and sell electronically and find customers among millions of geographically dispersed superhighway users. Virtual craft fairs, seminars, and interactive counseling sessions would be available through the network.

Consumers can also expect to receive extensive company information over international network connections. But they will have one advantage they don't possess with television or radio ads. They will be able to interactively customize the information they receive. An ad might start by describing a new sushi knife from Japan, but the consumer might want a tea set instead and could relay the request to the Japanese company which would bring forth the multimedia tea set offering.

Shopping could become far more interactive than the Home Shopping Network or browsing through the Sunday newspaper. From their superhighway console, consumers could find the best prices, location, and quality of the products and services they seek. They

> *Two-way consumerism will replace passive advertising and will be the predominant economic style of the superhighway.*

could choose to investigate further, take delivery, or
travel to the location.

For big-ticket items such as automobiles, DEC's
Alpha test drives are a good model. Instead of seeing an
ad for Chrysler's new Neon automobile, users will be
able to take a virtual test drive by tapping into their
auto dealer's computer simulations. They could also test
drive different versions of the vehicle with different features or try out as-yet-unmanufactured models, providing feedback to help the company determine
consumer preferences.

Financial transactions might be one of the first and
easiest services to become available on the superhighway. Instead of Automatic Teller Machines (ATMs)
on every corner, ATM access could be provided to every
home. The accounts available through the ATMs could
be accessed for on-line purchases of advertised items.
Banks could use their extensive international networks
to manage monetary exchanges for foreign purchases.

Travel, hotel, and car rentals are another set of services easily transferred from telephone orders to superhighway offerings. These would have the added feature
of customizable multimedia advertisements that would
allow consumers to experience the trip before commit-
ting to the purchase.

Vice President Al Gore is fond of talking about how
government should strike a deal with business to make
sure that the information superhighway reaches every
classroom in America, no matter how isolated the school
district. When we achieve that goal, every school child
will have the world's storehouse of information at his or
her fingertips and it will be up to the teachers to guide
the student's access to information into a journey to
build knowledge.

What might be found in the highway's information
banks? Imagine a student's science project on the inside
of the earth or the shape of the universe, based not on a
ten-year-old encyclopedia, but on quotes and images
from leading researchers. New theories on all major subjects would be open to the student through direct communication with major universities and research centers.

Much of NASA's data, the National Weather Service, Library of Congress, and records from the Smithsonian and the White House are already available on-line via one of the dial-in services or the Internet. In the coming years, the superhighway will make access to these sources of knowledge available instantly in a customized form.

Beyond these resources will be access to international information on culture, customs, geography, and language. Learning about distant lands will change from a sterile one-way reading experience to interaction with living representatives of other countries. Schoolchildren from Asia and America will teach each other about the nature of their worlds.

The key that will bring about this change is an easy-to-access, affordable information system connected to the highway available in every classroom and, eventually, on everyone's desk.

While information and learning might be the greatest benefits of the information superhighway, entertainment may be the biggest reason for its initial popularity and monetary success. As a society, we are more willing to spend money on movies and distractions than we are on schools and knowledge.

Perhaps the best known and most talked about entertainment service of the information superhighway is video-on-demand, which will provide custom access to movies, sitcoms, and documentaries. Consumers will experience two levels of entertainment applications for the superhighway. First, they will have instant access to the programs they know and love — being able to watch the last episode of "M.A.S.H." or the first episode of "90210" anytime they wish. Second, a new wave of interactive programs will become available. Led by game shows and discussion programs, these will be multimedia experiences that place the viewer at the center of the action in a fantasy environment.

Entertainment will be a key entry point for the superhighway because the ubiquitous television console will be the model for the multimedia access device. The combination of television's accessibility, telephone's interactivity, and the computer's richness of programming are the attributes of the superhighway console, which will still have a large screen and probably a remote control as well as a keypad and speaker/microphone.

Another factor leading to entertainment's strength as the killer superhighway application is economics. The companies most likely to make the connections and programs a reality are already seeing financial advantages to partnerships that will form the superhighway's basic business foundation.

The six-month-long takeover battle for Paramount Communications, which ended in February 1994, stunned many analysts because the $10 billion price Viacom, Inc. paid was 17 times the cash value of the company. The explanation: Paramount is well-positioned to feed the superhighway with programming. It owns rights to 880 films and controls many of the top movie and TV programming studios. Its offerings and resources are ready and waiting for another pathway beyond the standard channel selections of current TVs and the VCR/video rental business. The superhighway could support programming through user fees and the opportunity to expand the advertising audience for any given show.

On the network/hardware side, cable TV companies and local telephone companies are looking for ways to burst out of their regions and match the reach of their national rivals, while nationwide phone companies want to penetrate local markets to expand their services. New phone and cable connections are getting fewer and fewer as the nation becomes saturated with current services. So new services with additional features are required to drive business growth and peak consumer interest.

New technologies, such as personal communications devices and wireless systems, will broaden our communications options and make superhighway access very different from today's Internet connections.

Marriages between phone firms, which have the reach and switching technology, and cable firms, which have the fiber optic networks and access to the programming, will usher in the entertainment applications of the superhighway. In the first such marriage, U S WEST, the

Western Regional Bell Operating Company (RBOC), acquired 25% of Time Warner, which has a cable network as well as other entertainment-related properties.

As applications begin to move from test beds to deployment across the networks that are now in place or those that will be built in the near future, a number of issues must be resolved.

- How can equitable access be provided to all citizens, regardless of their ability to pay for services or for access equipment?

- How do we safeguard the privacy of our personal communications?

- How do we make sure that individual intellectual property rights — ideas expressed over the superhighway — are not open to unauthorized usage?

- How do we deal with the rapid spread of misinformation?

Future technologies will broaden our communications options and make superhighway access very different from the Internet connections of today.

Universal access could be a significant line of demarcation between the superhighway and the Internet and other on-line services. Current Internet use is limited to those with the technical inclination or ability to afford such services. The applications are also geared to predominant types of users, so technical information still makes up the bulk of the material available on-line today.

Eventually, developers will reduce the ease-of-use problems with the Internet through interfaces such as the World-Wide Web and Mosaic. These advancements will accelerate the merger of the Internet into a larger superhighway that also includes video servers and commercial on-line services.

If the superhighway is to become a true tool to provide government services, a facilitator of a more interactive community, and a significant political conduit, then everyone must have the option to be on-line.

Two forces will shape movement toward universal access. Government will have to use its regulatory and financial vehicles to channel deployment into universal directions. Businesses will devise the most cost-effective methods for spreading the superhighway out to the widest possible population to provide the maximum number of users for products and services.

The problem is not insurmountable. Models for nearly universal access at an affordable price are right in front of us — the telephone and the TV or radio. Many corporations, given sufficient incentive, have no difficulty providing universal access to their internal networks for hundreds or even thousands of employees distributed throughout the world, and many of these have extended this access to include the Internet as well.

Unlike universal access, which can be solved primarily through regulatory and marketplace means, privacy will require technical solutions that don't close out interaction in favor of control on information. Security will be important for financial information, personal exchanges, and even for patterns of superhighway usage. Much can be determined by the kinds of information we seek and the frequency with which we seek it. Insufficient privacy could be like having a monitor on your TV that broadcasts to anyone who cares to notice what your viewing habits are, from which they might infer other personal details.

Privacy in political matters is also extremely necessary. One only has to think about the late-Fifties McCarthyism to envision a society where political affiliations are known and used against individuals. Even more well-known is the image of state control called up by George Orwell's *1984*. Big Brother could take the shape of a prying government with access to all superhighway transactions.

The Clinton Administration recently fanned the flames of such fears by introducing a standard encryption chip that would be on everyone's systems, but to which only government would have the code. The uproar from individual-rights groups caused the administration to back off from its position and seek other alternatives.

Nevertheless, banking transactions, military communications, and other highly sensitive conversations today will all need to be protected by various methods of coding or scrambling the electronic information. These techniques can be transferred to the superhighway from current government and business systems. An investment of time and money will be required to make this happen, as well as an investment in compromise to settle who should hold the keys to secure systems.

Intellectual property rights can best be protected by strong penalties for abuse just as the laws protect us against abuse for misuse of written or spoken information. The electronic nature of the communication will make it more difficult, because the free flow of information is harder to follow. There are no hard-copy documents to use as evidence. The courts are already struggling with these issues with regard to computer software and legal solutions will eventually emerge.

Preventing misinformation from becoming common belief and having that belief lead to mistaken action is perhaps the hardest matter to resolve. Unlike today's media where some level of credibility is assumed of the distributors of information, who usually state their sources or the foundations for their conclusions, the superhighway will be open to anyone's opinion and ideas. This is not a bad thing in a democracy, although it does place a burden on the recipient of the information to determine how to weigh the credibility of its source. But a worldwide information flow will cross the borders of democracies, dictatorships, and other forms of society as well. How do we prevent a Saddam Hussein, for example, from broadcasting his views to every home in the United States on a regular basis?

With universal access and the desire to have open information pathways, the superhighway could be abused by hostile users, who could spread rumors of atrocities by certain ethnic groups, or promote financial disasters through malicious rumor. This problem will require the forces of government agencies and technology to solve, as well as responsible action by the majority of superhighway users in identifying and refusing to circulate or respond to negative and false information.

The Superhighway and You

Now is the time to prepare yourself and your children for the information superhighway. Luckily, the task isn't as daunting as it sounds. Using the latest computer technology, it is easy to get on-line and glimpse what our multimedia future holds. If you can get comfortable with on-line services today, you'll be able to tap into the power of the superhighway tomorrow.

More than 30 years ago, a businessman in the movie *The Graduate* approached Dustin Hoffman's character and whispered a magic word into his ear — "Plastics." At that time, the secret to the future was, indeed, plastics. The subsequent 20 or so years saw everything imaginable crafted out of plastic — from kitchen containers to car parts and even clothing. This was due in part to America's infatuation with this new material and a desire to explore the limits of its applications. It was also due to the fact that it was less expensive and more versatile than wood or metal.

If *The Graduate* were filmed today, that businessman would likely whisper a very different magic word — "Multimedia." If current trends play out, everything in the foreseeable future of the entertainment, education, and information industries will move toward multimedia. Our movies and television programs, the books we read and the games we play, and a host of new experiences will be composed from this new magic substance. So what is it?

Multimedia, according to Waring Partridge, chief strategy officer for AT&T's Multimedia Products and Services Group, is defined as "the integrated use of two or more media — meaning, in everyday terms, the simultaneous communication of voice plus handwriting, data, fax, and video images." Partridge states in an AT&T strategy report that, "Our challenge is to make two-way multiple media at least as easy to use as voice — using voice and familiar voice telephone interfaces such as a touch tone pad and existing telephone numbers."

Multimedia is easy to see but hard to explain. Consider for a moment the senses involved in interacting with another person. You see them move and absorb the essence of their gestures and mannerisms. You hear them speak, breathe, or cough. You can touch them and even taste them. You take in their unique scent and associate it with other scents in your surroundings. All of this sensing occurs simultaneously, and without conscious thought or effort. The input to each of those senses changes as you interact with that person, instantly passing along differences and new information to stimulate your actions and

> *If current trends* play out, everything in the foreseeable future of the entertainment, education, and information industries will move toward multimedia. Our movies and television programs, the books we read and the games we play, and a host of new experiences will be composed from this magic substance.

reactions. This is truly a multimedia experience, involving many senses — not just one or two.

Until now, our electronic interactions have been more like looking at a still picture of that person you were just interacting with. It engages your senses one at a time, most frequently using the visual sense, and from positions and content that are usually controlled by the "photographer" rather than the viewer. This is what happens today when we move from direct interaction with people to using the telephone, watching the television, or sending e-mail on the computer. Telephones require us to listen and to interact verbally, but nothing else. Televisions allow us to use our vision and hearing, but there is no interactivity. Computers require touch, vision, and occasionally hearing.

Multimedia contains more food for our senses than any previous form of indirect human interaction. It will incorporate still and full-motion video pictures; voices, music, and other sounds; and a variety of touch-based devices to help us interact. Eventually, we will even be able to speak with the multimedia images we interact with. These images will be able to react based on our interaction, as well. Short of smell and taste, multimedia will engage many of our senses.

Multimedia has become possible because many previously separate pieces of hardware — such as the phone, television, and computer — are moving toward the use of a single technology called digital. Digital simply means representing information by numbers. This technique dates back to the first human beings adding and subtracting using the digits on their hands and feet. All computers do is combine different digits, much the same way as we do by hand. The key difference is the computer's superior speed and memory. Today's computers are more powerful than ever, and it is their ability to process tremendous amounts of computations with near-lightning speed that gives us the capability to represent voices, moving pictures, and sound digitally. This digitization of voice, sound, and picture is at the heart of the multimedia revolution.

Is calling it a "revolution" overstating the matter? Take a look at these headlines, all of which appeared on a single day in May 1994:

Industry Experts See TV-PC Hybrid by End of Decade
(*The Fort Lauderdale Sun-Sentinel*)

TCI To Buy Smaller Bay Area Cable Rivals
(*The San Jose Mercury News*)

Electronic Redlining Alleged in Plans for Video Dialtone
(*The Associated Press*)

Scientific-Atlanta, Apple, IBM to Design Set-Top Boxes
(*San Jose Mercury News*)

Radio Shack to Sell IBM Personal Computers
(*Reuters News Service*)

Digital Convergence Buzzwords at Comdex Convention
(*Orlando Sentinel*)

TV Junkies Are Channeling into Their Computers
(*San Jose Mercury News*)

IBM Forms Plan To Boost Its Presence in Interactive Arena
(*The Wall Street Journal*)

Microsoft's Tiger May Help It Catch Up to Video Rivals
(*The Wall Street Journal*)

Can't Get Enough of Book? Buy a CD-ROM
(*The Wall Street Journal*)

Clearly, the forces of industry and technology are gearing up to fight on the front lines of the multimedia revolution.

USA Today's headline for that same day, however, sums up the primary reason why many of us have only a faint awareness of multimedia, the information super-highway, and computers in general: "The PC Curse: Breakdowns." The fact remains that personal computers are hard to use. They break down (usually at the worst possible moment), and they're relatively expensive.

The *USA Today* article cites a finding that nearly 25% of 45,000 personal computer users surveyed reported problems with their computers. Thirty percent said their computers broke within a month of purchase

and 7% were damaged even before they were plugged in
for the first time. Recalls were also reported: in 1994,
63,000 Dell personal computers were recalled by the
U.S. Consumer Products Safety Commission because
they could overheat and cause fires. In November 1993,
IBM recalled its Thinkpad 500 notebook portable personal computers because they had faulty batteries.

Between the problems that have to be repaired and
the learning curve that needs to be experienced to make
a computer a truly useful tool, many people have chosen
not to use them. Up until now, this has been an under-
standable attitude, since the benefits that the average
person gained from computer use were minimal at best.
But as we move into a multimedia-oriented society, this
attitude will become increasingly less practical.

Previous generations faced the same types of
choices. When telephones replaced telegraphs, there
were those who refused to use one. When television
replaced radio, many were reluctant to bring them into
their homes. There were even those who thought plastic
was a bad idea. The end result was that the people who
accepted and learned how to use the new appliances
were a giant step ahead of those who did not.

Now, it's our turn to deal with a major technological
chain reaction. In the past 10 years, personal computers
have appeared in every corner of work, home, and
school life. In the last 5 years, these computers have
been combined into networks, making them even more
powerful and opening up a world of new possibilities.

In the next 5 years, personal computers, or, more
precisely, tools that allow us to manipulate a variety of
media digitally, will dominate our communications systems. The senses involved in using these new computers
will be the same ones engaged by our new telephone and
television hybrids, until they eventually merge into a
single type of appliance that has multimedia and network abilities at its core.

This evolution will give us many benefits in
enhanced entertainment, education, and interaction.
But the transformation will be less like simply adding
another appliance in our homes and more like acquiring

a new language or way of life. Those who refuse to become acclimated face the danger of feeling like foreigners in this new culture. They will miss much of what's going on and be isolated from the greater society until they learn the language and begin to understand the culture.

We are fortunate to be able to start our learning process now. We can make the multimedia world accessible to ourselves and our children, and so get ready to deal with the future products of industry and technology. If we learn how to operate in this new landscape, we will be able to participate in shaping the future, rather than simply reacting to it.

The way to start is by getting on-line. This means acquiring a personal computer and a modem. Since most of us are already quite familiar with the interaction and sensory input involved with the use of the telephone and television, becoming acquainted with the techniques of networked computing will move us well along the learning curve to our future.

Learning to interact with a computer and network is the foundation of learning the new multimedia language, just as learning to construct sentences is the basis for learning any foreign tongue. And, as with other languages, understanding the new multimedia language will provide insights into the multimedia culture as well.

In the future, you'll be able to walk into a department or consumer-electronics store and buy an appliance that contains computer intelligence and that either has its own color video screen, sound input and output, or that has the ability to work with a television monitor that has those capabilities. Manufacturers are aiming for a $300 price tag for these devices.

You'll be able to take this appliance home and plug it into your wall, where a connection has been installed to connect to your cable or phone company network. You won't need separate software, disks, or CD-ROMs because everything you need to start will be preinstalled and the network connection will supply the rest. Multiple media, ranging from videos to interactive conversations and eventually involving voice, will be

> *Those who refuse to become acclimated face the danger of feeling like foreigners in this new culture. They will miss much of what's going on and be isolated from the greater society until they learn the language and begin to understand the culture.*

instantly available to you. You'll pay a one-time fee for the appliance and a monthly charge to the phone or cable company for the services you use. Billing and payment for services might even take place through electronic banking conducted on your appliance. You could authorize the bank to subtract the fee/usage charges from your account and the bank would credit the network provider's account. Today's on-line services charge your membership fee and service-usage time to your credit card, which you authorize as you navigate through the "welcome" screens.

But why wait? Today, you can walk into a department or consumer-electronics store and purchase a $2,000 personal computer with a modem that runs multimedia programs. You'll have to pay about another $50 for each multimedia program you want to purchase. These are sold like other computer products or video recordings in the same store.

If you can learn to use a bank machine (sometimes known as an ATM, which is not to be confused with asynchronous-transfer mode ATM that will be discussed later), a touch-tone keypad on your home or office telephone, a computer application, or a computerized cash register, then you can learn how to use a personal computer at home. You just have to be willing to form a passing acquaintance with some technical essentials and you're up and running. And even then, the only time these essentials will really matter is when you make the actual computer purchase. After that, they're largely in the background while you become familiar with the programs you want to use.

You can reduce the amount of technical information you need to learn by buying one of the new, easy-to-use multimedia personal computers (like the Compaq Presario). Many of these are equipped with:

- A speedy processor, such as Intel's 486SX;
- 8 megabytes (MB) of RAM (Random Access Memory);
- A 200MB hard drive;

- A CD-ROM drive;
- A 3.5" floppy drive;
- 1MB of video RAM;
- A 16-bit stereo sound card and speakers;
- A 9600 bps modem;
- A SVGA monitor.

Remember, the only difference between a computer and counting on your fingers is really speed — so speed really counts when you're buying a PC. You want the fastest (or close to the fastest) processor you can afford; but don't forget that within at most a couple of years, even faster processors will be available for the price you paid. Don't waste your money on a processor that's considered slow by today's standards (like the Intel 386) because it will ultimately waste both your time and your money. Not only will it be slow, it will also be less capable of handling the increasingly immense amounts of data that are needed for true multimedia applications, leading to its quick obsolescence.

Once you've got a system with the basic elements to run multimedia programs, all you need to do is become acquainted with the software — the programs themselves.

Whether you buy a PC or a Mac, most systems today come with pre-installed software, something only the Apple Macintosh — long recognized as the easiest-to-use computer — used to do. After you physically set up the computer (plug it in and attach the cables), a system startup routine will require some minimal involvement from you. Then, the software loads itself and you're ready to go.

Many multimedia PCs start with Microsoft Windows, a host of accessories, games, and integrated programs for word processing, calculation, record keeping, and electronic mailing. Windows is easier to use than its predecessor DOS. (So if you stopped using a computer because of DOS, you can rest easy — DOS is usually hidden from view.) But Windows still has a learning curve. The major thing you need to know is that you can access any program by clicking on its icon (a picture representing the program) or the commands that appear below it. You can also get out of anything by clicking on a menu and finding the commands to close and leave it. Whatever you open can be saved and closed in the same way, by choosing the appropriate command from a menu.

Finally, you get to the fun part of the computer — using multimedia. The key is your CD-ROM (Compact Disc-Read Only Memory) drive, which reads and processes the digital storage version of the audio CDs commonly used for music (most will also read and project the regular audio CDs through the PC's speaker, for an extra benefit). CD-ROMs are handy because they let you pack enormous amounts of digital information in a small space. For example, the entire 26-volume *Encyclopedia Britannica* can be stored on a single CD-ROM, complete with sight, sound, and indexes. CD-ROMs hold as much digital data as 1,500 standard disks. Access to information on CD-ROMs is extremely fast, because it is read by laser rather than by the physical movement of disk-drive magnetic heads. The only real drawback to this CD-ROM technology today is that it is read-only; the technology that will allow you to write data to a CD-ROM on your home computer is not yet available.

What are the benefits of CD-ROM over traditional books? Here's an example. A recent book, *The Halderman Diaries*, written by one of President Richard Nixon's former aides, was also released on CD-ROM. The book was edited down to 1,000 pages. The CD-ROM version contains all 2,200 unabridged pages, including 45 minutes of home movies. Computer searching allows far greater access to its riches than a reader could obtain through the printed word.

There is an ever-increasing range of interactive programs available on CD-ROM, many of them for kids.

There is an ever-increasing range of interactive programs available on CD-ROM, many of them for kids. You can design your own comic strip or your own home, or learn and listen to a foreign language.

CD-ROMs let you interact with the program to obtain information, play a game, run a video. More important, they get your senses used to experiencing entertainment and information based on your own interaction with the program. You learn how to use program cues and search strategies to get what you want and, along the way, develop likes and dislikes for various navigation tools and techniques. This will be especially useful when you have to choose your connection to the information superhighway.

You'll also start to see some of the benefits of this new world, which can provide you with new ways of learning, playing, and thinking. And all of this is only a tiny fraction of what the multimedia revolution offers.

The powerful combination of multimedia and networks will make the information superhighway most people's route of choice for many daily activities — from shopping to conversing, and from banking to playing and learning.

The easiest way to get started on a network is by buying a personal computer that has access software for an on-line service, such as America Online, pre-installed. Assuming your computer has a modem, America Online's program, for example, sets up all the communications requirements for you. It lets you dive right in to its list of services. CompuServe, Prodigy, and other on-line services offer similar programs or have associated software you can load to make the connection easily.

How expensive are these connections? Well, in mid-1994, CompuServe, which has the broadest range of services, cost $8.95 a month, plus $9.60 per hour for extended services. Prodigy charges $29.95 per month and $3.60 an hour after the first 25 hours. America Online, the easiest to use, costs $9.95 per month for up to 5 hours of connect time. An additional $3.50 per hour is charged after that. All these services are more expensive than the Internet, which can be accessed for about $20 a month for 30 hours of service.

America Online is a good example of one of these services. It has a Windows-like interface and, therefore, uses an icon-based menu system from which you can select from eight "departments":

- **News & Finances.** This lets you search by topic through major publications and wire services, and provides daily reports in real time on U.S. and world news, business and finance, technology, sports, stocks, and the weather. There's even an opinion "page."

- **On-line Magazines.** You can read the current (and back) issues of magazines including: *Time, Omni, Windows, The Atlantic Monthly, Disney Adventures, Chicago On-line, San Jose Mercury Center, Compute, Consumer Reports, The New Republic, Wired,* and *Worth.*

- **Lifestyles & Interests.** There are more than 40 clubs and special interest forums. These are electronic conferences and message boards centered around hobbies or topics of common interest (like sports, travel, parenting, computers, education, and so on).

- **People Connection.** Live electronic conferences (like a multiparty telephone call), classes, and "chat rooms" are featured here allowing free-form, real-time interaction with other network users.

- **Travel & Shopping.** American Airlines reservations can be made in this area, and you can purchase goods and services by responding to electronic advertisements.

- **Games & Entertainment.** This area features multi-player on-line games and trivia as well as entertainment industry news.

- **Learning & Reference.** Live education services, encyclopedia information, on-line access to the Smithsonian, Library of Congress, National Geographic Society, CNN, and a Career center are available here.

- **Computing & Software.** More than 50,000 software programs are available for you to download (save on your computer). Computing advice, on-line access to *PC World* magazine, and other industry information are also available. In addition, this area offers live technical support for users, deals with billing issues, and handles other service-related questions.

You can access the Internet through America On-line's Internet Center at no additional cost. Users can send and receive messages from other America Online members or millions of Internet users.

Tapping into the power of the network is easy once you get comfortable with menus that feature icons and text descriptions of information. It's easier if you've spent time with Windows on your personal computer.

On-line multimedia services are still a few years away, largely because of the limited capabilities of the telephone networks used to connect to on-line services and the Internet. However, there are many benefits to investing in an on-line service or Internet connection now — well before the superhighway brings video to your doorstep.

As a learning tool, these services help prepare us for the future. Think about how you share information now. For most people, the response is "over the telephone in two-way, voice-only conversations with one person at a time." America Online chat and conference areas and Internet's "Usenet" newsgroups are simultaneous con-versations with any number of people. Just imagine the number and variety of opportunities for interaction.

The Internet also has mailing lists where you can subscribe to listings or "conversations" on a certain sub-ject. Subscribers automatically receive mail from other subscribers on the topic, and can respond to that mail individually or in a *posting* that the entire group will receive. For many of these groups, subscribers have the option of receiving the information in two ways — as the other subscribers generate and mail it, or collected auto-matically by the network into a single large file, called a *digest*, that they receive once a day or once a week. For many, this is a way of keeping current on a topic, con-necting with peer groups from all over the world, or of having a large, always-available support system.

Although the future multimedia world will allow video as well as voice and writing, today's network chats, newsgroups, and mailing lists are all conducted through writing.

With most of the forums offering chatty, informal styles, the on-line systems offer us a way to express ourselves in writing without the high pressure of a formal letter or document. They are encouraging literacy through writing, but without much of the pain that has been associated with writing in the past. Just as storytelling encouraged the development of language centuries ago, electronic information sharing has the potential to foster the development of written communications.

Network chats and newsgroups are also a good way to get used to the simultaneous availability of multiple respondents, each of whom may have something interesting (and completely different) to say. The groups are open to anyone who cares to respond to — or just read — the exchanges. This dual ability to "listen in" as well as join in provides a broad audience for the information expressed.

Private messages, known as electronic mail or e-mail, are also facilitated by on-line networks. This is like using the telephone except messages are written and the receiver might take more time to respond. In many cases, it's probably like leaving a phone message with virtually unlimited length on an answering machine. But many users comb through their e-mail frequently and reply quickly.

On-line networks allow both targeted and random contact with strangers from around the world. Neighbors and associates in the same region or area can get involved. Many people find it a good way to stay in touch with scattered families. Since more and more colleges are providing on-line access for their students, it's a way for college students to "call home" without sending the long-distance telephone bill into orbit. It's also a way for worried parents of college students to leave a message that might get answered, rather than hearing the dormitory phone ring for days before someone eventually picks it up.

The most basic, and least challenging, form of on-line service is written communication. You'll master it quickly and want to move on to other challenges. The networks make it far simpler to find and use materials than it is to visit your local library or bookstore. By using a technique known as *keyword searching*, your computer can search through the storage space on other computers attached to the network to find things pertaining to a specific word, phrase, or topic. It doesn't care whether the material it is looking for is a straight-text file, a picture, a video clip, or a program, as long as it contains the word or phrase you want. Plus, it does this search in what's called *background* mode — it operates behind the scenes while you browse other areas of the network, edit a file, or take a break and watch TV.

One of the biggest benefits of this type of search is that you'll probably find material that you didn't even know existed. Your search could browse through a database at the Library of Congress, for example, and identify not only commonly available materials, but rare holdings that pertain to your topic. Try doing that by hopping in the car or picking up the telephone.

There is, however, one problem with this type of search. If you haven't structured your search well or defined your keywords carefully, you could end up with much more material than you will be able to go through to find the information that will be useful to you. For example, if you are researching *kidneys* because you want to know about kidney stones, you should be careful to restrict your search — otherwise, you'll end up with everything from scientific studies about kidney development in the embryo through in-depth information on surgical techniques involved in kidney transplants. In the wealth of material you'll receive, it will be hard to find the 10 articles about kidney stones and their treatment written for a lay audience. So it is important to plan your search carefully, and start with more restrictive search criteria than you think you might need — it's easier to expand your search if you don't get what you want on the first pass than it is to figure out what to cut out of an overabundant one.

Once you've found the information you want, usually in the form of one or more files of written text and/or program code, you can download it onto your computer's hard drive and use it when you're not connected to the network. It's yours for keeps, provided you follow whatever copyright or ownership limitations are specified in the material. Usually, on-line materials are freely accessible as long as you don't try to distribute or make money from them.

Keyword searching may save you travel time, but its real benefit lies in its ability to make the information from news reports and publications (both common and obscure) accessible and usable. You don't have to scroll through an entire newspaper or magazine to find information on a specific topic that you think was reported on that publication date. Your search will locate the specific reference to multiple articles on your keywords, or will indicate which article has the most *hits* (successful matches) for your keyword. This lets you concentrate your efforts more effectively. It also makes it easier to search for specific pieces of information, like whether a friend of yours was involved in an event that was reported in the news. To do this, simply search on your friend's name, or on attributes (like organization membership, place of employment, age, and so on), and only within reports about the event.

Receiving information electronically lets you get the news and data you want in the format and order you need.

This is one of the key differences between receiving information via your computer system and through printed magazines, newspapers, books, and even television. You can't customize the printed or broadcast formats. You have to take them as is or leave them. But by using your computer system to design your own searches and pick your own topics, you can reorganize generic news and information into your own news and information.

This ability will also be a key attribute of the multimedia/superhighway future, so the more you learn about it now, the farther ahead you'll be when it becomes widely available as part of interactive services.

You can also complete financial transactions such as shopping, buying stocks, and making travel reservations while you're sitting at your computer. It's also a prime time for checking out classified ads and real-estate offerings. In fact, much of what you'd like to do can be done anytime you want. The networks don't close for business at 5 p.m. Many users like to get on-line late in the evening after their work and family time are over. In addition, telephone rates and connect-time charges are lower in the evenings.

Not all users of on-line services are doing serious business in their evening encounters, though. Many, in fact, are seeking pure entertainment, similar to that they find on television. The *San Jose Mercury News* reports the following sampling from some of the on-line services on the subject of television trivia — a topic certain to keep you up at night.

America Online features a group of fans known as "Place-mats" who follow the plot twists of "Melrose Place." "Seinfeld" and "The X Files" also have their own groups. Soap opera summaries and other fan-based groups are available as well. There is also an area devoted to NBC. Hosted by the network, it features message boards, star biographies, photos, background info, a live-chat auditorium, and a multimedia library. The network will answer viewers' questions posted to the "Talk to NBC" area.

Prodigy offers "Total TV" — a database of nation-wide program listings. "Star Trek" (and its sequels and spin-offs) is getting its own bulletin boards to host around-the-clock talk by aficionados. CBS and 25 cable channels run their own bulletin boards, program listings, and answering services for viewer mail. Jerry Seinfeld and Jay Leno have served as guests on the services, fielding about 10,000 questions each during the month they were on-line.

CompuServe runs soap opera summaries and also offers expensive "extended services," featuring the Showbiz Forum and Entertainment Drive. The Showbiz Forum focuses on celebrities — with particular attention to their love affairs. Entertainment Drive is used heavily by CBS employees and includes a private area, known as Section Zero, which is exclusively used by the stars and starmakers of the network.

The TV networks are using the on-line services to get feedback from viewers about their programming. But they would be better served by working on bringing interactive technology to the TV screen. Today, that mission seems to be in the hands of the movie and video-making industry.

The entertainment-oriented services I've just described are only a shadow of the thousands of newsgroups on the Internet and hundreds of other bulletin boards around the country that offer a new virtual community for entertainment and information exchange. The passport to them is your computer system and a willingness to shift your senses to new visual and communication media.

The changing nature of our business world is an important reason to invest the money, time, and energy to get a multimedia system and set yourself up on a network. Many companies have invested millions in developing internal networks to connect their regional offices and plants. But as businesses move toward partnerships with different companies and try to connect more directly with their consumers, they need networks that connect with those outside their walls. Many companies also provide their employees with on-line access for telecommuting and electronic mail.

The Internet, which has always been a platform for collaboration, has increasingly become a forum for work groups and task forces composed of different people. You might, for example, find manufacturers, marketers, distributors, regulators, and consumers of products joining together to resolve common issues.

Using networks and personal computers to collaborate on projects both within the company and outside its boundaries is a major trend in business computing. If you work for a company or do business with one, sooner or later you'll be asked to collaborate with other specialists on a project of mutual interest. If you reply "What's e-mail?" when asked if you can join in the e-mail conversation, your business partners have two choices: invest time and energy bringing you up to speed with the computer revolution, or find a different, network-literate partner. With speed being one of the most essential elements in business, your partners are likely to look for another specialist. You can prevent such embarrassment by getting involved now.

If you have or are planning to have children, they're another powerful reason to move to personal computers and on-line access today. Their future will be dominated by the information superhighway, featuring more advanced services than we can even imagine. With scores of educational programs, games, and communications tools, there is no reason not to start them on the digital path as quickly as possible.

Of course, many schoolchildren will receive some exposure to computers in school, and more schools are focusing portions of their curriculum on computer usage. However, it remains true today that most of the computers in today's schools are not networked (with each other or with any on-line services) and do not have multimedia capability. Classes on computer use still focus largely on keyboard mastery and basic skills. So, to a great extent, it remains up to you to widen that focus for your children to help them obtain the skills and comfort with computers that will make them valuable in tomorrow's workplace.

The text and icon-based world of interactive systems and the power of accessing people and information throughout the world are things that your children should become familiar with just as they learn math, the metric system, or how to use a microwave or television.

If cost is an issue, you can always start with a less expensive system that lacks multimedia capability and add the multimedia components later. For less than $1,000 you can purchase a high-quality personal computer that runs most major software and includes a modem. The additional purchase of a communications program or software for on-line services such as America Online, CompuServe, or Prodigy will give you a fairly inexpensive access point to the on-line experience. The investment is worth it and really not that much more expensive than Nintendo, Sega, or the video game system you got your child for Christmas.

Multimedia add-ons, such as CD-ROM drives, can be purchased for $500 to $800 and prices are likely to drop in the future. So too will the price-tags on CD-ROMs themselves; they are hot commodities right now because they're in the "just arrived" stage, but within the next couple of years they'll become much less costly.

Computing technology is changing at a supersonic pace. What is considered state-of-the-art today will be tomorrow's old news. But it's critical that you and your children master today's technology, because it will give you a necessary foundation to the technologies that you'll face in the near (and not-so-near) future.

Mobile computing is developing quickly, in the form of smaller, less-expensive computers that can be taken anywhere and in networks that don't need wires, communicating instead over radio frequencies. Cellular phones are the first instruments to become widely available in this wireless world. Wireless computers are already the talk of the computer industry. They will make home and work, networking and collaborating, easier. In short, this trend is creating or adapting digital technology to human needs and attributes.

There is an AT&T television commercial that dramatizes the attributes of this new age. It shows a woman walking around in her apartment, not paying particular attention to her computer. A little dog appears on the computer screen and tells the woman that a transaction she has requested went through okay. He also informs her (in a squeaky little voice) that he is still searching through publications for the information she requested. This 60-second commercial ends with the woman saying "good boy" to the dog.

This ad shows the future. The dog is a computer-generated personality, like Max Headroom, from the 1980s. But unlike Max, who was a TV fantasy, the dog is an intelligent agent who can perform network transactions and keyword searches at the verbal command of the computer's owner. This agent can probably also "fetch" videos and interact with other intelligent agents to schedule meetings, arrange for exchanges of information, and so on.

So you can see that it's time to get up to speed in the present, because our future is looking stranger, but also more promising, by the day.

Infotainment

Entertainment and information services will be among the first superhighway offerings available to consumers. Multimedia, virtual reality, and interactive networking are the foundation — the technologies upon which these applications will be built. Test beds for these technologies are already fully-operational, and experimental demonstrations of infotainment services are given in public everyday.

T he place to catch a glimpse of the information superhighway is Orlando, Florida. As the home of Disney World — including the Magic Kingdom, Epcot Center, and MGM Studios theme parks — Orlando is the host to the latest infotainment technology: the combination of information and entertainment using multimedia presentation.

Add to this concentration of infotainment — exhibiting everything from the history of communications to the latest Disney adventure fantasy — the presence of Universal Studios, with its virtual-reality movie simulations, and there is more than enough opportunity to submerge a visitor into a mind-expanding present or future fantasy.

Just as the Internet is the testing ground for worldwide access to data and two-way communication with anyone, anywhere, the Orlando area is the test bed for the multimedia and virtual-reality technologies that will support future information superhighway applications for information and entertainment.

It is also the location of one of the most ambitious interactive networking experiments outside of the Clinton Administration's National Information Infrastructure Test Bed. Time Warner Cable plans to provide its customers in the Wekiva, Sweetwater, Lake Brantley, and Spring Lakes Hills sections of Orlando with access to an interactive network through their television cable systems. By the end of 1994, 4,000 cable users are expected to be a part of what the company calls the Full Service Network.

Time Warner and its business partner U S WEST plan to upgrade 85% of Time Warner Cable's 7.2 million customers in 36 states to the Full Service Network by the end of 1998. That's more than six million consumers. And Time Warner is only one of several companies creating networks of this nature.

The Full Service Network will allow customers to navigate along "an electronic superhighway lined with entertainment, shopping, information, education and communication opportunities," the company states.

The home of Disney

World and Universal Studios, Orlando, Florida, is the test bed for the multimedia and virtual-reality technologies that will support future superhighway applications for information and entertainment services.

Time Warner is being very quiet about the details of its Full Service Network until its formal unveiling late in 1994. But descriptions of the basic services and technology have been released. One of the company's scenarios describes a family of four on a typical Saturday in a quiet Orlando neighborhood.

10 a.m.: Mom goes grocery shopping, browsing the televised aisles — placing her order with a click of the remote.

Noon: Tommy wins a video game against his best buddy Bill — neither has left their home.

2 p.m.: Dad goes shopping for his new car, gets all the information he needs on the latest models, and even arranges for a test drive — without leaving the living room.

4 p.m.: Nancy joins her classmates for the weekly seminar on Advanced Algebra — comfortably ensconced on the family couch.

7 p.m.: The family relaxes together, ordering a pizza and watching "Free Willy" — without an unnecessary trip to the video store.

All these applications are accessed via a television connected to Time Warner's cables. Their materials go on to say:

Customers receive a new smart cable box, a simple remote control, and a color printer to print out material accessed through the television. Then the fun begins.

All the services are accessed by using the remote control to navigate through graphic displays that make choices simple. Turn on your TV, and a town center will appear, with identifiable buildings representing available services. Using the remote, you can fly through town — animation gives viewers the feeling of flying — to the theater and select the evening's movie, by title, stars, or themes. When shopping, you can handle the merchandise, using the remote to turn a box of cereal to examine its ingredients.

The graphics presentation used to navigate through the services was still being revised in July of 1994 and the final form may be different than this description, but the idea of accessing shops, games, conversations, education, and movies from your couch using your TV and remote control is the essential goal of the Full Service Network. It's the information superhighway as a cable company would have it.

The full menu of services include:

- Enhanced analog cable television.

- Video on demand: a service allowing each customer immediate access to motion pictures and other digitally stored television programming, along with the ability to pause, rewind, fast forward, and even stop the movie to make a popcorn run.

- Video games accessed by the customer from central digital storage that can be played with another user in the system, whether the opponent is next door or across town. Rather than using dedicated video-game machines, these applications only require the navigation and network connections that are part of the cable-based system.

- Interactive video shopping at "stores" including Spiegel, Eddie Bauer, Warner Bros. Studio Stores, the Auto Mall, and your local grocery or drug store. The service provides access to full-motion video of merchandise with immediate ordering available through the keypad.

- Distance learning through interactive educational instruction, allowing full-motion video coverage of the participants in a classroom exercise to be transmitted between two or more locations. It also includes access to such video from homes, either in real-time or in digitally stored courses.

- Access to libraries and library services.

- Banking and other financial services.

- Driver's license renewal or tag registration.

- Videoconferencing, offering full-motion video that connects and displays participants from two or more conference sites.

- Access for homes and businesses to long-distance telephone service.

- Personal communications services, such as mini-cellular communications devices. These would work with the computer technology in the "smart" cable box, providing network access through that entry point.

- Full-motion video picture phone service on full-sized TV screens.

- Medical imaging.

- High-speed data transport for business.

Many of the services being offered will require regulatory approval, such as the ability of a cable firm like Time Warner to offer telephone services. But the applications are all feasible, and many are being tested elsewhere. There are the telemedicine, remote learning, and research applications in test implementations sponsored by government agencies, universities, and telephone companies throughout the country. Congress is also examining legislation that would remove regulatory barriers to these services.

How much will this Full Service Network cost to customer? While not yet quoting prices, Time Warner answers the question this way: "The traditional cable service for Time Warner Cable's customers will not change as a result of the Full Service Network. Initially, customers will not be charged for the special equipment. Customers will only pay for each service used — the movie watched, the groceries or clothing bought, the games played."

The company says that the movie access will be priced in the same range consumers now pay at the video store. In addition, cable subscribers who choose not to use the Full Service Network will not incur any additional charges.

The initial 4,000 consumers of the Full Service Network will be chosen from among 5,200 subscribers in the test neighborhoods, based on their interest in the services. Families with children and those who are willing to allow the company to track the services they use will be the most likely candidates.

This initial test will be used to discover how well the technology works, what consumer preferences are for various services, and to create a platform for future service concepts, the company says.

While the company has installed the cable and tested the video-on-demand service, one question that consumers will have to answer is whether the system has any limitations. For example, only 1,000 people can order different movies simultaneously in the current design. This means that only about 25% of the 4,000 consumers testing the system can be accessing different movies simultaneously. Time Warner plans to follow usage trends closely to avoid having any customers "receive the video version of a busy signal."

Providing sufficient capacity for simultaneous access to network applications may be one of the tougher problems to solve — even the Internet bogs down when too many users try to get information from the same source. However, the access systems and content for applications are already quite well-developed. The infotainment vehicles exist in abundance, but they have yet to get onto the highway of a broadly accessible network.

Just a short drive from the Time Warner test site in suburban Orlando, Universal Studios and Disney World offer many opportunities to experience the future. Unfortunately, consumers must pay a premium in terms of money and time to see them. Travelling to Orlando, paying the admission fee, and waiting up to an hour for the major attractions are all part of the experience.

While many of the attractions are only accessible through "rides" in a fantasy vehicle, such as a boat, car, or train, some of the most interesting allow visitors to walk in and explore the technology at their own pace and depth.

AT&T's multimedia display at Universal Studios provides an excellent opportunity to view the kinds of multimedia applications and access systems that will likely be available on the information superhighway.

> *Even the Internet bogs down when too many users try to get information from the same source. Providing sufficient capacity for simultaneous access may be one of the tougher problems to solve.*

Called "AT&T in the Movies," the display connects the future with the past. It starts by giving visitors an opportunity to record their own voices on a vibraphone — an early version of the phonograph. At the same time old movies — such as the silent version of *Frankenstein* — are playing across the room, creating an atmosphere of nostalgia.

This reference to the past sets the stage to allow visitors to see how far technology has progressed as they walk into the next room and find eight personal computers — all accessed by touching the screen rather than a keyboard. One system is even armed with voice-response technology, letting users touch the screen and hear the computer speak the words and phrases they select.

Other systems are connected to video cameras, which take pictures of the visitors that are immediately transferred to the computer screen. At the touch of command buttons on the screen, the computer jumbles the picture and reassembles it. A similar system applies "make up," such as hats, beards, and mustaches, to the visitor's on-screen image.

Movie quizzes and puzzle portraits of famous movie personalities are available on other touch-screen computers. The whole display is far more interactive, informative, and entertaining than the vibraphone and old movie clips. In short, it's good infotainment.

My four-year-old son, Chris, is especially enthralled with an "Electronic Fingerpainting" computer that allows him to touch the screen and copy images of E.T., colored circles, lines, and other shapes anywhere he wants on the screen. The montage he creates is automatically projected onto an overhead screen. The simple method of touching an object, then touching the screen, which reproduces the object, delights Chris, giving him a sense of control and magic.

All these applications could be stored digitally and made available over a network. The receiving computer would need touch-screen, voice-response, and video-camera capability — not quite your average TV, or even a TV with a special set-top box. But the network for delivering these applications could well be the cable company's new fiber-optic system.

The AT&T display also has a giant telephone for making calls and a normal-sized AT&T Public Phone 2000, which provides a keyboard and menu options including computer and data services, information services, travel reservation services, telephone communications services, special devices for the deaf, and a help option.

More informative infotainment with more advanced access systems can be found in the last room of the display, which AT&T calls "Touch the Future." In addition to the opportunity to examine actual microchips under microscopes, the room provides five more touch-screen personal computers, each with three telephone receivers attached. Up to three visitors can pick up the receivers and listen to digitally stored videos that stop, start, and change in response to touch-screen commands.

The most impressive interactive system is contained in the two computers at the back of the display — called "The Dawn of Sound." Each features a slow-moving timeline containing black-and-white photographic reproductions of key events in movie and communications history between 1912 and 1962 — from early silent films to satellites.

The visitor touches the screen and the timeline stops on the year and runs a short video of the event, complete with the sound of the actual participants. The sound can be heard over the attached telephone receiver. Then the visitor is given the option to go deeper into the topic by touching a list of menu items, one offering related events, which are also displayed on the screen. The visitor can go backward or forward in time, drilling down to related events or staying with the flow of the timeline.

The combination of a valuable multimedia presentation, interactivity, touch-screen access, and actual video and sound clips make the system informative and very easy to use. These techniques could easily be used for other applications — education, shopping, or creative expression.

The other three personal computers in the room provide in-depth touch-screen video clips on the "Giant Computer," a child's-level explanation of early computers; "Microelectronics," a description of the past, present, and future of microcircuits and optical (laser-based) systems; and "The Microchip," a close-up look at the components of a personal computer.

Each display has its own "personality." The Giant Computer story is told via colored drawings of metaphors, such as a house to represent the size of the computer. The Microchip sets a spaceplane into motion, zooming into different planets and galaxies that contain descriptions and images of the components. The Micro-electronics system shows actual laboratory, home, and office settings where microcircuits and fiber optics are in use.

The display includes discussions of future develop-ments, such as an optical computer that will use photons rather than electrons and that will be based on optical components rather than microchips. It also described the 1992 effort to lay a 4,000-mile cable from the United States and Canada to the United Kingdom, France, and Spain. The undersea cable contains six strands of fiber-optic lines capable of handling 80,000 phone conversa-tions simultaneously. The cable also allows data to be transmitted at incredible speed and capacity. The equiva-lent of the *Encyclopedia Britannica* can be sent across the ocean in less than one second!

The technology in AT&T's display shows what is possible with today's systems. They also show that it will take time for us to adapt to the many choices technology offers. On the one hand, you can easily become frus-trated with the slow-moving timeline in the video dis-play and wish for a broader selection of film clips and the ability to see events beyond 1962. On the other hand, people are often slow to grasp the interaction required by the technology when it is different than they customarily expect. For example, phone receivers in the display are designed for listening to pre-recorded infor-mation rather than interactive conversation. And yet, people walk up to the phone receivers and yell, "Hello!" into them.

These are some of the issues the world of infotainment will confront. But human history is clearly marked by our ability to adapt, especially when it comes to technology and communications. This theme is wonderfully developed in another AT&T Orlando display — the "Audio-Animatronics" story of communications, which takes place inside "Spaceship Earth," the signature geosphere that marks the entrance to Epcot Center.

Known as one of the wonders of the world, the sphere, which represents the Experimental Prototype Community of Tomorrow (EPCOT), was designed as part of Walt Disney's vision of a domed, pollution-free city. Today it houses a multimedia display of the growth of human communication ability.

Holographic images of cave men, combined with moving mannequins, tell the story of the discovery of fire, the first writing of symbols on cave walls, the discovery and use of papyrus by the Egyptians, the creation of language by the Phoenicians, Greeks, and Romans. The Dark Ages demonstrate a decline in knowledge, technology, and communication among humanity. Then the visitor emerges into the Renaissance, the invention of the Gutenberg printing press, and moves quickly through early newspaper to radio and television — where video clips show old and new movies and TV shows.

The future is only brushed upon by a model of AT&T's national control center and a suggestion that computers, telecommunications, and television will converge.

Although visitors to Epcot experience this display by riding in a vehicle that carries them up and down the 17-story sphere, it is easy to be unaware of the reality of your circumstances. Total darkness, except for the lighted display, causes a feeling of traveling in a timeless, motionless space, where the events of the past parade before your senses.

Countless other experiences at Walt Disney World have the same effect. The simulations are so real and the vehicles used to travel through them are so simple and unobtrusive — except maybe the flying ship in "Peter Pan" — that you easily forget the reality and fall into the fantasy.

This ability to be submerged in a sensory experience can easily become an attribute of superhighway applications. Beyond movies, multimedia applications for creative learning, shopping, and communicating will be major breakthroughs in our use of technology and communications. Add the ability to interact with, change, and create new images within these applications, and the superhighway can become an even more powerful platform for our development.

Epcot offers a number of interactive worlds that allow visitors to sample different experiences. One of the most intriguing is "The Living Seas," a simulated undersea laboratory complete with a tank full of exotic creatures, including sharks, dolphins, and manta rays.

Visitors enter the display by taking a ride on cars that give the impression that they are entering a space within the tank. They then take an elevator down into the lab. This elevator doesn't actually travel, but the illusion is quite real. During this trip, the captain welcomes visitors, and crewmembers can be heard conversing about the business of the lab.

Unmanned exploration vehicles inside the tank and huge coral mountains and hills give the impression that the "sea" outside the lab is broad and deep. It has a dimension and reality that feels much larger than a fish tank.

Multimedia displays, videos, and models of lab gear — like diving suits and the talking Jason undersea robot — as well as markings of the different levels of the lab complete the illusion. Visitors take the elevator again to exit and emerge on a different side of the park.

Similar experiences are available through visits to the "countries" of Epcot. Eleven nations are represented, complete with native performers who speak the language and wear appropriate attire. Visitors can immerse themselves in virtual representations of England, France, Germany, Norway, Morocco, Mexico, China, and Japan.

England is a Tudor-style village with street performers and shops. France features a fountain, salon theatre showing panoramic views of the countryside, the Palace of Versailles, Notre Dame, and the Riviera. A French restaurant serving escargot and other delicacies completes the fantasy.

> *Multimedia applications for creative learning, shopping, and communicating will be major breakthroughs in our use of technology.*

Morocco's street musicians and native dancers call visitors to shops selling oriental carpets, silver, gold, brass plates, and other treasures. A waterwheel irrigation system feeds a well connecting the display to Epcot's central lagoon.

The Mexican and Norwegian venues include trips that bring visitors through the mythology, ancestry, and virtues of the cultures, connecting the past with the present. Toltec images and temple scenes are linked with celebrations of modern Mexico. A distant volcano spews smoke and lava, while an enormous altar raised to the gods is prepared for a sacrifice. These are followed by fireworks celebrating current culture with children playing during a festival.

Viking exploration and courage is tied to the images of today's Norway. A scary troll ride is followed by images of Viking voyages and struggles against the sea overlaid with modern fishing and drilling rigs battling the same elements.

The key to all of these experiences is multimedia. Each exhibit focuses your attention on videos and dioramas of the display, helping you absorb the messages with all your senses, rather than simply using one or two of them.

All these exhibits bring visitors into and through real images and cultures that either once existed or still do exist. These images are available at Epcot and Universal Studios through a significant investment of time and energy, and they are offered at a premium. The information superhighway will allow these images and cultures to be transported over a worldwide network, giving users a similar level of complete access and experience.

Disney World's Magic Kingdom and MGM Studios are filled with another kind of image, too — the fantasies created by animators. Few places have the ability to touch childhood memories the way Disney's stories and characters can. A trip to Magic Kingdom and MGM is a trip into a child's mind — everything from the honor and wonder of children in "It's a Small World," to the parade of characters, and stage performances of movie scenes; these are all examples of the way a young mind encounters the world.

The same techniques of immersion in fantasy make the characters, scenes, and situations seem real. Fed by the reality of Disney that many of us have grown up with, the displays tap a powerful legacy that we access as part of the total experience.

These fantasies, too, could be available through the information superhighway in multimedia applications that offer up Disney-on-Demand, complete with the power to deeply experience the fantasy world.

Although they are both in Orlando, many miles and different views of technology separate Time Warner Cable and Disney World. To Time Warner Cable, the access system and network are the central elements. To Disney, content is everything.

Let's imagine our own virtual experience for a moment. Suppose the images, content, and technology of Disney World were available on the Time Warner super-highway system. For good measure, let's imagine that the superhighway is connected to an Internet-like worldwide information system. What would a typical suburban family's experience be like in such circumstances?

7 a.m.: The kids, Tommy and Anne, wake up because it's Saturday morning and they are allowed access to the information superhighway console at 7, until their parents call them down for breakfast. Anne uses her remote control to select an animated version of *Cinderella*. She then switches on the system's touch-screen and stops the video in mid-motion. By selecting different touch-screen menu options, she begins to create her own animation, where Cinderella starts off living in the castle with the Prince and then proceeds to travel the world seeking adventures, encountering fantasy charac-ters of Anne's own creation.

Tommy goes on an African Safari. Using a console in his room, he uses the remote to select live videos of a trip down the Nile. The screen shows the view from the a boat's bow and pans the riverbank where zebras, ante-lope, and gazelles are feeding. Suddenly, Tommy spots a movement and uses the touch-screen to zoom in on the high grass behind the animals. A lion is crouching low, getting ready to pounce.

10 a.m.: Mom and Dad are awake and send a flurry of communication using their voice-activated consoles. Mom contacts the shopping network to see what today's bargains are, then sends a message to her friend telling her about a special sale. Dad checks the restaurant and entertainment catalogue to see what looks good for that evening. He then makes reservations, after receiving messages from the neighbors that they'll join them. Payment is automatic through a bank authorization code Dad reads into the console.

11 a.m.: The family switches gears to educational and cultural pursuits. Once a month they have a live video conversation with a "sister family" in another part of the world. The families and countries change every six months, although many still keep in touch. This session is with a French family outside Paris. Last month, it was an Indian family near Bombay. Dad activates the family's main multimedia console in the living room and the images of Henri, Claudette, and their children, Jacques and Estelle, appear on the screen. Though both families are working on each other's languages, they are far from fluent and rely on the translation system on the network to make complex statements that the other family can understand.

The families talk about what life is like in their own cultures and discuss common problems, such as how to manage the multiple demands of family activities and household organization. The children talk about what they're learning in school. The exchange is part of the school's cultural education program and they get credit for reporting on what they learn from the sessions.

Noon: The family talks about their activities of the morning and makes plans for the balance of the day. After a quick lunch with the family, Mom accesses the financial network to check on the family's investments and to move money between accounts to take advantage of interest-rate and stock-value changes. Using the food service network, Dad examines menus for the week's meals and selects the ones that are most appealing. He then automatically places an order for all the ingredients that will be needed and authorizes payment upon delivery from the grocery store.

Tommy and Anne do their karate and dance exercises by tuning into lessons on the regional network for sports and artistic expression. Through voice-response feedback, the participants respond to the instructor's questions or ask questions of their own. They can also activate the video camera to send an image of their movements to the instructor's view screen.

2 p.m.: Concerned about persistent shoulder pain, Dad accesses the health network and studies text and video images of shoulder-related problems. Not satisfied, he commands the system to connect with the on-line 24-hour clinic, where he has a conversation with an on-call physician who prescribes medication that is instantly ordered at the pharmacy. The bell rings and the grocery order arrives. Dad asks for help to carry in the goods. A short time later, the pharmacy order is also delivered to the door.

While the kids help Dad, Mom relaxes in the family's jacuzzi which is surrounded by a video screen showing a calm forest with green leafy trees and soft breezes. She changes her mind and switches to a flowered garden sanctuary. This still isn't right. So she accesses the relaxation network one more time for a gentle beach scene, where the waves can be heard as they brush against the sand.

4 p.m.: Mom and Dad get ready for a night out, while the kids plan their interactive video game. They are part of a neighborhood team exploring a wilderness on the game network. So far, no one in their area has found the hidden Aztec treasure buried among the ruins of a temple in the South American jungle. The role of team leader rotates each week so each participant gets a chance to lead the party to success or disaster. It's Anne's turn tonight and Tommy gives her his best advice even though two weeks ago he took a wrong turn and had the team trapped in quicksand for the first hour of the evening.

6 p.m.: The sitter arrives. Mom and Dad head out and the kids' game begins.

8 p.m.: Jean, the sitter, makes sure the kids end the game and accesses a calming tour of the wonders of the

world for Tommy and Anne. The children fall asleep after the description and panoramic views of the Sphinx and before the introduction to the hanging gardens of Babylon.

11 p.m.: Mom and Dad return and check a detailed weather report customized for their outing to the mountains in the morning. The forecast looks favorable, so they set the console alarm to wake them at 7 a.m. and turn in.

This may someday be what interactive, multimedia applications will be like on the information superhighway. In fact, these applications may only be a small portion of what will be available. Experts predict that initial infotainment applications will become available for interactive TV programming very gradually, beginning next year. Within two years, we are expected to be past the experimental stage. Within five to seven years such programs will be common.

Whether the applications are stand-alone, or single network applications of international systems that allow video connections and touch-screen control, depends on the advancement and merging of parallel technologies. Interactive TV itself can advance as cable firms like Time Warner build the networks and set up the receiver systems. In other words, TV technologies with local cable networks can and will start the ball rolling.

But advancements in computer technology that make touch-screen and video-camera systems affordable, compatible, and available to the average consumer must also take place. Certainly, these technologies are available today in laboratories and certain high-end markets. But when they will be a reality for everyone is impossible to predict. In short, a time will come (and quickly) when computer consoles will make better access devices than televisions; however, no one can predict when they will be priced attractively enough and available widely enough to make them a sensible alternative for the everyday consumer.

Likewise, the networks themselves must advance. As companies lay more and more fiber-optic lines, will they inevitably connect with each other like the Internet

Experts predict that initial infotainment applications will become available for interactive TV programming very gradually, beginning next year. Within two years, we are expected to be past the experimental stage. Within five to seven years such programs will be common.

networks do today? Probably. But when it will make sense to do that depends on the business climate.

Trials in underway by GTE in Cerritos (CA) and Newton (MA); by GTE and AT&T in Manassas (VA); by Microsoft and TCI in Seattle (WA); by Pacific Telesis in Milpitas (CA); by Viacom and AT&T in Castro (CA); by U S WEST in Omaha (NE); and by Time Warner in Orlando (FL). These trials will be the proving grounds that will shape the future of interactive television. Consumers who live in these test areas should not take these experiments lightly. You are the pioneers — the first test drivers on the information superhighway.

You can expect to see programs from AT&T, such as "Clickity Corners," a spelling game for children based on interaction with screen images, and "Power Brain," a trivia game that has different users on the network challenging each other's ability to answer questions.

A current television program that already experiments with interactive capabilities is "21st Century Vaudeville," which is broadcast in Boston by WMFP, Channel 62. Developed by a company called Telemorphix, the show consists of five-minute segments in which people who call in perform improvised skits by taking on the role of animated characters.

The characters can be selected from the show's database or created by the callers, who send in pictures or describe the character to the show's computer animation artist. The animated characters, with voices provided by the callers, interact with the show's computer-generated host, M. Jack Steckel.

While early interactive applications may seem less useful than what they could be, it will be important to remember the history of communications as we take our first steps onto the information superhighway. Cave drawings seem like a child's fingerpainting to us, but to the cave dwellers they were far superior to verbal tales of the hunt dependent on an individual's memory.

The image of monks creating manuscripts by hand to produce copies of documents or the use of stone tablets or papyrus to record information seem unimaginable to us today. How could these primitive forms of communications really help advance a culture and communicate ideas?

Morse code and early silent pictures also seem strange leftovers of another age, but at one time they were society's cutting-edge technology. With less than a century of electronic communication behind us, the least we can do is have patience with our baby steps into the future.

The *Dream* *Makers*

The Clinton Administration's
information superhighway agenda
is two parts promotion and one
part deregulation. The government
sees the superhighway as a tool
that the country can use to remain
competitive worldwide economically,
technologically, and educationally.
It also sees the superhighway as a
vehicle that will enable and
encourage proactive approaches
to solving domestic problems such
as healthcare and public safety.

President Clinton and Vice President Gore have a vision of the information superhighway: no less than an essential tool to keep the United States competitive economically, educationally, and in health-care. Yet the early government-sponsored applications are mostly in the research arena. Take the case of Terry.

Terry, an oceanographer from Seattle, needs to know why, where, and how the salmon population is declining in the Northwestern U.S. Before the advent of a special system, called Earth Data, she could only obtain bits and pieces of information about a region from its local computer systems and by talking with fish-ermen. Her quest for concrete answers to the fish problem would have to take the form of a detective's investigation: trying to solve a mystery with very few clues. The effort would take several months, at least. But the fishermen and environmentalists need answers immediately so they can take appropriate action before the salmon population is further compromised.

But thanks to a federal information superhighway initiative called the National Information Infrastructure Testbed, Terry can use the Earth Data System (EDS). EDS is a multimedia application that gives users at nine locations throughout the country instant access to 20 years of environmental information, stored at major research installations around the world. This informa-tion bank includes satellite images of land, oceans, weather, and coastlines, river data, and information on water quality and fishing yields.

Using EDS, Terry collects the land and ocean images for the area she is concerned about by using a navigator called the EDS data browser. This browser retrieves the data transparently — Terry doesn't need to know what information came from which part of the network, or even from which locations throughout the world. She accesses coastline and river data in the same way, even if they're collected and stored at different institutions.

The result? Her first finding after studying the selected information is that certain streams show silt emerging from their mouths, causing the destruction of plant life. The changes in ocean temperature and fish levels match the activity observed in the stream mouths.

> ## The vision of the
>
> Administration for the superhighway is not centered around entertainment and recreational applica-tions, such as video-on-demand and home shopping services, or even one full of Internet news and on-line chat services. They see it as a way to maintain our com-petitive edge.

Using EDS' on-line collaboration services, Terry consults with an expert on data analysis at a distant location. Terry is quickly able to give the expert a full view of the data drawn from the system, even though the expert is only connected with her through the network. Terry and the expert together build a model of what the stream damage is doing to the surrounding environment and a forecast of how it will affect the fish population in the future. She passes this information on to the fishermen and environmentalists.

The information EDS relies on resides at The College of Ocean and Atmospheric Sciences, Oregon State University; The Department of Energy/Sandia National Laboratories, University of California at Berkeley; The Institute for the Study of Earth, Oceans and Space at the University of New Hampshire; and the Smithsonian Astrophysical Observatory.

AT&T and Sprint provide the long distance communication networks, Digital Equipment Corp., Hewlett-Packard, Network Systems Corp., Sun Microsystems, and SynOptics Communications provide the computer and local communications systems.

EDS is only the first application to be built by the National Information Infrastructure Testbed, a consortium of government, business, and universities. The Testbed's mission is to develop and test superhighway services for later deployment. A key feature of the application is that it relies on existing computer products, so new applications can be built using the same technology. The next Testbed application is planned for this year in the healthcare arena.

In another part of the country, BellSouth has partnered with the State of North Carolina to create the North Carolina Information Superhighway. Connecting 106 locations statewide, the superhighway includes applications like these:

Distance learning. Students anywhere in the state can participate in classes located in major research or population centers. For example, students in Lincolnton, a little town in the foothills of the Blue Ridge Mountains (in the western part of the state), are taking an Oceanography course offered out of Wilmington, on the eastern coastline. In another example, students at different Charlotte high schools are learning Japanese together from an instructor at the University of North Carolina, hundreds of miles away in Chapel Hill.

Students from both rural and urban North Carolina locations are also taking *video field trips*, where they use the network to meet and interact with distant sites of interest. In one such trip, Wilmington students took a video tour of the New Hanover Regional Medical Center.

Research. North Carolina boasts the Microelectronics Center of North Carolina (MCNC). This research facility, aimed at developing new technology, is also on the superhighway and its Cray supercomputer is available to the state's school system.

Healthcare. In healthcare applications, patients at a Roanoke geriatric facility will be able to visit with geriatric care specialists nearly 100 miles away at the University of North Carolina Hospitals in Chapel Hill for remote examination and diagnosis. For many of these elderly and fragile patients, this will bring state-of-the-art medical attention without the discomfort and danger of a long ambulance ride.

Plans are also in place to make patients' medical records available to healthcare professionals over the network to save time.

Public Safety and Government. Government applications include tracking diseases as they break out across the state to better link them to environmental causes. State agencies can share information electronically and hold meetings through videoconferences to cut down on travel.

Public safety applications may eventually include video arraignments to save the time and cost of transporting prisoners. Law enforcement officers will have better access to records databases containing warrant information. Prison inmates will also receive medical treatment over the network and be able to participate in remote classes.

In all, the North Carolina Information Superhighway includes 52 secondary schools, 24 universities and colleges, 11 medical facilities, 4 state government agencies, 3 public safety institutions (including the state prison), and the research facilities at the Microelectronics Center and Research Triangle Park.

The $69-million project includes 116,000 miles of fiber-optic networks and key network switches from Bell-South, Carolina Telephone, and GTE. It uses a new technology called ATM (asynchronous transfer mode), which allows the simultaneous transmission of voice, data, video, and images. BellSouth plans to extend the superhighway into the eight other southeastern states it serves.

The Testbed's Earth Data System is meant to solve complex problems through information access and collaboration; the North Carolina Superhighway has its mix of distance learning, telemedicine, and remote government services. Both are good examples of what President Bill Clinton, Vice President Al Gore, and Commerce Secretary Ron Brown are talking about when they describe the Administration's desire to make the dream of the information superhighway a reality.

Theirs is not a highway centered on entertainment and recreational applications, such as video-on-demand and home shopping services, or even one full of Internet news and on-line service chat lines.

"If we do not move decisively to ensure that America has the information infrastructure we need, every business and consumer in America will suffer," Vice President Gore told technology managers attending a February 1994 Government Technology Conference. "Systems of regulation that made sense when telephones were one thing and cable another may just limit competition in a world in which all information can flow interchangeably over the same conduits. To understand what new systems we must create, though, we must first understand how the information marketplace of the future will operate."

Gore describes the key players in the new information marketplace as follows:

Owners of the highways. Those who will build the superhighway. "Unlike the interstates, the information highways will be built, paid for, and funded by the private sector," he said.

Makers of the information appliances. Like telephones, televisions, computers, and new products that will combine all three.

Information providers. Local broadcasters, digital libraries, information service providers, and millions of individuals who will have information they want to share and sell.

Information customers. Everyone who wants access. According to Gore and others, they should have it along with privacy, affordability, and choice.

Gore goes on to say,

> At some point in the next decades we'll think about the information marketplace in terms of these four components. We won't talk about cable or telephones or cellular or wireless because there will be free and open competition between everyone who provides and delivers information.

The long-term vision, then, is of a totally open market where consumers can buy information services from whomever they please and be able to receive them on affordable, accessible, secure systems.

Getting to that stage is the hard part, Gore said.

> It is during the transition period that the most complexity exists and that government involvement is the most important. It's a phase change — like moving from ice to water; ice is simple and water is simple, but in the middle of the change it's mush — part monopoly, part franchise, part open competition. We want to manage that transition.

> And so I am announcing today that the Administration will support removal — over time, under appropriate conditions — of judicial and legislative restrictions on all types of telecommunications companies: cable, telephone, utilities, television, and satellite.

According to Gore, this deregulation is based on five principles:

> *The long-term vision is of an open market where consumers buy information services from whomever they please and are able to receive them on affordable, accessible, secure systems.*

1. Encourage private investment.

2. Promote and protect competition.

3. Provide open access to the network.

4. Avoid creating a society of information haves and have nots by requiring universal access.

5. Encourage flexibility.

"The challenge is not, in the end, the new technology. It is holding true to our basic principles. Whether our tools were the quill pens of the Declaration of Independence or the laptop computers being used to write the constitutions of newly freed countries . . . better communication has almost always led to greater freedom and greater economic growth," says Gore.

In March 1994, Gore extended this vision to include a worldwide information superhighway or "Global Information Infrastructure." He traveled to Buenos Aires, where he spoke these words to the International Telecommunications Union:

> In this decade, at this conference, we now have at hand the technological breakthroughs and economic means to bring all the communities of the world together. We now can at last create a planetary information network that transmits messages and images with the speed of light from the largest city to the smallest village on every continent.

> The President of the United States and I believe that an essential prerequisite to sustainable development , for all members of the human family, is the creation of this network of networks. To accomplish this purpose, legislators, regulators, and business people must do this: build and operate a Global Information Infrastructure. This GII will circle the globe with information superhighways on which we all can travel.

Gore's pronouncements have been closely followed by a number of government initiatives designed to get the ball rolling in private investment, deregulation, and detailed analysis to determine the most important steps to ensuring that the principles he listed are carried out.

Two significant arms of the Administration's efforts are the Information Infrastructure Task Force (IITF) and a 27-member Advisory Council. IITF is charged with describing and implementing the vision for the superhighway, which the Administration calls the National Information Infrastructure (NII). The task force includes high-level representatives of federal agencies that play a major role in developing information and telecommunications technologies and policies.

Chaired by Commerce Secretary Ron Brown, the IITF is working to make real the information superhighway's goals: private investment; universal access; technological innovation and new application development; seamless, interactive, user-driven operation; security and reliability; and protection for intellectual property rights.

While the main task force is responsible for developing policy statements and legislation on these issues, the Advisory Council is working on building a consensus of its members, which represent numerous industry segments, on the following questions:

1. How will today's technologies be affected by the information superhighway?
2. What national interest is being served by the information superhighway?
3. What are the private interests involved?
4. What are the public interests involved?
5. Where do the interests meet and how can they be accommodated?
6. What are the international implications?

The group has created three Mega-Projects around which to build consensus. The projects are: The Visions and Goals of the NII; Access to the NII; and Privacy, Security, and Intellectual Property.

Work began in April 1994 to address these projects, and an interim report is due in December. Those involved in tackling Mega-Project One include: Morton Bahr, President of the Communications Workers of America; Dr. George Heilmeier, CEO of Bellcore; Alex Mandl, CEO of AT&T's Communications Services Group; and John Sculley, former Chairman of Apple Computer.

This project is aimed at defining how real the Administration's vision is and whether it is achievable by the year 2000. To do this, the members are examining application areas such as education, healthcare, electronic commerce, and public safety.

While Administration officials and the Advisory Board take the high road and discuss the broad principles and potential applications of the information superhighway, the only direct action so far by government is a series of bills making their way through Congress.

These bills are concerned with the nitty-gritty issues of present regulations that fail to recognize changes in technology that allow a large number of different service providers — cable, phone, computer, and communications companies — to offer similar services wherever the consumer interest can be found. Limitations on competition prohibit phone companies from participating in certain businesses, control cable contracts, and safeguard outdated monopolies. So far, the legislative agenda to address these problems looks something like this:

In November 1993, Rep. Ed Markey, Chairman of the House Telecommunications and Finance Subcommittee, introduced HR 3636 which would drop restrictions on competition in the territories of local telephone companies, allowing long-distance carriers, entrepreneurs, and others to set up phone service to compete within the current monopoly areas of the Regional Bell Operating Companies (RBOCs).

In the same month, Rep. John Dingell proposed HR 3626, which would lift the antitrust restrictions imposed on AT&T and the RBOCs as part of the breakup of Ma Bell. The Administration has added its own proposals to this plan. In February 1994, Sen. Ernest Hollings introduced S 1822, the Senate version of these House bills.

In March of the same year, the House bills were considered in hearings with an eye to combining the Markey and Hollings plans. In the next phase, the Senate and House will attempt to work out the differences between their proposals so that one bill package can be considered by Congress. Before the year ends, President Clinton is expected to sign a final bill, allowing the broadest telecommunications reform in more than 60 years.

In January 1994, Larry Irving, Assistant Secretary for Communications and Information for the Department of Commerce, described for the House Committees why legislation reform is needed now and how it is relevant to the goals of the information superhighway.

> *"We cannot become a nation in which the new information age acts as a barrier, rather than a pathway, between Americans — a nation divided between the information rich and information poor," says Secretary Brown.*

First, in an increasingly competitive world trade environment — which will become even more open with the implementation of NAFTA and the GATT — we simply must ensure that our telecommunications capabilities remain the best in the world. Because information transmission increasingly is the lifeblood of all our industries, archaic rules that inappropriately retard innovation by telecommunications firms have a negative impact on the international competitiveness of the private sector in general by inhibiting industrial productivity and job creation. Legislation that lifts these outdated structures will enhance competitiveness and spur creation of good new jobs.

Second, the existing regulatory structure has been altered on an ad hoc basis over six decades to meet perceived problems of the moment. This has created an uneven playing field that artificially favors some competitors over others, and that in some instances unnecessarily discourages investment and risk-taking. These effects, in turn, inappropriately skew the growth of industry sectors and retard development of the NII itself.

Third, we need to be sure that our telecommunications policies are fully responsive to the needs of the American people as a whole, and in particular, poorer and disadvantaged Americans. As Secretary Brown stated, we cannot become a nation in which the new information age acts as a barrier, rather than a pathway, between Americans — a nation divided between the information rich and information poor. Yet, while the universal service provision of plain old telephone service has long been a national goal, the existing regulatory structure may not be sufficient to ensure that all Americans benefit from the broader range of information services that will become available under NII.

The Administration's solution to these problems follow the framework of Gore's five principles — private investment, competition, open access, universal service, and flexibility. This is the Administration's policy mantra for the information superhighway.

To encourage private investment, Irving told the Congressmen and Congresswomen, we must lift "the artificial regulatory boundaries that separate telecommunications and information industries and markets." Gore and Irving argue that distinctions are blurring, if not outright disappearing, between local and long-distance telephone companies, cable providers, and other transporters of information, as highlighted in this quote:

> Technology enables virtually all types of information to be represented and transmitted as bits — the ones and zeros of computer code. Thus, rules which artificially distinguish among different types of bit transmitters based on old historical understandings will no longer serve a socially useful purpose.

This desire to recognize this convergence of information transmissions caused the Administration to include a review of broadcast policies in its deregulation plans. It also means that the government supports competition in the *local loop* (the local connection between a telephone user's home and the RBOC's telecommunications switch). "Competing providers will have the opportunity to interconnect their networks to local telephone company facilities on reasonable, nondiscriminatory terms. Local telephone companies will also be required to unbundle their service offerings so that alternative providers can offer similar services," Irving said.

Irving also said that competition should lower prices, but in the event prices spike in the short term, the Federal Communications Commission (FCC) and state regulators may act to prevent *rate shock* from affecting any class or group of customers.

Cross-ownership of cable TV firms and telephone companies would be allowed by removing restrictions in the 1984 Cable Act. This ownership structure would allow phone companies to provide video services. But this is a double-edged sword: the phone companies cannot prohibit video providers from offering competing local telephone services, according to the Administration's proposal. The proposal also would prohibit phone companies from acquiring cable companies in their local exchange area for the next five years, to prevent quick mergers that would eliminate local competition.

Most of the legislative proposals advocate fostering private investment and competition through deregulation of the monopoly held by the RBOCs, and by easing the business limitations currently placed on them.

The Administration suggests that the FCC be assigned the task of developing rules to address open access to superhighway programming — allowing multiple companies to compete in offering services over the same network and systems. In this scenario, the FCC is also charged with developing new regulations for hybrid firms that are neither phone nor cable: the expected product of future mergers. In addition, the FCC would have the authority to not implement the regulations if the situation changes and they no longer serve the planned purpose. Likewise, the FCC and individual states are empowered to iron out the details of providing universal service.

For all the Administration's efforts, its information superhighway policy is troubled by contradictions. The goals of vast national and global networks accessible by everyone, providing highly sophisticated services, are lofty. But the cash to fund them is low.

More than $200 billion was spent on roads by the federal, state, and local governments from planning to construction. An equivalent amount will be required for the information superhighway.

To date, the Administration has budgeted $26 million for NII, with another $100 million requested in fiscal year 1995. The National Telecommunications and Information Administration is responsible for using this sum as part of a grant program to support information superhighway applications. The program is called the Telecommunications and Information Infrastructure Assistance Program (TIIAP). More than 7,000 requests for grants have already been submitted.

Realizing that deficit-reduction and other programs claim the bulk of federal resources, the Administration has made private investment its number one priority for the information superhighway. But this requirement poses a problem. It is problematical for the government to dictate the scope and requirements for the NII, even if they are in the national interest, when it is companies and individuals that will foot the bill for its development and implementation. The need to leave the field open to competitors and to provide service to all — no matter how expensive this may be — runs counter to the profit needs of the telephone, cable, and computer companies who will fund the highway.

The industry and some legislators are considering charging residents who can afford to pay them some fees for new connections to their homes (like switching from traditional analog phone lines to digital lines that can support multimedia), thus creating a subsidy fund for those who cannot pay. The subsidies would be administered by the companies, who would provide the service out of their revenue.

Industry executives are concerned, however, that such a subsidy program could get out of hand. "The government should say [to business] go into whatever market you want without creating any red tape or regulations," said U S WEST's Tom Pardun.

Despite the debate over regulations, or perhaps because of it, the telephone companies are going ahead with ambitious experiments like Sprint's and AT&T's involvement in Testbed applications, BellSouth's North Carolina Information Superhighway, U S WEST's trials with Time Warner, and Pacific Bell's initiatives in California. The jockeying for position has already begun in an as-yet-undefined competitive landscape.

One thing is clear: business conditions are very sensitive to government action around superhighway issues. Take the case of Bell Atlantic and TCI. The failed merger, blamed by some on a change in cable regulations (a seven-percent reduction in rates) by the FCC, caused a wave of caution regarding the superhighway to ripple through the industries involved.

For its part, the Administration continued to sound the clarion call despite this setback. In May 1994,

> *Despite the debate over regulations, or perhaps because of it, the telephone companies are going ahead with ambitious experiments. The jockeying for position has already begun in an as-yet-undefined competitive landscape.*

Assistant Secretary Larry Irving gave a speech before the Association of Local Telecommunications Services Conference. The talk was titled, "The Death of the National Information Infrastructure, or Don't Believe Everything You Read."

> I am here to tell you that media reports of the demise of the NII are greatly exaggerated. Perhaps the biggest telecommunications news story last year was the proposed merger between Bell Atlantic and Tele-Communications, Inc. (TCI). To many, the announcement of the deal was like distant thunder on a humid summer night, a signal that, after many years of waiting, the deluge — technological innovation and market convergence — was at last upon us. Cable and telephone companies alike scrambled to find partners with which to face an uncertain competitive future. People freely speculated as to which cable firms were natural allies of which telephone companies and vice versa.
>
> Then, early this year, the Bell Atlantic/TCI merger fell apart. Shortly thereafter, BellSouth terminated plans to acquire a substantial share of Cox Communications, a major media firm with extensive cable television holdings. In both cases, the so-called experts and in-house spin doctors cited an FCC decision requiring cable companies to reduce further their rates for basic cable service. The true story of the mergers' collapse was, of course, more complex. The firms involved faced a series of significant obstacles besides government regulation — accommodating different . . . personalities, melding two very different corporate cultures and, most importantly, negotiating a mutually agreeable sales price in a rapidly-changing market environment.
>
> In a speech at the National Association of Broadcasters' annual convention, the Chairman of Bell Atlantic acknowledged that differences over price killed the Bell Atlantic/TCI deal, not government regulation. Nevertheless, press accounts typically assigned most of the blame to the FCC. And that is, perhaps, not surprising. If respected newspapers like the *Wall Street Journal* continually parrot the companies' line, it does not take long for a somewhat self-serving story to become unvarnished truth.

One of the most intriguing aspects of this entire story is the role that infrastructure development has come to play in the policy debate. I am concerned that, to some, the phrase "it will promote (or hamper) deployment of an advanced telecommunications infrastructure" has become a "killer" argument, sufficient in and of itself to justify adopting one policy prescription, or rejecting another. Moreover, given the vehement reaction to government action that would allegedly hinder infrastructure development, I can envision members of a future House Un-American, Anti-Infrastructure Committee asking witnesses a modern version of an infamous question: Are you now or have you ever been responsible for delaying deployment of the NII?

The Administration, of course, strongly supports wide-spread availability of an advanced telecommunications and information infrastructure. However, as the Vice President and Secretary Brown have pointed out, the NII must be developed according to the public interest. I believe that the public interest will be best served if we remember that infrastructure is simply a means — a resource that can help U.S. businesses compete more effectively in the global marketplace and the American people live more productive, comfortable lives. Infrastructure development is not an end, to be pursued at all costs.

I am therefore concerned about the level of invective hurled in the aftermath of the FCC's cable rate decision. Putting aside the fact that the FCC is complying with a mandate from Congress, there was considerable evidence indicating that basic cable rates had increased to excessive levels since wide-scale rate deregulation in December 1986. In the view of many, those rates were no less excessive merely because cable systems devote a portion of the resulting profits to upgrading their networks. Put another way, it is questionable public policy to suggest that cable subscribers should be forced to subsidize construction of the NII. Indeed, it would be ironic if those consumers were sacrificed on the altar of an infrastructure that is supposed to make their lives better.

This is not to say that cable firms should not receive a reasonable return on their investments. Because they are entitled to no less, government regulations must not be confiscatory. More importantly, however, government agencies must provide the regulatory certainty that encourages regulated firms to make efficient investments of all kinds. The only point to be made here is that we should not be quick to condemn a regulatory framework — such as the FCC's cable rate order — merely because it may reduce the cash flow of regulated firms.

Even if we assume that government should promote aggressive investment in infrastructure development, however financed, it is not clear that major mergers (with a resulting increase in industry concentration) are necessary for such development. There is considerable reason to be concerned about alliances between the dominant providers of video to the home — cable operators — and their most prominent potential competitors in local markets. Congress apparently shares this concern because all pending telecommunications reform bills contain provisions limiting to a substantial degree mergers between cable and telephone companies.

Nor is it clear that collapse of the various cable/telephone company mergers will have a significant adverse effect on infrastructure development. Many of the new telecommunications facilities and services brought to market over the past three decades were not introduced by large firms, either individually or in combination with each other. For many years, MCI's growth was attributable to the vision and audacity of a single man — Bill McGowan. The revolution in customer premises equipment was fueled by the efforts of a host of individuals entrepreneurs and small businesses, from Tom Carter (of Carterfone fame) on.

The continuing revolution in computer hardware and software is being driven by a host of small- and medium-sized companies, such as Apple, Microsoft, and Sun Microsystems. The laws of physics dictate that as big bubbles get bigger, little bubbles burst. The exact opposite seems to be true in business, particularly the computer business. The fastest growing telecommunications network in history — the Internet — is a vibrant, decentralized amalgam of individuals, organizations, and institutions, each of which has considerable influence over the nature of the network and the services available over it.

The Administration believes that the best way to spur investment in the NII is to promote competition in all telecommunications and information markets. The long-distance market provides a powerful illustration of the potential benefits of competition in this area. Since the AT&T Consent Decree removed the final barrier to full long-distance competition in 1984, prices have fallen more than 50 percent, while services and service options have increased at a dizzying rate.

Competition's impact on infrastructure development has been equally profound. All major facilities-based long-distance companies now have laid fiber optic cable throughout much of the country; currently, there are no fewer than four nationwide, state-of-the-art transmission networks. This transformation has occurred much faster than anyone expected. In 1987, for example, AT&T projected that 95 percent of its long distance network would be digital by the year 2010. In fact, AT&T's network was virtually 100 percent digital by the end of 1991, after investments in excess of $6 billion were made in response to actions by MCI and Sprint.

Competition is having similar effects in local exchange service markets. In the growing number of states and cities where local competition is allowed, this group's members and others have prompted local telephone companies to reduce rates, improve customer service, and accelerate deployment of advanced network facilities. This trend will surely continue as more and more states open their markets to competition.

Make no mistake about it, competition and open entry will eventually become the norm, rather than the exception. The FCC has, of course, a long-standing commitment to facilitating competitive entry in interstate service markets. In recent months, it has taken action to expand competition in the provision of the local exchange access services subject to its jurisdiction.

Similar actions are being taken at the state level. Beginning with the New York Public Service Commission's landmark interconnection order in 1989, an increasing number of state commissions have opted for competition as a means for reducing rates and promoting network modernization. Less than a week ago, the Maryland

> *The Clinton Administration believes that the best way to spur investment in the NII is to promote competition in every information and telecommunications market.*

Public Service Commission authorized Metropolitan Fiber Systems (MFS) to provide a full range of local and long distance services within the state. MFS will receive its own blocks of numbers, thereby ending its subservience to Bell Atlantic for the customer "addresses" essential to communications. Perhaps more significantly, MFS will receive from Bell Atlantic some form of number portability, thus enabling subscribers to switch between the two carriers without incurring the inconvenience and potential cost of giving up their telephone numbers.

Although the pro-competitive activities in many states are encouraging, more can and should be done. That is why the Administration is committed to enacting telecommunications reform legislation in this session of Congress. The reform bills now pending in the House and Senate (HR 3636 and S 1822) would establish a national policy favoring competitive provision of local exchange services, most explicitly by generally preempting states from restricting entry into telecommunications service markets. The bills would also require all local exchange carriers to offer alternative providers nondiscriminatory access to a wide range of network facilities and functions, thereby lowering economic barriers to entry by competing providers. Finally, both bills require local exchange carriers to implement number portability as soon as technically feasible (and, on the House side, economically reasonable).

You can count on steadily increasing opportunities to compete with incumbent local telephone companies to provide a wide range of local services. Those opportunities will be accompanied by several obligations and challenges. Let me mention two. First, competing providers will be expected to contribute, on a competitively-neutral basis, to the preservation and advancement of universal service. If the NII is to be a tool for improving the lives of all Americans, all Americans must have access to the features and capabilities of the NII. Although the market rivalry among competing service providers will go a long way toward achieving universal service goals, some degree of subsidies will be inevitable. Alternative providers cannot fairly expect the right to compete for telephone company customers, unless they are prepared to assume some portion of the companies' universal service obligations.

Second, you must be prepared for the deregulation that must surely follow local competition. As local competition takes hold, local telephone companies will be able to make an increasingly compelling case for freedom from the regulatory strictures now imposed on them. As regulation is relaxed, the local companies will need to be able to respond more quickly and more aggressively to your market activities. That may not be a pleasant thought, but it is a fundamental feature of the competitive marketplace that you have worked hard to create. The regulators' task, to paraphrase Secretary Brown, is to ensure that the rules governing the transition from regulation to competition are fair to all market participants and, most importantly, to consumers.

What does this all mean? It means, among other things, that the world's most famous Canadian Mountie, Dudley Do-Right, was wrong when he said: "If it's in the newspaper, it must be true." Reports of the NII's demise are indeed greatly exaggerated. Pro-competitive policies will promote rapid, efficient infrastructure development. As a result, we need not pursue infrastructure development at any cost.

By choosing deregulation instead of direct funding to foster the creation of the superhighway, the Clinton Administration is tackling a legacy of mixed results in telecommunications rulemaking. It will take many small barrier-breaking steps to realize the Administration's vision through this route.

Telemedicine

The information superhighway will provide new healthcare services such as remote diagnosis and the "on-line doctor." These advances will challenge the traditional medical model. However, they will also lead to a more efficient healthcare system — one that provides better care for a larger percentage of the population, and at far less cost.

D octors and patients alike are often annoyed by aspects of the everyday healthcare experience. Doctors are increasingly pressured to increase the number of patients they see each day, leaving patients irritated at not receiving enough time with their doctor. The result is long lead-times for appointments, long waits in the office before being seen, and a general feeling of dissatisfaction for both doctor and patient.

One factor that contributes to the time deficit is patient information (or the lack of it). Today, doctors cannot easily access information about their patients; most is stored in handwritten paper archives. So doctors (or their office assistants or nurses) must not only find the paper files, they must also decipher the handwriting of whomever attended the patient in the past. Gaps must be filled in by the patient's verbal account and memory of previous office visits. If they have seen a specialist for a condition, that specialist will often not be available quickly for a consultation on the results of the visit, and the records kept by the specialist are not usually available to the primary-care physician. All of this results in doctors treating patients without proper information, or in someone spending time to find and reconstruct the patient's records.

Payment for healthcare service is another set of problems altogether. Insurance companies and doctors' offices devote countless hours identifying exactly what service was delivered and determining who should pay how much for it. Patients often experience delays in treatment or receive bills that cause undue anxiety, when their insurance will actually cover the service.

Hospitals are overloaded with emergency room patients and have trouble funding the costly long-term care of those needing extensive attention but lacking extensive resources.

Clearly, this is a system in need of reform. Fortunately, help is on the way. The Clinton Administration is aggressively pushing healthcare reform on two fronts — through legislation in Congress aimed at reforming how services are offered and funded, and through advocating healthcare applications as a key component of the information superhighway.

The medical profession can use the super-highway to strengthen traditional ways of doing things by simply automating current procedures, or they can break new ground and create better, more efficient systems.

President Clinton and Vice President Gore frequently cite hospitals and clinics as part of the list of essential facilities that must (along with schools and libraries) be included, when they challenge communications companies to develop the highway's high-speed networks. In addition, a number of companies and research facilities are testing healthcare applications that will benefit patients and providers through the use of interactive multimedia networked systems.

Like the use of computers in other areas, however, information superhighway applications in medicine can go in one of two directions. They can be used to strengthen traditional ways of doing things by simply automating current procedures and tasks, or they can break through old barriers to create new and better ways of accomplishing goals.

Fortunately, the planning of the superhighway is occurring at a time when healthcare is widely perceived to be in a state of transition. There is broad agreement that the old way of doing things is no longer satisfactory. This circumstance increases the likelihood that superhighway applications will be used to pave a new path, rather than to bolster traditional, poorly designed systems.

Prior to the mid-1980s, the healthcare industry suffered from a limited perspective of how to manage treatment for patients. The system was based solely on what services the patient required. The more services needed, the higher the cost of treatment, and the greater the payback for participating medical professionals and institutions. This led to a focus on performing tests, treatments, and therapies at ever-increasing costs with little regard for the overall health and satisfaction of the patient. There was no sense of value for services rendered.

This began changing in the 1980s when companies providing medical benefits wanted to control rising healthcare costs. Simultaneously, health maintenance organizations (HMOs) came into prominence as lower cost providers of medical coverage. In addition, the federal Medicare system instituted diagnosis-related groups (DRGs) that specified preset fees for various medical treatments and hospital admissions.

These efforts to control costs helped somewhat, but they have not solved the healthcare problem. Government healthcare legislation is trying to address the cost spiral, while also making sure that everyone has equal access to medical treatment.

While Democrats and Republicans argue over who will pay for universal service and the cost of healthcare reform, the healthcare community is slowly moving along a path for patient treatment that will be greatly enhanced by the development of the superhighway.

This path involves focusing treatment around the patient as a whole person. The diagnosis, treatment, and recuperation for medical problems will be based on the person's total needs — his or her emotional and environmental well-being as well as the immediate health problems.

The key to this new form of treatment will be information. Doctors will need all the information they can get about their patient's past, present, and future physical and emotional states, as well as background about the environment he or she is in. They will also need quick, reliable access to the records and diagnoses of other medical providers and specialists who worked directly with the patient, or who could lend useful information based on similar cases.

It is true that these information resources are available now through old techniques and technology. Paper files, stand-alone computer systems, telephones, and x-rays provide a great deal of information. It would theoretically be possible to construct the complete patient profile and related information using these techniques. But it is difficult to imagine a physician seeing a parade of patients at 15-minute intervals on a daily basis having time to collect the appropriate material. It is also hard to imagine the support staff accomplishing this task, when they are equally concerned with scheduling and processing the appropriate payment and insurance forms.

Networked computer systems could accomplish the task easily, bringing together the required information extremely fast. Not only could the physician then access information from a number of different areas — hospital records, clinical databases, and demographic profiles, but also the information recorded about the patient a week, a year, or five years ago would be accurate and available, thus allowing continuity of care rather than an isolated reaction to the presenting problem.

It will take years to completely change the record-keeping and cultural nature of the current healthcare system, but many facilities are already experimenting with systems that will support advanced access to medical information.

In an article in MIT's *Technology Review* magazine, Jerome Grossman, CEO of Boston's New England Medical Center, discussed two examples of how physicians at the teaching hospital are using decision support systems. One, the Acute Cardiac Ischemia Time-Sensitive Predictive Instrument (ACI-TIPI) provides doctors with fast answers to determine whether a patient is experiencing a heart attack. This computer-based system allows the physician to enter information about the patient such as age, gender, and level of chest discomfort, and allows an electrocardiogram (EKG) to be generated.

The program analyzes the information and computes the probability that the patient is suffering from a heart attack. The system works in minutes, compared to the hours a traditional blood test requires. This works in two ways to benefit hospitals and patients. First of all, about 20,000 heart-attack victims each year are sent home without treatment due to misdiagnosis. And, each year, only about half of the 1.5 million patients admitted to coronary care units are actually experiencing a heart attack. These unnecessary admissions cost our healthcare system over $3 billion a year.

"A two-year study of an ACI-TIPI prototype found that its use reduced unnecessary coronary care admissions by 30 percent," Grossman states "Projected to every U.S. hospital, that figure would translate into 250,000 fewer admissions each year, as well as savings of perhaps $1 billion in unnecessary healthcare costs. The latest version of ACI-TIPI, which is easier to use than the prototype, is now undergoing clinical trials on some 15,000 patients at 10 hospitals around the country."

> *It will take years to completely change the record-keeping and cultural nature of the current healthcare system, but many facilities are already experimenting with systems that will support access to medical information.*

A second set of systems use artificial intelligence with the help of MIT's Laboratory of Computer Science. Like early medical programs that analyzed simple variables based on a system of rules developed with a medical expert, these systems quantify the risks and benefits for the medical and financial consequences of treatment decisions. Using decision trees, the systems provide doctors with a wholistic view of the possible ramifications of their decisions. These systems forecast the consequence of surgery and drug treatments and are being enhanced to include individual patient preferences.

Both of these applications give the physician much-needed information at critical points in treatment. But they are far less powerful than those that will be achieved using the combination of sophisticated computer programs and networks. Expert systems will be able to use a single patient identifier, such as a name or code number, to search the physician's office network, related hospital systems, and the databases of other doctors or specialists to create a customized profile of a patient in a matter of minutes.

Physicians could consult this profile before treatment and add their own observations and treatment recommendations. In this way, patients' histories are recorded, updated, and available at their request or at the request of those they authorize to access their data.

Many of us have had the experience of being in the hospital. Chances are good that you will change departments at some point in your hospitalization. And, along with the change, you suddenly find yourself having to re-explain all of your situation, your preferences, and your needs to a new set of hospital personnel. Using the network model, the various departments in a hospital will be able to share patient records so that they are all working with the same information as a patient passes through their departments. This will give both the hospital and the patient a universal view of their relationship.

This type of information will also help hospital administrators assess the effectiveness of various services and the way they are delivered to the patient population. They'll be able to look at patient groupings to assess differences in efficiency, cost, or quality of care. They can choose to look at the same hospital population, segmented in a variety of ways — by gender, race, age, illness, length of stay, and so on. They may find that there are unnecessary procedures for certain patient groups, or that others are missing some services the hospital could provide. Overall, the data would give the hospital administration a real-time sense of the hospital's strengths and weaknesses, and of the nature and volume of patients passing through each department.

This same information could be used by consumers, regulators, and physicians to gauge which hospitals to go to for specific types of procedures, to judge where patients should be sent, and to monitor adherence with government requirements. It's not that such information doesn't exist today. The problem is in gathering it quickly and providing broad, real-time access to it.

Grossman also cited an early version of such systems called HELP (health evaluation through logical processing), which was developed at Salt Lake City's Latter Day Saints Hospital. The system automates the dispensing of antibiotics by the staff. It provides reminders to give antibiotics before surgery and issues orders to stop the antibiotics when the therapy period is over, notifying the physician and the pharmacist. The system can also provide decision support to help the physician select the right antibiotic and can recommend cost-saving alternatives.

HELP has selected the right antibiotic 94 percent of the time — a better success rate than that of the average physician.

Moving beyond a single networked hospital, we encounter the more powerful links that medical facilities can have with each other — around the country or around the world. National and international organizations of physicians and administrators do exist today, but they cannot begin to approach the level of real-time communication of everyday issues that is possible when facilities throughout the world are linked.

All facilities — not just those with advanced research facilities or those with the most high-powered specialists on staff — will have access to the best treatment methods, hospital management techniques, and cost-saving policies. The superhighway can act as an equalizer for facilities in remote locations.

Additionally, this type of system will allow a person to gain instant access to their medical records anywhere in the world that they might need treatment — an important benefit with today's increasingly mobile patient populations. This will help the patient receive appropriate treatment, in the context of any chronic conditions that might be present, even if they have never before been seen by that doctor or medical facility. This will also help to quickly assess the spread and exposure of populations to disease.

Networks are also having an effect on equipment purchasing. Until recently, hospital equipment was acquired through single providers of proprietary information networks. In the future, a cooperative network of equipment suppliers will offer their supplies jointly on a common system, allowing hospital administrators to select whatever brand is desired using a single system. Known as OnCall EDI, the system is expected to reduce ordering costs and keep prices up-to-date for all suppliers' products.

Among the most powerful medical uses of the information superhighway will be interactive video applications. These multimedia systems will usher in the age of telemedicine. Consultations among doctors, lectures on medical knowledge, even patient exams or self-diagnoses will be facilitated by networks that allow all these interactions to happen no matter where the doctors, students, or patients are located.

Sophisticated equipment and expertise will no longer be the province of certain facilities, localities, or systems. They will be accessible to all kinds of network users with an interest in healthcare. Group consultations among physicians scattered across the country or around the world will also be possible.

One of the first telemedicine trials is BellSouth's and the State of North Carolina's Information Network. This system, part of the state's superhighway initiative, allows rural hospitals to tap experts at research facilities. This instant communication of data, video images, and conversation allows patients to be treated close to where they live, avoiding sometimes-hazardous travel to a more sophisticated facility.

In another example, First Lady Hillary Rodham Clinton, who is championing the administration's healthcare initiatives, viewed a demonstration of telemedicine at Syracuse University in New York. The application allowed doctors separated by 50 miles to simultaneously view and discuss an ultrasound image of a child's heart.

Bell Atlantic Corp. and Oracle Corp. are teaming up with Kaiser Permanente Health Plan, Inc., a health maintenance organization in Maryland, to provide multimedia services to examining rooms and patient homes. Michigan State University's Center for Applied Medical Informatics uses a network that allows physicians and residents to share patient data from locations in six regions around the state. Videoconferencing is the key to this application.

At the University of Minnesota, videoconferencing over a high-speed network lets students participate in medical lectures without leaving their facilities. This reduces travel time and allows a single expert to provide consistent information to a regionally dispersed group of students.

> *The next breakthrough in telemedicine will be patients' access to physicians and medical information from their homes.*

The next breakthrough in telemedicine will be access to medical information and physicians in the home. With the superhighway allowing a direct path from the hospital, research facility, or doctor's office into individual homes, there are many opportunities for electronic "house calls" or self-diagnosis with the help of medical knowledge.

This trend was anticipated by J.C.R. Licklider, a computer science and engineering professor at MIT. He also served as director of the Advanced Research Projects Agency of the Department of Defense in the 1960s. In a 1979 essay on *Computers and Government*, Licklider identified the use of computer networks to establish continually updated individual medical histories that would be available to a doctor's office. Records of this kind for the whole population would help public safety experts respond to trends in diseases, as well. Licklider wrote:

> If and when every residence and every doctor's office are "on the net" and there is a microcomputer in every bathroom scale, it will be possible for an individual to build up a much more detailed medical record than is feasible at present. It will include daily values for each variable that can be measured as part of the morning routine, monthly values for each variable that can be measured automatically in the doctor's office, as well as yearly values for each variable that requires the doctor's personal attention. If, in addition, effective computer system and network security has been developed, sophisticated programs will be continually examining and analyzing the medical records of the entire population, discovering which patterns of values predict which kinds of troubles and detecting epidemics before they affect large numbers of people.
>
> If the progressive "denaturalization" of our way of life continues, the threat of additives in the diet, exposure to synthetic chemicals, and so on could conceivably make it necessary to augment individual medical records to include an item for almost every ingestion of or contact with food, drink, drugs, textiles, and living creatures. That would require identifying and keeping track of every package bought in the supermarket and every menu item in restaurants, as well as complete appointment schedules, attendance lists, and so on — a mind-boggling prospect. It is to be hoped the future of pollution, contagion, allergy, and terrorism will not force us to any such science-fictional extreme, but it is by no means certain that we are not well along the way to it already. If we have to adopt such a system, the government will surely play a role in creating it and perhaps also operating it.

While the tracking of all our consumption and contact might be far-fetched, the ability to communicate directly with the doctor's office to view and update our own medical records and to allow our conditions to be monitored remotely are very appropriate and likely information superhighway applications.

Perhaps the members of society who will take the most advantage of this instant access to medical information and exchange in the home will be the elderly, disabled, or immobile. Licklider again foresaw this circumstance:

In the near future it will be possible to equip a hearing aid with a digital processor that can transform sounds in ways not feasible with analog circuits, to customize the processor for a particular ear, and to optimize it dynamically for various listening situations. Reading machines for the blind are already in a fairly advanced stage of development, and the next decade could see them become affordable enough for wide use. Microcomputers may open the way to a whole new technology of prosthesis for manipulation and locomotion.

Another area that is obviously ripe for development is the monitoring of patients. Computerized devices are already in limited use for monitoring indicators like heart rate, but they could be applied to almost any significant condition. Automated monitoring also promises to be useful for baby-sitting and looking in on elderly people who can care for themselves except in emergencies. The monitoring computers might be sensitive to sounds caused by breathing or other movements, to speech, to the adjustment of light switches and faucets, and the prearranged "I am OK" signals — which the computers might prompt whenever they suspect trouble, at which time they would communicate with sources of help: relatives, friends, neighbors, special quick-response centers, or local police. With the aid of a network, the arrangements for calling for help could be quite sophisticated, the monitored situation could be checked out before anyone rushed to the scene of the alarm, and in many instances the whole problem could be taken care of remotely. Indeed, there is no real need to wait for a network before developing this notion, for quite a lot could be done with a telephone dialer, an intrinsically simple device though rather an expensive one in the absence of a mass market.

Suitably organized, networking will give immobilized people a chance to participate actively in on-line meetings, projects, and competitions, to avail themselves of essentially unlimited education and training, and to work — to be employed. For some, special consoles and special ways of interacting with computers will have to be devised, but for many immobilized people only a standard console and a network connection will be needed. Indeed, even present networks like the ARPANET (a government network set up by the Defense Advanced Research Projects Agency of the Department of the Defense) or Telenet could do great things for paraplegics in the Veterans Administration hospitals: teleconferences, tele-games, message services, learning to program and help-ing others learn — an "on-line" community in the best sense of that term.

Some of these notions, and others that they may suggest, may be developed even without governmental stimulation and support, but it seems unlikely that anything like their full potential will be realized in the absence of govern-ment involvement.

Other uses of healthcare applications in the home include instructional programs with interactive videos showing the proper way to administer medication.

Grossman described a 1991 project in which the New England Medical Center and IBM conducted joint research to develop interactive home-based support for the care of children with leukemia. Designed as a user friendly educational resource, the system provides clini-cians with progress reports directly from the patient.

Videos are included to provide instruction on changing bandages or catheters. There are also discus-sions by other families and caregivers on the clinical and emotional aspects of the illness.

Ease of use is provided by touch screens and directo-ries of stored information on symptoms, care, and emo-tional, and family issues. Future services may include a network linking patients with similar conditions, a hos-pital-based bulletin board for news, and full-motion video transmissions between doctors and patients.

The benefits of the program include giving the family of the patient information to allow them to participate directly in the patient's care. It reduces the number of trips to the hospital to check on the patient or give out information (which can be especially traumatic for

children). It allows for a feedback loop in which the staff
is better informed of the patient's condition and compli-
ance with treatment.

In addition, the close contact between the staff,
patient, and family helps alleviate emotional concerns
about how treatment is proceeding. Grossman states:

> And contrary to what one might expect, the technology
> actually humanizes care by addressing the emotional
> needs of the patient and family, and by easing the fami-
> ly's anxieties about tending to their ill member.

> The link between the homecare patient and the caregiver
> will soon become even stronger: schemes now under
> development for providing patients with instruments con-
> nected to a home computer that is in turn linked to an
> information network. If the patient needs regular electro-
> cardiograms, a mobile machine at home would transmit
> the readings in real time to the EKG lab and the physi-
> cian's office. A patient whose blood pressure must be
> monitored could insert one arm into a cuff attached to a
> computer, which would immediately read results in the
> medical record and flag any exceptional readings for the
> physician's urgent attention. Technologies like these will
> be a major step toward establishing the continuity of care
> that eluded the medical profession for so long.

These technologies will not be put in place without
some cultural changes and investments. "For many
hospitals and physician practices, sophisticated information and networking systems are simply too expensive," says Grossman.

Fortunately, government and business initiatives to
build the information superhighway are rapidly creating
opportunities for healthcare providers and consumers to
take advantage of new network and multimedia technologies. These initiatives will make high-speed networks capable of multimedia application widely
available. Corresponding efforts will continue to lower
the price of computers and television hybrids.

In addition, early studies indicate that medical facilities can obtain rapid payback for these kinds of investments. Grossman cites a study conducted by the Tiber
Group, a Chicago-based consulting firm that looked at

healthcare systems in Minnesota and Virginia. Electronic filing of healthcare claims yielded savings of $307,000 a year in savings for small hospitals and $1.4 million a year for larger hospitals. Physicians' practices netted $13,000 a year for small practices and $183,000 for larger practices.

Start-up costs for the automated systems were $11,000 to $12,000 for hospitals and $4,000 to $13,000 for medical practices.

The studies concluded that $4.7 billion a year could be saved if 85 percent of all healthcare transactions were accomplished electronically.

> *With the advent of technology to disseminate information, the knowledge monopoly of the medical profession has been thoroughly smashed. The doctor is no longer a god.*

The other major issue besides cost is culture. Grossman says:

> Technological change also runs up against human barriers. At first people may be intimidated by new computer systems, regardless of how user-friendly they may be. In some instances the new information systems will change the essence of people's jobs, for better or worse.

> For example, hospital staff who monitor the quality and cost of care now spend much of their time poring through reports to identify incidents that fail to meet specified criteria. With new systems that automatically flag variances, the staff occupy themselves with the more challenging task of analyzing the causes, effects, and solutions.

In his 1990 book, *Power Shift*, Alvin Toffler describes the end of "God-In-A-White-Coat," which he describes as the end of the traditional role of doctors because of the advent of information and the technology to disseminate it. Toffler states:

> Throughout the heyday of doctor-dominance in America, physicians kept a tight choke-hold on medical knowledge. Prescriptions were written in Latin, providing the profession with a semi-secret code, as it were, which kept most patients in ignorance. Medical journals and texts were restricted to professional readers. Medical conferences were closed to the laity. Doctors controlled medical-school curricula and enrollments.

> Contrast this with the situation today, when patients have astonishing access to medical knowledge. With a person-

al computer and a modem, anyone from home can access data bases like Index Medicus, and obtain scientific papers on everything from Addison's disease to zygomycosis, and, in fact, collect more information about a specific ailment or treatment than the ordinary doctor has time to read.

Copies of the 2,354-page book known as the *PDR* or *Physicians' Desk Reference* are also readily available to anyone. Once a week on the Lifetime cable network, any televiewer can watch twelve uninterrupted hours of highly technical television programming designed specifically to educate doctors. Many of these programs carry a disclaimer to the effect that "some of this material may not be suited to a general audience." But that is for the viewer to decide.

The rest of the week, hardly a single newscast is aired in America without a medical story or segment. A video version of material from the *Journal of the American Medical Association* is now broadcast by three hundred stations on Thursday nights. The press reports on medical malpractice cases. Inexpensive paperbacks tell ordinary readers what drug side effects to watch for, what drugs not to mix, how to raise and lower cholesterol levels through diet. In addition, major medical breakthroughs, even if first published in medical journals, are reported on the evening television news almost before the M.D. has even taken his subscription copy of the journal out of the in-box.

In short, the knowledge monopoly of the medical profession has been thoroughly smashed. And the doctor is no longer a god.

This case of the dethroned doctor is, however, only one small example of a more general process changing the entire relationship of knowledge to power in high-tech nations.

It can be argued that, rather than benefitting society by spreading medical information around, the dissemination of healthcare information has simply flooded the market with too much technical material that needs explanation and (possibly) an expert to apply it to individual cases. Also, the availability of the information may be dangerous to untrained readers who may take their interpretations of problems as the appropriate treatment when they should still consult a physician.

However, public access to medical information has somewhat demystified the medical profession, allowing for close examination of what actions doctors recommend and whether they are the best course. Overall, it increases consumers' ability to control quality and helps progress toward cost control.

The information superhighway will both enhance the trend of making medical information more widely available and simultaneously reconnect the patient or consumer with the healthcare expert who can best recommend how medical information should be applied to an individual case.

Unlike the technologies of one-way television, unassisted database searches, or other forms of distilled interpretations of medical information by the print media, the superhighway networks and applications will allow access to medical information when and how it is most relevant to individuals. Besides having instant access to the material that applies to their case, consumers may also use an expert system that can provide a superficial diagnosis.

Armed with analyses based on medical videos and expert-system advice, the consumer can then schedule an in-person or videoconference appointment with the physician. The session can be interactive and can include a database report of the consumer's condition and medical history that both the doctor and the consumer can reference during the conference.

Short conferences of this nature, where the patient has done most of the background work, will permit shorter, but more effective, consultations and help physicians focus more energy on implementing appropriate treatment, rather than simply trying to diagnose the initial problem.

In addition, second or third opinions will be easier to obtain through similar videoconferences. In fact, physicians can be consulted anywhere in the country or the world, allowing the consumer to seek out the most qualified specialist for the job.

Costs should also be reduced because less time and money will be wasted on procedures and diagnosis, or even on office visits. Remote monitoring and at-home consultations such as the IBM/New England Medical Center leukemia project will reduce the time and need for hospital stays as well.

Information superhighway applications in medicine can accomplish two goals of President Clinton's troubled healthcare reform strategy. Telemedicine, which allows remote access to doctors and patients, can extend healthcare's reach to patients in rural locations who cannot afford to make a trip to a major medical facility. This capability advances Clinton's major principle — providing access to healthcare for every citizen. This is also the one area where he refuses to compromise in his healthcare plans.

All the patients will need to do is travel to a nearby site or have a two-way video camera set up in their home or at the local clinic so that doctors can examine them from their offices in distant cities. Electronic stethoscopes and other devices allow examination of a patient's heart, lungs, eyes, and throat via video images available on the doctor's monitoring screens.

The second area where these applications will advance the national healthcare reform agenda is in driving down cost. According to a 1992 study by consultants from Arthur D. Little company — one of the largest management consulting and research firms in the United States — these applications can reduce the cost of healthcare by $36 billion nationally. Efficiency achieved through electronic exchange of patient information will be responsible for the bulk of the savings. Electronic claims processing, inventory management, and telemedicine will bring about the rest of the cost savings.

Full implementation of these applications will mean a challenge to the doctors and medical staff that will be far greater than Toffler's view of the replacement of medical control of information with open access. Healthcare professionals will have to change the way they work altogether, opening themselves up for partnership with knowledgeable patients to solve medical problems using a host of new technologies and interactions.

Of course, a co-responsibility falls on the patient to learn about their own medical needs. Perhaps improved health training in the schools and special public-service workshops will be created to discuss this issue and educate the public on such matters.

Grossman states that such changes should not be done haphazardly:

> Designing and installing new systems must be a cooperative venture between developer and user. As much as possible, the new products should take into account the user's needs and habits. The ACI-TIPI system for identifying heart attacks, for example, was originally designed in the form of a calculator, which is not a standard part of the physician's "toolkit." Incorporating the system into an electrocardiograph made it more palatable. In the past, the conservatism of the healthcare community has caused it to lag behind other industries in applying information technology to help manage production processes. But now we must surge ahead. The Congressional Research Service has estimated that about half the growth in healthcare expenditures is controllable — that is, unrelated to general inflation or population changes. As the emphasis in medicine shifts from inputs (services provided) to outcomes (treatment results and patient well-being), the incentives are growing for physicians to provide high-quality, cost effective care. Advances in information and networking technology can accelerate this trend by helping care providers determine the most direct, most effective, and least costly means of diagnosing and treating patients. Such technologies offer the tools to redefine and restructure healthcare in our time.

Although Grossman's view may be among the more progressive in the medical establishment today, most major healthcare organizations are implementing new computing technologies to decrease costs and improve the quality of their services. This trend will form a natural foundation for the telemedicine applications of the superhighway.

Remote Learning

Schools of the future will have information superhighway services that encourage and support interactive education, distance learning, and self-teaching. Funded by the government and private interests, these services will challenge current teaching methods that have been in place for almost 100 years. To children of this generation, networks and computer technology will be a commonplace tool. Learning will no longer be limited by the confines of the classroom.

Teaching hasn't changed much over the past 100 years. Printed textbooks, which have been available for centuries, are the primary sources of information. Teachers use lecture, dialogue, and example, much as the Ancient Greeks, like Socrates, did in the early years of modern civilization.

Teaching today largely relies on an individual's ability to express ideas and connect with the students. Learning is often based more on receiving input and replying with appropriate information, rather than active participation in a process.

The information superhighway enables a new medium that can transform education from a passive, one-to-one experience into an interactive, many-to-many process. Already, computers and videos are used as largely passive tools in America's classrooms. But according to education researcher Arthur Melamed:

> U.S. schooling is a conservative institution, which adopts new practice and technology slowly. Highly regulated and financed from a limited revenue base, schools serve many educational and social purposes, subject to local consent. The use of computer technology, with its demands on teacher professional development, physical space, time in the instructional day, and budget . . . has found a place in classroom practice and school organization slowly and tentatively.

The Clinton Administration, through the U.S. Department of Education, is determined to speed up the pace of technology application in America's schools. Both President Bill Clinton and Vice President Al Gore have been quoted as challenging the companies that are creating the superhighway "to connect all of our classrooms, all of our libraries, and all of our hospitals and clinics by the year 2000."

The Department of Education issued a white paper in May 1994, entitled "A Transformation of Learning: Use of the National Information Infrastructure for Education and Lifelong Learning." The paper outlines the potential impact of the superhighway on public schools and on adult education. This white paper states:

Teachers who make use of the superhighway will have access to more information and a new medium that will help transform education from a passive, one-to-one experience into an interactive, many-to-many process.

The National Information Infrastructure will be the vehicle for improving education and lifelong learning throughout America in ways we now know are critically important. Our nation will become a place where students of all ages and abilities reach the highest standards of academic achievement. Teachers, engineers, business managers, and all knowledge workers will constantly be exposed to new methods, and will collaborate and share ideas with one another.

Through the National Information Infrastructure, students of all ages will use multimedia electronic libraries and museums containing text, images, video, music, simulations, and instructional software. The infrastructure will give teachers, students, workers, and instructors access to a great variety of instructional resources and to each other. It will give educators and managers new tools for improving the operations and productivity of their institutions.

The infrastructure will remove school walls as barriers to learning in several ways. It will provide access to the world beyond the classroom. It will also permit both teachers and students access to the tools of learning and their peers — outside the classroom and outside the typical nine to three school day. It will enable family members to stay in contact with their children's schools. The infrastructure will permit students, workers, and instructors to converse with scientists, scholars, and experts around the globe.

Workplaces will become lifelong learning environments, supporting larger numbers of high skill, high wage jobs. Printed books made the content of great instruction widely and inexpensively available in the 18th Century. The interactive capabilities of the infrastructure will make both the content and interactions of great teaching universally and inexpensively available in the 21st Century.

The creation of a "Lifelong Learning Society" is the goal of the government's efforts. Results of these efforts may include:

- Professionals and students of all ages will be able to tap into the knowledge of well-known experts and teachers remotely, as well as talk with each other about common interests.

- Students with disabilities will have fuller access to educational and reference materials and the ability to participate interactively in class.

- Multimedia interactive learning programs delivered to homes of immigrant children and their parents will facilitate learning English as a second language.

The possibilities outlined in the white paper include the following:

> The Administration's National Information Infrastructure initiative can trigger a transformation of education, training, and lifelong learning by making new tools available to educators, instructors, students, and workers and help them reach dramatically higher levels of performance and productivity.

> The impact of this transformation in teaching and learning is inestimable, but clearly enormous. Knowledge drives today's global marketplace. The infrastructure will permit us to take learning beyond the limitations of traditional school buildings. It will take our educators and learners to worldwide resources. Learning will be our way of life.

Already, there are many examples of new resources for teaching and learning available via on-line networks — the precursors to the information superhighway. These applications involve: video-based instruction, remote information gathering, communications via electronic mail or bulletin boards, teaching to and from remote locations, and using networks to send communications software and simulations between sites.

With three-quarters of America's schools having access to cable television, the potential for interactive applications and access to distant databases is great. Cable firms are among the first companies experimenting with high-speed networks and advanced services beyond television programs.

Half the country's teachers use videos in their courses. They obtain them in the academic equivalent of the video rental store or library. How much more powerful their instruction will be if they can obtain educational videos on demand, similar to the service phone and cable companies are providing for consumers.

Instead of the school's budget and video library limitation, teachers will have a nearly unlimited choice of videos to use as instructional aids, making available topical material at the appropriate point in the curriculum, and providing unlimited access to such popular programming as PBS' "Reading Rainbow."

Collecting information using computer networks is directly supported by the Department of Education, which uses a computer system connected to the Internet to provide access to educational research information. Services available on the Internet include AskERIC, an educational research database, Cable News Network (CNN) programs, and the Educational Testing Service (ETS). Lesson plans on space flights and science topics are provided by NASA's Spacelink through the Internet, as well.

Also, two-way communication is being used in test cases throughout the country. Texas teachers have access to the Texas Education Network for sharing information, exchanging mail, and finding sources. Inter-school or regional networks can increase the consistency of academic offerings and keep everyone informed of the latest techniques and resources.

Even more powerful than teachers exchanging information is the concept of distance learning, where students gain access to teachers who may be located miles away. Rural areas are particularly well-suited for this application.

Despite the potential, government researchers conclude that: "Compelling applications that will become indispensable to teachers, students, and workers are not yet available. All the capabilities of computer-based instruction and multimedia instruction can be distributed using the National Information Infrastructure facilities to schools, workplaces, homes, libraries, museums, community centers, store fronts — wherever and whenever people wish to learn. Yet the infrastructure and applications to support this level of accessibility for education, training, and lifelong learning uses have yet to be developed."

Efforts are underway to correct this. For example, BellSouth's efforts to connect North Carolina's schools with government and research institutions, and Pacific Bell's commitment to link all California schools, colleges, and universities will begin the process of application-building in those states.

The government's role in this is likely to be twofold: direct support of publicly funded superhighway applications for education purposes and the removal of regulations and administrative barriers to such efforts. The regulatory and administrative role will likely have a greater impact since limited government funds are available.

The Clinton Administration's white paper on educational applications of the information superhighway reports that the private sector will have to "make 75% to 95% of the nation's investments in applications development for education and lifelong learning."

The private sector is expected to build the networks between school systems and research institutions, but state and local governments will continue to shoulder the burden for hardware, software, professional development, and support services just as they currently fund 93% of the investment in elementary and secondary education (and support higher education as well).

The federal government, according to the white paper, will facilitate private investment in bringing the superhighway to educational institutions by creating incentives, removing regulatory barriers, establishing standards, supporting research, evaluating, testing, and seeking out "visionary benchmark applications."

The Departments of Agriculture, Commerce, Defense, Education, Energy, Housing and Urban Development, Interior, and Labor, as well as the Federal Communications Commission, NASA, and the National Science Foundation are all working on initiatives to advocate educational applications of the information superhighway and many are planning to fund the creation of public access networks that provide agency information to schools and universities.

A multi-agency program known as the High-Performance Computing and Communications Initiative is developing the National Research and Education Network (NREN). This high-speed network is meant to provide advanced network products such as servers and security at an affordable cost to research and education facilities.

State government efforts to build local versions of the superhighway also will benefit educational applications. The Iowa Communications Network (ICN) includes 2,600 miles of fiber-optic cable linking 15 remote learning centers, 3 universities, and Iowa Public Television. There are 63 courses offered over the network, any of which students can "attend" without leaving their locations. In addition to these distance learning applications, ICN hosts workshops, seminars, and town meetings which anyone in the state can "attend;" distance is no longer a barrier. Iowa, which has spent more than $100 million on ICN, plans to connect every college and high school statewide.

North Carolina has a school technology commission studying the needs of the state's schools and is considering a $350 million investment in technology for education. These efforts are in addition to the North Carolina Information Highway, which BellSouth has developed in conjunction with the state to connect public and educational institutions.

Ohio has the Ohio Educational Computer Network, which is working on connecting students in grades Kindergarten through 12 to educational applications statewide. The Ohio Academic Resources Network is charged with linking colleges and universities.

Already, federal grants, computer company donations, and affordable Internet access have brought new dimensions of learning into rural and urban schools. These applications are the forerunners of the superhighway.

For example, the *New York Times* recently reported on the Ralph Bunche elementary school in Harlem and its computer-based mini-school where 250 students use the computer network as a learning tool. Jump-started by $100,000 worth of Apple Computers and a $15,000 per year National Science Foundation grant for a high-speed network connection, the program is increasing students' interest in school, making it possible for them to learn directly from researchers, and increasing their overall performance on standardized tests.

These Harlem students have exchanged e-mail with Australian researchers, listening to and developing a multimedia report on whale sounds, and videoconferenced with researchers at Cornell University. Their use of computer networks helps the students control their learning experience and gives them a chance to seek knowledge from an endless array of sources around the world.

The challenge of the program is guiding the students smoothly through the Internet and other difficult-to-navigate computer and networking access vehicles. To overcome this, the teachers at Ralph Bunche have designed their own software to overcome these problems, hiding the difficulty from the students.

Across the country, Glenbrook North School in suburban Chicago possesses more than 300 computers, including laptops that the students can take home. The students access the Internet for academic assignments. The school also provides them with a computer-equipped television studio.

Despite these leading examples, only one in eight American classrooms has a telephone line for linking to a telecommunications network and only one in 25 has a computer armed with a modem or other technology to send and receive information.

This low incidence of computer network availability is the spark for the Clinton Administration's advocacy of educational investment in the information superhighway. While local communities will have to wrestle with how to get computers and network-connection equipment into their schools, the Administration is hoping new telecommunications laws will prompt companies to provide the high-speed networks for school access.

Legislation before Congress calls for reasonable or preferential rates for schools, leaving interpretation of what rates should actually be charged to the Federal Communications Commission. But assurance of low-cost access for schools is one of the stipulations the government may place on any companies wishing to build information superhighway systems.

Rep. Edward Markey, chairman of the House Telecommunications Subcommittee, says that schools should be charged as little as a penny a minute for access to the highway. The George Lucas Educational Foundation, a nonprofit group, is calling for free services for schools.

The bottom line issue behind the cost of access is whether the superhighway will help bring equality to the educational system or continue the disparities that exist today between schools in wealthy locations and those in poor areas. The networks of the highway could be a great equalizer, providing all students the same level of access, just as the students in Harlem and suburban Chicago have equal access to the worldwide Internet information bank.

Of course, problems of vandalism and lack of parental support "prevalent in some school districts" would have to be addressed to effectively balance the availability of the technology with the students' ability to access it. Only then would these computer systems truly have an equalizing effect.

There are two big unanswered questions. The first is: can the companies that build the superhighway network afford to provide equal access for all schools without government funding? The second is: how will poorer districts pay for the software and hardware they'll need to bring the network and information to all the students in their schools. The government's white paper addresses this, as well:

> *Computer technology is unevenly distributed in our schools today. The top fifth have nine times as many computers as those in the bottom fifth of all school systems.*

> Computer technology is unevenly distributed in our schools today. The top fifth have nine times as many computers as those in the bottom fifth of all school systems. Computer density in the schools is not strongly correlated with socio-economic, racial, or ethnic patterns, however. Lower than average computer densities are found in large schools, urban schools, both private and parochial schools, and schools with large numbers of Hispanic students.

The report also states that the majority of schools use older computers not suitable for multimedia applications. Video technology, though, is better placed. In fact, schools in rural and poor areas have more VCRs, satellite, and cable systems than in other areas. Networks themselves are more prevalent in Northeastern and suburban schools. Despite these limitations, the proliferation of computers with information superhighway capabilities is inevitable. In fact, it has been anticipated by futurists and experts for many years. Nine years ago, in 1985, Marvin Cetron wrote in his book, *Schools of the Future*:

> Computers and videodiscs can serve as extensions of an individual's mind to communicate information and data (text, graphics, speech, and picture). These emerging interactive literary technologies will include telephones, televisions, monitors, and computers that students will use for reading, writing, computing, and even drawing. And the artificial intelligence of the new computers will assist students to progress through their own individualized educational programs.

> If the new learning technology is properly used, schools of the future will take on an entirely new look. The formal learning environment will not be confined to a single building. Instead, it will extend to the home, the public library, the museum, and even a college campus hundreds of miles away . . .

> By 2000, computers will be available to 25% of the poorest school districts on a ratio of 1 per 8 students. In contrast, 25% of the most affluent school districts will have 1 computer per 4 students. One-tenth of primary school students and one-quarter of secondary students may use interactive television to study at home 1 or 2 days per week.

> In the year 2000, the learning environment will combine automatic teaching in a variety of settings to accommodate many learning styles, allow new definitions of literacy, and foster life-long learning skills. Nine-tenths of all homes will be wired with new laser technology, many will receive interactive cable and computer on-line networking. Students will be able to direct-dial their encyclopedias and other resources for homework, individual research, and study. The advent of this technology will

make research, study, and communications skills the new basics of education.

Other experts see even more profound changes in the way we teach and learn. Alvin Toffler states in his 1990 book, *Power Shift — Knowledge, Wealth, and Violence at the Edge of the 21st Century*:

> In the case of education, the reconceptualization now required is so profound, reaching so far beyond questions of budgets, class size, teacher pay, and traditional conflicts over curriculum, that it cannot be dealt with here. Like the Second Wave TV networks (or for that matter all the smokestack industries), our mass education systems are largely obsolete. Exactly as in the case of media, education will require a proliferation of new channels and a vast expansion of program diversity. A high-choice system will have to replace a low-choice system if schools are to prepare people for a decent life in the new Third Wave society, let alone for economically productive roles.

The convergence of trends in communications and computers indicate that these predictions are not far from reality. It is almost certain that the government will require that some kind of upgraded network services be provided to public facilities in general, and to schools in particular. Students will have access to these networks either through low-cost systems based on a hybrid of televisions that have computer "smarts," or through personal computers themselves. These will be easier for school districts to acquire if the prices fall to the level of consumer electronics. In addition, it is likely that computer companies will continue to donate systems to schools to enhance their reputations and encourage brand loyalty at a young age.

Programs to run across these education superhighways will be the next major challenge. Certainly many of the CD-ROM multimedia packages now designed for the home will be adapted for school use. In fact, it is conceivable that students will be able to (or even be required to) access the same programs via the network from home and school giving them a continuous and consistently progressing learning experience.

But the engagement of computers and networks deeper into the educational system can go beyond anything that has presently been achieved. Whenever technology has been introduced, whether it be in marketing, manufacturing, or record-keeping, the first impulse is to use it to do things exactly the way they were done before — only faster. This is a disservice to the capability of the technology and robs us of an opportunity to open new vistas that computers can create.

This conflict in education's use of computer technology was foreseen by MIT mathematics Professor Seymour A. Papert in a paper on "Computers and Learning," published in December 1979 in *The Computer Age: A Twenty-Year View*, Michael Dertouzas, Editor (MIT Press). Nearly 15 years ago, Papert identified and understood the basic revolution in curriculum and learning expectations that we will face as we bring the superhighway into the classroom. He wrote:

> Faced with a computer technology that opens the possibility of radically changing social life, our society has responded by consistently casting computers in a framework that favors the maintenance of the status quo. For example, we typically think of computers making credit decisions in an otherwise unchanged banking system, or helping to teach children to read in an otherwise unchanged school system. We think of computers as helping schools in their task of teaching an existing curriculum in classrooms instead of confronting the fact that the computer puts the very idea of school into question. The invasion of computer technology into education is inevitable. By operating with a limited and deformed vision we are increasing the ultimate social cost of correcting the mistakes we are now making, mistakes that grow out of our collective resistance to coming to terms with what the computer is going to mean in our lives.

Papert goes on to criticize "drill and practice" programs that simply make the computer an electronic substitute for the teacher, but that add no value beyond that. He argues against uses of the computer that keep the student limited to coming up with prescribed answers based solely on memorization.

He urges us to consider programs that use the computer as a tool for discovery. These forms of learning

> *We often think of computers as helping schools teach an existing curriculum instead of confronting the fact that the computer puts the very idea of school into question.*

help students come to the answer in their own way so they can relate to the knowledge they gain. Computers, because they enable individualized experiences, allow each student to discover their own right answer and may even allow them to redefine the problem and develop new ideas that add to the teacher's knowledge.

Papert cites the LOGO computer language, which at that time was part of a computer-based learning environment at the MIT Children's Lab. The lab featured children interacting with computer-controlled devices that respond to natural language commands. One such device, "the turtle," traces lines over a distance specified by the child, such as "FORWARD 100" or "RIGHT 50." The turtle memorized the commands for certain distances associated with shapes, so that the command "SQUARE" would yield the same results as the distance commands in consecutive order to make a square. Papert describes the children's experiences:

> For young children, the operation is conceptualized as teaching the computer a new word, and how to teach becomes not only a metaphor for how to program but a theme of the child's activities in the learning lab. Suppose the child wants to program the turtle to trace out a circle and he asks us what to do. Instead of telling him what instructions to write, we say "Stand up, walk in a circle," and perhaps after a few false starts the child proposes to the teacher that what he is doing is turning a "tiny tiny bit and moving forward a tiny tiny bit." The child then tries that with the turtle ... This is the way the child will develop many programs of his own invention.

> The child is learning by being brought into relationship with his own intuitive knowledge structures, in this case of his own body. He is learning to see formal mathematics as a symbolic language, a different style or articulating and elaborating what he already knows ...

> The teacher becomes a partner with the child in a joint enterprise of understanding something that is truly unknown because the situations created by the child are totally new ...

> Just as marked as the change in the child's relation to himself and to the teacher is the change in his relation to

knowledge. Knowledge is now a source of power to do what he could not do before. One sees this most dramatically when a child moves from simple programs designed for a mechanical turtle that traces patterns on the floor to programs for a "light turtle" that operates on a TV-like display screen. Compared with what was possible with paper and pen, new possibilities offered by the complexity, precision, and animation on computer-generated graphics seize the imagination. Children are fascinated by doing things with lines, light, color, and animation that they have never done before, but beyond the novelty experience is the awareness that they themselves are able to do something such as animation that they previously associated with television, something they watch as passive observers... The question is no longer right or wrong, gold star or not, for the steps in a little exercise but a goal that might be reached only after several weeks' time.

Papert's experiences offer the computer as a tool that goes far beyond the traditional memorization/drill curriculum and his findings are based on a single program and learning environment. Imagine what experiences of discovery await the child who has access to unlimited learning environments via the information superhighway.

If the teacher stays out of the way by not leading the students through their network experiences, but letting them drive the direction of the communication, then a new form of learning will emerge. Teachers can stand by as flight instructors, showing the students the controls, and then letting them solo.

Some students may choose to use a multimedia interactive learning environment from the school's library or may sample ones from other schools or universities, national research centers, or even other countries. Other students may conduct extensive electronic conversations to learn from other students or citizens of other parts of the country or other parts of the world.

Schools could provide multiclass or multischool problem-solving programs, encouraging students from different locations to work cooperatively and simultaneously on the same problem and act as a team to develop a solution.

The key, besides putting the technology and access in the students' hands, is letting the learners run the learning, letting them set their own pace, and driving the curriculum in whatever direction fosters the most interest, enthusiasm, and knowledge gain. Papert foresaw that such a role might be difficult for teachers:

> The traditional teacher can scarcely avoid being ambivalent about such a changed relation to the child. Much as he might envy the situation in which the child does not need to be "motivated," he can scarcely face with equanimity the possibility of the child really taking off on his own . . . . Quite obviously, if part of what is supposed to happen in a classroom is getting children used to accepting authority, they have to believe that the teachers "know." This points to the way in which this project goes beyond suggesting how computers can be integrated into schools and becomes one of rethinking what our society expects schools to do.

For its part, the government recognizes the need to address teacher training as a critical factor to the usefulness of the information superhighway in education. The white paper states:

> Investment by all levels of government in research, development, and evaluation, implementation, and technical support will increase dramatically. The investments will include professional development and technical assistance for teachers, school administrators, instructors, and managers in the use of information technologies.

> Providers of professional development and technical assistance will be encouraged to offer quality, easily accessible services in a variety of ways. A majority of teachers will have access to personal telecommunications devices and networking services to support continuing professional growth and interchange of professional information.

The government's long-term goals for the superhighway in education include:

Access. Both the school and home will have convenient and equitable access to all relevant applications. "Affordable workplace and home access will give all learners resources whenever and wherever they are needed, will enable family members to be fully involved in the education of their children, and will allow workers to participate in a productive, lifelong learning society."

This access will be fostered by high-speed networks available to all locations so that interactive transmissions of voice, video, data, and multimedia applications can be received.

Ease of use. Exploration tools, directories, and highly intuitive and interoperable interfaces must be developed for educational purposes. In addition, the government wants users to connect to the superhighway as easily as they now connect their telephones.

Security. Security will also be a concern, to protect the privacy and confidentiality of sensitive information, and to protect intellectual property rights.

The government expects the superhighway's educational applications to impact the workplace as well as the school system, as shown in this quote from the white paper:

> We have found that technology is the key to making training accessible and affordable — especially for small-to-medium-sized firms with few resources of their own to devote to producing and implementing the training and lifelong learning their workers need and for workers who, on their own, are attempting to improve their skills or transfer them to new areas of endeavor.

> Finally, in preparing students for the workplace, we have learned that interactive, high-performance technology can produce immersive, real world instructional environments. These environments can smooth long term school-to-work transitions while helping to meet the immediate objectives of both schools and workplaces. Our efforts to develop this capability have been fragmentary at best.

Job training and Papert's view of the discovery process of learning will receive a tremendous boost from virtual reality applications. These are expected to follow on the heels of network access and multimedia into schools, workplaces, and home learning environments. Instead of reading about computer manufacture, repair, or program development, trainees will be able to experience it (very likely at home during their own time) by working with a simulation available on the network.

Instead of watching the "turtle" device make shapes in response to keyed commands, students will actually *be* the turtle, moving in different ways to manipulate a computer image. More of their senses will be involved in learning and experiencing information.

History will be discovered by giving students access to actual diaries, videos, and documentaries from the period being studied. Students will be able to interact with computer recreations of historical personalities. Computer simulations will also help them learn about science. Chemistry, biology, and physics will be revealed not as abstract concepts or formulas, but as everyday realities that have their own internal laws. Simulated experiments in mixing chemicals or testing the effects of objects will be available over the superhighway.

Students will access programs that allow them to experience being inside the human body. Disney World already offers this type of attraction that allows information about the body to be absorbed as part of the virtual environment.

The possibilities extend far beyond the basic communications and information retrieval services now offered by the Internet and on-line services. These services will likely upgrade their educational components as higher speed networks and multimedia applications become more prevalent.

Like many aspects of the information superhighway, these future educational services are barreling down on us now and will be commonplace in the next five years. The wisest strategy for the average family is twofold. First, any and all opportunities to encourage your children's schools to acquire personal computers with modems and multimedia capability should be explored. Often, educators hesitate to install technology because it doesn't "fit" the curriculum. Take Papert's advice. Computers offer a replacement for the curriculum and forward-looking schools should come to grips with this new kind of learning.

Second, as I advised you earlier, acquire your own information superhighway vehicle. The experience you and you family gain today will be invaluable in the future. There are numerous educational programs available right now. Your children should already be learning the power of discovery through communicating with other people on the Internet and on-line services, using programs available on the network, and by using the computer at home for writing, math problems, research, science, and experiencing the world of multimedia.

This generation of children will be the pioneers. They will experience networks and computer technology as a pervasive phenomenon just like the children of earlier generations who were the first to see the phone as a commonplace tool for communication, the automobile as the essential way to travel, and the television as a primary vehicle for entertainment and information.

But unlike these previous technological changes, the information superhighway will bring profound changes within school systems that have been doing business the same way for hundreds of years.

Beyond Buggy Paths

One of the keys to the future of the superhighway will be who builds it. The government and communication companies are focusing on the infrastructure; the entertainment, computer, and consumer electronics companies are concentrating on technology and applications. Unfortunately, it won't be that simple. Companies will have to join forces, government must rewrite regulations, and constituencies will have to band together to accomplish the construction of the superhighway.

The information superhighway — it's a national obsession. The big thing isn't that we're going to have new electronic roads; the main attraction will be the world of exciting services and events those roads will bring into our homes. Preoccupation with the superhighway is like our predecessors staring at the dirt horse trails and getting excited about asphalt. We should be paying attention to the vehicles that will be the automobiles of the superhighway.

Fortunately, while the federal government and communications businesses concerned with the electronic roads have been dominating public attention, companies in other industries have been thinking about the vehicles we'll use to ride on them. The consumer electronics and computer hardware companies are working on access vehicles in their laboratories and test beds. The entertainment and news providers and computer software firms are thinking through programming and content issues, testing partnerships, and developing deals of their own.

The most confusing aspect of all this policy-setting and deal-making is that we are living in a world where there are rudimentary examples of what the superhighway will be like, but where no concrete model exists for it. It is hard for the experts, let alone the average person, to see how the superhighway will blossom out of the seedlings we have available to us now.

It was probably much the same at the end of the last century when horses were the vehicles and roads were the networks that connected cities and towns, neighbors and friends. There were automobiles available well before Henry Ford struck upon the Model T and mass consumption. But they were seen as far less viable alternatives for getting around than the reliable stallions and mares of the time. The horse and carriage had been suitable, highly functional transportation for hundreds of years. Brand new, noisy, hard-to-operate "motorcars" were more of a nuisance — or toys for the elite or mechanically gifted.

But automobiles did emerge as the dominant vehicle and new highways were created to support them. From 1921 to 1965, the number of cars grew to 80 million.

> ## *Our obsession*
> with the superhighway is like our predecessors staring at the dirt horse trails and getting excited about asphalt. We should be paying attention to the vehicles that will be carrying us on the superhighway.

Sixteen million buses and trucks were also placed on the road. Three million miles of roads were constructed and 40,000 miles of interstate superhighways were built.

This new mode of transportation wasn't cheap. State and local governments spent $173 billion on roads and the federal government spent $43 billion on highways from the late Twenties through the early Sixties. The public sector provided the pathways, supported by taxpayer investment. The public sector also provided the vehicles, supported by consumer expenditures and relatively free of federal and state regulations.

Those who refused to believe in the value of the car were soon swept up in a movement that allowed faster travel and a wider range of destinations than any horsebound traveler could have imagined.

In a relatively short span of history, we have changed from a society where the vast majority of people never traveled more than 15 miles from their place of birth, to a society of global (and even stellar) travelers. The changes that this has brought about in our society range from geographically dispersed families, global business enterprises, to new methods of communication — including the information superhighway.

As we approach the next century, the parallels are even more numerous. The superhighway promises to serve functions that today are served by the telephone and television. Both of these existing networks are accessible nationwide. Both provide information and entertainment. But both are destined to become as obsolete in their present forms as the horse and buggy are today. What their 21st-century counterparts will be is as difficult for us to predict as it would have been for a person in the 1890s to foresee the space shuttle.

The superhighway will provide information and entertainment in much richer ways and with more variety and freedom of choice than either the TV or telephone do now. How will it accomplish this?

The common answer to this question is captured by the term "convergence." The core of this idea is that the computer will merge with the telephone, which will in turn merge with the television in some super-technology hybrid that will both provide access to and operate the superhighway.

Yet convergence is the wrong way to think about this change. The automobile did not merge with the horse and buggy — it totally replaced them. New technology came along and superseded the prior technology by virtue of its superior capabilities.

What, then, is the replacement that will serve our information and entertainment needs?

Futurist George Gilder puts his finger on it better than anyone else. He says that the information superhighway will be spearheaded by the personal computer network. The personal computer, in a more consumer friendly form, will be the access instrument that knocks the telephone handset and television monitor and console out of their dominant places in American life.

The reason for this shift, besides the fact that it mirrors the historical model of the prior century, is simply function. Television and telephone networks function much the way a railroad does. The TV viewer becomes a passenger who climbs aboard the broadcast network and is taken wherever the train is headed along with all the other passengers. Viewers can choose different channels to get to other programming just as passengers can buy tickets for different trains.

Telephone users are in a similar predicament. Though they can pick their destination, they still must travel down a single track and take only one trip at a time. The phone resembles the private train on a railroad. Wealthy passengers can hire it to go down any track they like, but only down one track at a time. They also have to know something about where they are going, much the way a phone user needs the number and information about the party at the other end of the line.

Personal computers by themselves give you access to a wide variety of information and help you create information and entertainment experiences at will, using hundreds of varieties of software you can buy at department, computer, and discount stores. The only limit is the nature of the software available (there are far fewer compact disc multimedia packages than traditional programs, for instance) and your budget. This is already much more than you can do, in terms of choice and customizing, with either the television or telephone, even with today's video stores and extensive networks. Television is a passive experience compared to personal computers that require user participation. Telephones are limited by voice-only services and one call at a time (although videophones and multiparty calling are becoming more generally available).

But when the personal computer is linked to a network it has many more functions than a single preprogrammed track. In fact it's not limited to a single track at all. You can use other computers on the network as resources. You can broadcast information to multiple computers and their users simultaneously. You can use programs installed on other computers on the network, gain information, or participate in entertainment. Many of these functions can be available even if there are no other users present on the network at that time. For example, you can search another computer's files, run a software package, or send a message without anyone being there at the other end. Try that with a telephone and see if you can get beyond voice mail or an answering machine!

Like the automobile, the personal computer lets you choose where you want to go and how you want to get there and it lets you get there fast. It also allows you to travel to multiple virtual destinations at the same time.

You might ask, if the personal computer is so wonderful, why hasn't it already overtaken the telephone or television? There are three basic reasons:

1. Like the early automobiles, it is hard to use. Until recently, only technical experts found the personal computer accessible.

2. Also, like the early cars, the personal computer is relatively expensive. Though its price has come down considerably in the past few years, it is still many times more expensive than the television and 30 times more expensive than the telephone.

3. The true power of the personal computer and its full functionality are not apparent until it is part of a network of other computers. Networks are growing and more personal computer users are signing on. However, network services represent another learning curve for the user and the easiest to use are also the most expensive.

The builders of the networks — the telephone companies — are planning upgrades. Their voice-oriented conduits have limited capacity (called bandwidth) that allows the flow of voice communications or data (relatively slowly), but not both simultaneously. Fiber-optic networks have greatly increased bandwidth that can carry simultaneous multimedia programming and communication.

These upgraded fiber-optic networks will be well-suited for upgraded televisions (with only slightly enhanced functions) or personal computers (with far greater capabilities). So the evolution and availability of the networks will not be a function of technology growth. The key will be the ability of each network provider to justify the expense of installing or acquiring new fiber-optic cabling. How much money the communications firms can earn in building and enhancing superhighway networks depends greatly on the ultimate nature of the Clinton Administration's regulatory plans and the laws Congress passes in this area. If the firms are allowed to collect sufficient profits without experiencing overwhelming competition, then the networks will be upgraded.

Many telecommunications providers have already set to work installing or adding to their fiber-optic networks. The following figure shows that telephone companies plan to deploy more than 5.5 million miles of fiber-optic cable at a cost of more than $15 billion. And that's just for starters. Many million miles more of cable and many billions more dollars will be required.

Partnerships with cable-TV firms that already have fiber-optic networks and television programming are shortcuts for phone companies to establishing a presence in this upgraded technology arena.

Comparison of Telephone Company Network Infrastructure

	Access Lines (millions)	Access Line Growth (91/92)	% Lines Served by Digital Switches	Miles of Fiber (thousands)	Capital Expenditures ($ billions)
Bell Atlantic	18.2	2.4	63	1,160	2.2
Bell South	19.0	0	67	1,000	3.0
Ameritech	17.0	0	53	590	2.3
US West	13.3	3.2	41	800	2.4
Nynex	15.5	0	67	810	2.5
Pacific Tel	14.6	2.0	43	300	2.4
Southwestern Bell	12.8	3.2	39	580	1.7
GTE*	16.8	4.0	82	90.6	0
Sprint	5.8	3.9	95	195	0.7
SNET	1.9	1.0	43	2.0	0.3

* This represents GTE's US telephone operations only.
Source: LINK Resources Corporation, 1993.

Television is a different story. If it is to be modified as the primary information superhighway access vehicle, we must live with its limitations. And, for the time being, that is exactly what many companies intend to do. Much of the new development when it comes to creating access devices for the information superhighway is in building TV set-top boxes like the video game systems from Sega and Nintendo.

These boxes have the advantage of a $200–$300 consumer friendly price, compared to the $2,000–$3,000 a personal computer and software costs. They also will work directly with the installed technology — your current color TV — thus preserving that investment.

But functionally, they will have the limits of add-on programming — only having the capability to play videos from a central system on the network or only able to obtain information from select databases.

So, we are first likely to see something with the functionality and horsepower of a bicycle rather than the richness of a race car. Consumer electronics companies will prefer this approach because it doesn't make their present business obsolete and because it gives them a new revenue source. Program providers — the major networks and cable companies — will also like the additional audience time and user fees they can obtain for offering slivers of programming across a TV set-top system linked to a fiber-optic network on one end and a television at the other.

One development effort underway involves Oracle Corp., a computer database and application development tools maker. The company recently contracted with several manufacturers of set-top systems to build interactive TV systems.

The deal comes on the heels of a multi-year agreement between Oracle and Bell Atlantic Video Services Co. (a subsidiary of one of the Regional Bell Operating Companies) to produce commercially viable interactive services by the end of 1994. Services are expected to include movies-on-demand and interactive home shopping.

The interactive capability of the information superhighway will supersede anything a set-top box can ever provide.

ABC, the television network owned by Capital Cities and the *Washington Post* newspaper, which also owns *Newsweek* magazine, has struck a deal with Oracle to use the company's database software to create customizable news, video, and publication services. Oracle recently produced software that allows computers to store and retrieve still pictures, video, sound, and text.

While deals like these may mean that 500 channels will eventually be available, as well as video-on-demand, it still falls short of the vision of the information superhighway that can be realized by the single act of hooking up modified personal computers in everyone's home to a nationwide fiber-optic network. Full two-way interactive capability will supersede anything a set-top box can ever provide.

The prominence of the set-top boxes will last only as long as the personal computer cannot overcome the three hurdles mentioned earlier. Fortunately, things move fast in the computer industry and the personal computer has already made huge advances in ease-of-use, price reduction, and power increase. Work is still underway, but attention is also being applied to the cumbersome interaction of the personal computer and networks.

A good place to start with personal computers is software. At one time, the operating system software — the system that runs the computer by managing files, allocating memory, and providing a platform for applications — was usually based on DOS. Using this operating system requires that you know the way a personal computer looks at the world. The system prompt — an informative C:\ — and the commands it understands are essential parts of what you need to understand in order to operate a computer using this system. You have to know where the application is stored in the computer, which drive to use, and how the program is listed. All in all, this is a very non-intuitive approach.

Unfortunately, many early users' first experiences with computers was with DOS and its similar, one-time competitor CP/M. Understandably, this turned them off, just as many people in the 1920s first experienced the automobile as something you throw your back out trying to crank by hand.

But cars now operate at the turn of a key and a little pressure on the gas pedal, and most personal computers now run using either Windows or the Macintosh operating systems. Windows, which comes from Microsoft Corporation, and Macintosh, which comes from Apple, are graphical user interfaces, sometimes called GUI (pronounced like "gooey"). They rely on icons, which are pictures of objects familiar to you (or easy to learn), to replace cryptic commands. In the case of Windows, DOS is still there, working behind the scenes. But Windows translates your wishes into DOS commands without your intervention, simply by using an electronic pointer and then clicking a button on a mouse or trackball to select an item. Much simpler, and much more intuitive.

Applications — the information databases, word processors, and games — are also easily accessed via this point-and-click method. Windows has become pervasive in a little more than 2 years. It is not the easiest program from a technical perspective because it runs relatively slowly and requires a great deal of storage space on the computer. Developers can do better and they are busily working to simplify the interface even more while adding functions and capabilities. Also on the hardware side, IBM and Apple are delivering a product called the PowerPC in 1994 that will run multiple operating systems from different vendors.

Today, computer users can buy a personal computer that is ready to run when they bring it home from the store. It comes with a full suite of software for business, educational, and entertainment needs and operates using Windows or Macintosh applications, allowing easy, consistent access and the ability to run multiple tasks simultaneously.

Perhaps the next step in ease-of-use is a solution that IBM and other computer vendors are working on — the ability of the computer to recognize voice commands. Personal computer software can be installed that recognizes the speaker's voice and translates it into text on the screen and/or system commands. Systems already available that allow VCRs to respond to your voice are a parallel development in the home market.

Price is another issue separating set-top units from personal computers. But personal computer prices have been dropping about every three to six months. What you bought for $6,000 a few years ago now costs half that. Why? Because personal computer makers are delivering smaller, faster, easier to handle systems. The core processor — the memory chip — is becoming cheaper to produce and more powerful. When a new chip design is delivered, the old one falls off a cliff in terms of price. The same thing will happen with personal computers adapted for the superhighway. The price will start high, then decrease until the price reaches an acceptable level for a mass market.

Henry Ford realized that mass-production manufacturing techniques would allow him to build a car so cheaply that he could greatly reduce the going price. As computer makers find opportunities in the consumer field, the forces of competition and innovation will likely bring forth a similar breakthrough.

The biggest hurdle the personal computer faces as an access medium is its clunky ability to deal with networks.

Networks and the interoperation they require are both the
bane and the glory of the computer industry. As observed
earlier, networks turn personal computers into resource
powerhouses able to go anywhere and share anything
with other computers. That means instant, interactive
access to another household, institution, or country.

The Internet is the biggest and best example of what
networked computers can gain and what problems they
present. A worldwide interconnection of networks
largely based in government and research facilities, the
Internet works because of standards. Two standards
loom larger than the rest: TCP/IP (Transport Control
Protocol/Internet Protocol), the agreed-upon way of
handling information sent over the network from one
computer to another, and Unix, an operating system for
personal computers, workstations, and more-powerful
computers known as servers.

These standards enable a personal computer user
calling into the Internet using a phone line in China to get
a consistent response to messages and applications even if
dealing with a computer or user in Phoenix, Arizona.

Unix is popular on the Internet because it does basic
networking tasks well by virtue of built-in TCP/IP capability. Microsoft has promised to include such capability
in future versions of Windows. Still, Unix is not that
easy to use. It is powerful and reliable, having been built
in a university lab and modified by numerous vendors
and users over the years, but it requires more getting
used to than Windows or Macintosh. This limits the
Internet's use by the average personal computer user, let
alone the average non-computer user.

Despite this, the Internet is relatively inexpensive
($20 per month, and less than $1 per hour after the first
30 hours) and very powerful. It's like having a 10,000-
channel television (primarily in text-form), because it
helps you link with more than 10,000 other computer
networks with files to share. It's like being part of a large
telephone network (in text-form) connected to 20 million other people with whom you can exchange information. There are more than 5,000 formal discussion
groups and 2,500 newsletters.

But the Internet is poorly organized. *Time* magazine put it this way: "Instead of being surrounded by information, new users are adrift in a borderless sea." It is also open to security breaches. There is no direct control of obscene materials. And there are traffic jams stalling access to key sources of information.

So far, the Internet has been driven by a mixture of technical hubris and free-thinking anarchy. No single agency, industry, or organization put it together and no single entity effectively controls its growth or destiny. Internet cataloger Ed Krol has described it as "a Marxist State in a Capitalist Society."

Problems can be solved without the proper tools. But the superhighway developers should take a hint from the chaotic and complex nature of the Internet.

As such, its technological growth is governed by individual network engineers who have worked miracles, bringing whole countries on-line, but who have spent little time on ease-of-use. The capabilities of today's Internet are phenomenal and only limited by the available bandwidth — much of the Internet is dependent on computers that use traditional telephone lines to dial into larger computers. Without that restriction, even live television could be broadcast over this network.

Increased interest in the Internet has prompted the development of new sets of navigating tools. While some tools already allow users to search and find what they need quickly (with cute names like Archie, Gopher, Veronica, and WAIS), they are not easy for new users to master. A popular multimedia information browser called Mosaic, which is distributed free by the National Center for Supercomputing Applications (NCSA), is one of the first Internet tools with a point-and-click style similar to Windows. However, Mosaic is limited to direct Internet connections or dedicated high-speed phone lines and World-Wide Web servers.

Problems can usually be solved, even without the proper tools, but the information superhighway developers should take warning from the chaotic and complex nature of the Internet. Problems are much easier to solve when you do have the right tools for the job, so PCs meant for superhighway access should come properly equipped for the task. If network management is not virtually transparent to the consumers, chances are good that the application will not succeed.

For its part, the government recognizes these obstacles. Early work-in-progress statements from the Committee on Applications and Technology's Information
Infrastructure Task Force identify user friendliness and
interoperability standards as key issues:

> User-friendly hardware and software always have been
> important for mass applications of information technology.
> For National Information Infrastructure applications, such
> as those in healthcare or education, that are meant for use
> by broad segment of society, user-friendliness will be an
> important factor in user acceptance.

> Interoperability standards are essential to ensure that
> information can be transferred between different net-
> works, or different hardware and software systems, with
> accuracy, reliability, and security. Interoperability stan-
> dards are important to virtually all National Information
> Infrastructure applications, critically important to those
> that must function across a range of disparate systems in
> manufacturing, healthcare, and education, for example.

Who are the companies that will create these standards and create the networks, access systems, and programming? The most obvious choices are the major
corporations most affected: personal computer companies, telecommunications corporations, television manufacturers, and cable companies. Yet some companies are
moving faster and more decisively than others.

For example, AT&T, creator of the last great
national telecommunications infrastructure, recently
acquired McCaw Cellular, a leading wireless telephone
company with more than 3 million users. Although indi-
rectly off the track of the information superhighway,
McCaw, when coupled with AT&T's extensive tech-
nology-generation capability, positions the hybrid company to deliver voice, data, and video services without
traditional physical networks. This strategy would avoid
the regulatory issues confronting the other telephone
companies. For example, the government treats traditional telephone services as a utility, limiting rates and
markets. But the wireless world has, until now, been
treated more as a free-market system.

AT&T is especially wary of government intervention, having experienced it firsthand in 1982 when a

consent decree broke up the monopoly it held on telephone service in the United States. Now U.S. District Judge Harold Greene, who oversees the consent decree, is holding up the McCaw deal. He has challenged AT&T to prove that the acquisition is in the public interest and that the industry has changed sufficiently since 1982 to warrant a waiver of provisions that it not acquire any of the properties owned by an RBOC (other RBOCs have ownership interest in McCaw).

AT&T is also creating a slice of the information superhighway just for business: a high-speed data network called InterSpan, based on a relatively new technology called frame-relay, has more customers than it can service. Faster and cheaper than a standard phone line, InterSpan is growing by more than 1,000 user access locations per quarter, as of mid-1994.

The need to prove that the consent decree should be waived due to changes over the past decade could open the way for all the RBOCs to compete in new arenas such as long-distance services. This would accelerate the superhighway's development.

The RBOCs themselves have chosen to partner with cable-TV firms. But two of the deals have already fallen through. Bell Atlantic tried to acquire Tele-Communications, Inc. (TCI), one of the leading national cable firms, only to have the $33 billion deal fall through. As stated earlier, the main issue was a disagreement over price and cash flow. But new federal cable guidelines that trimmed rates were blamed for the demise of the pact. The firms had planned to connect 26,000 schools to an expanded interactive network. Despite the setback, Bell Atlantic plans to install an interactive network linking 1.2 million homes by 1996.

Similarly, Southwestern Bell acquired Hauser Communications, a Washington, D.C. cable company, for $690 million, but cancelled a $4.9 billion joint venture with Cox Enterprises to pursue interactive services because of "more stringent federal guidelines."

BellSouth has invested in a cable TV company in Texas and is putting in fiber-optic networks in its own region to support multimedia services. The company also backed QVC in its failed attempt to acquire Paramount Communications (Viacom won the bidding war).

Pacific Telesis spun off its cellular phone company to concentrate on plans to build a $16 billion interactive video network in California by the year 2000. U S WEST purchased 25% of Time Warner's entertainment and cable subsidiary, Time Warner Entertainment, owner of HBO, The Movie Channel, and Warner Brothers Studios.

But cable and telephone companies are not the only superhighway builders. Microsoft, flush with success from its Windows and other applications in the personal computer business, is working with TCI to develop interactive programming.

Oracle, already mentioned above, brings another dimension to the table — the software development tools organizations will need to build products to run on the superhighway.

Everyone involved in the invention of the superhighway wants something different. The government wants open access for users and competing service providers. It must, therefore, clearly define both universal service and the nature of the basic services it expects companies to offer.

> *Everyone involved in the invention of the superhighway wants something different.*

The RBOCs want to compete in long-distance services and interactive video, as well as to become major players in the information industry in general. To do this, they are willing to build new fiber-optic networks or form partnerships with cable firms that already have them. But regulatory issues have to be resolved before they can proceed full bore.

Long-distance companies want to reduce their competition in nationwide service and to compete in local telecommunications markets.

Cable television firms would like to add programs and services to increase their rates and reach. Recent rewritten Federal Communication Commission regulations are stalling their initiatives as well.

Computer companies want open access for their programs or hardware offerings on the superhighway.

Standards will be important to them. But their know-how in personal computer networking may be the telling factor in consumer acceptance of new superhighway access systems.

Media and entertainment companies ranging from newspapers and magazines to television and movie studios want to provide content for the superhighway. They would like the widest possible reach with the lowest possible investment in creating whole new services.

Other non-related businesses want access to the superhighway to increase the productivity of their employees and to offer their products and services to broad markets through a different medium. They also want future technological advances to find their way into corporate systems and networks; they need to make sure that their service providers don't ignore their needs because of excitement over consumer services.

There are also public interest groups with definite ideas about how the superhighway should evolve. The Electronic Frontier Foundation, founded by Mitch Kapor, who ran Lotus Software (maker of Lotus 1-2-3 spreadsheet software) wants to ensure that free markets are present in the superhighway. The foundation also seeks guaranteed access for private citizens and the opportunity to have electronic town meetings — connecting multiple community members simultaneously.

The users of current networks and on-line services — to say nothing of the providers — want to have their investments in systems and expertise respected by the new superhighway connections and applications. They have also learned valuable lessons about ease-of-use, standards, and open access that should migrate to the superhighway.

Members of Congress want to be seen as supporters of both businesses and consumers in their home territories and they are aggressively pushing forward legislation to take advantage of the administration's willingness to consider deregulation.

Fortunately, the Clinton Administration seems to be aware of these multiple constituencies. Commerce Secretary Ron Brown has formed a 27-member National

Information Infrastructure Advisory Council. Members include MCI Communications Chairman Bert Roberts, Black Entertainment Television Holdings' Robert Johnson, Esther Dyson (consultant and editor of *Release 1.0*, an influential computer industry newsletter), and other representatives of television, telephone, computer, and networking companies. Financial executives, representatives of labor unions, and people with disabilities are also members.

Such a mixture of representatives will no doubt breed numerous conflicting views. But the Clinton Administration thrives on consensus building, so the debate is likely to result in a final policy. The crafting of a superhighway with a combination of democratic access and capitalist funding requires no less than the attention of all segments of the population.

The White House began focusing public attention on the information superhighway when it announced The National Information Infrastructure: Agenda for Action in September 1993, calling for swift attention to the creation of vast electronic networks and services to enhance our competitiveness.

The next watershed event was a speech by Vice President Al Gore at the University of California at Los Angeles on January 11, 1994. Gore used the occasion to outline a series of legislative goals that will ensure that most Americans will have access to a network offering interactive communications and limitless television programming.

He identified the prime companies to create this network, which he calls the National Information Infrastructure (NII), as the television, telephone, and cable-TV companies. The new laws he proposed are aimed at freeing these firms from government regulations that prevent them from operating in each other's businesses or territories.

Vice President Gore also described the basic business trade-off that will form the framework for the superhighway. In exchange for allowances to get into the cable business, the phone companies must make their networks available to independent competitors and provide universal access to all Americans. Classrooms, libraries, hospitals, and other public facilities will get special attention in the government's plan, but rural areas are also targeted as locations where the deregulated firms must provide access.

The Vice President's promise of government support to jump-start the information highway was pre-empted by a flurry of legislation from Congressional representatives and Senators anxious to pave the road for information superhighway development.

President Bill Clinton gave the NII another push in his January 1994 *State of the Union* address, in which he asked for the speedy passage of the bills before Congress: "We must also work with the private sector to connect every classroom, every clinic, every library, every hospital in America into a national information superhighway by the year 2000."

All of this business and government activity has created a debate about competition among communications companies and the requirement for universal access. After all, most of the firms involved provide universal phone service in their regions, but they contend that it is only affordable because they have a monopoly.

There is no question that both the will and technology are present to create the information superhighway as Gore and the Clinton Administration see it. But how quickly the superhighway will come into being hinges on two key issues: In what manner businesses will be allowed by the government to compete to provide services; and when providers are positioned to offer equal access to everyone.

Teleputer Timetable

Computer technology, embedded in next-generation personal computers and cable television set-top systems, will be the primary on-ramp to the superhighway for the average person. How quickly and inexpensively universal access to the highway is realized depends on the timetable for adapting computer access hardware and software to the demands of the services. Computer, consumer electronics, cable, and telecommunications firms are all hard at work on this problem. Solutions will emerge over time though. There will be no big bang to usher in the superhighway, but there will be continuous evolution until one day we arrive at full blown access to a wide array of services.

M ore than anything else, the information super-highway is driven by the computer revolution. The superhighway will provide a platform for the continued business of nearly every manufacturer and supporter of communications and information services and equipment. Telecommunications vendors will be needed to enhance and maintain the network infrastructure, locally, regionally, and nationally. Entertainment, information, and news organizations will be needed to supply programming. Computer companies and consumer electronics firms will be needed to deliver the access equipment for homes, schools, and offices. Certainly, the government will be required to regulate and police the network, as well as to develop and support standard ways of transacting business and interacting with other countries.

> ## *It is not nationwide*
> effort that will turn the information super-highway on. Aspects of it will keep coming on-line gradually on a regional basis. Services will be added incrementally.

Locally, electricians, cable television installers, computer service dealers, and television and telephone repairers will have an opportunity to add new skills and develop businesses supporting small companies and organizations on the superhighway.

But when will this superhighway come into being? The answer depends greatly on which of the many industries and interested parties are able to best capitalize on the opportunities the superhighway offers. One thing we know for certain: The superhighway will not be turned on one day through some great nationwide effort. Aspects of it will keep coming on-line gradually on a regional basis. Services will be added incrementally.

The key player is not likely to be the federal government. For all the Clinton Administration's leadership and Vice President Gore's agenda for action, the government's powers are limited to spending tax dollars and regulating primary industries. Our economic environment is vastly different today than it was in the time when more than $200 billion state, local, and federal dollars were spent on the automobile superhighways. Enormous federal deficits and a public determined to shift support away from politicians who relentlessly increase the tax burden make the investment of huge governments sums unlikely.

In addition, while the automotive roads were built over a period of 44 years, the information superhighway is estimated to require that same $200 billion investment in just 10 years.

Regulation, then, is government's primary tool in this effort. The Clinton Administration recognizes this and is supporting multiple initiatives in Congress to free cable television and telephone companies from constraints that are preventing competition and new service development. To do this, they're offering the trade-off mentioned earlier — the easing of regulatory limitations in return for universal access. Like Clinton's healthcare initiative, which is negotiable except for the basic tenet of universal health insurance coverage for all, this access/regulation trade-off is the core of the federal information superhighway initiative.

But regulation, dependent as it is on the gradual movement of bills through Congress, is a poor stimulant for technological and economic innovation. Its primary role is to control or manage existing industries that have gotten out of hand, either through competitive issues or out of fairness or safety concerns with regard to consumers. It's difficult to imagine effective information-superhighway legislation before the highway itself even exists. Regulations only truly work within the context of a defined problem, because the outcome must be predictable. Creating rules for the superhighway at this point is dangerous, because their impact is extremely unpredictable.

The government's impact may be felt the most in federal dollars spent on creating government information superhighways for agencies and organizations directly within its sphere of control. Such initiatives are already beginning to take effect on the federal level, where Gore and other officials are mandating that government agencies sign up for information superhighway projects that will help them improve their services.

States, from Hawaii to California, are also creating their own superhighways for public services. These networks may be the first multimedia platforms on a large scale, accessible to significant segments of the population.

On the regulatory front, though, the jury is out on whether the Administration has chosen to focus on the right industry. Deregulation is probably helpful to create movement among the telephone and cable providers, but there are some drawbacks to pinning our hopes for superhighway-building on them.

Tony Rutkowski, the executive director for the Internet Society, says that the leaders of the charge will be found elsewhere. As a former executive with ITU (the International Telecommunications Union, responsible for worldwide communications and computer standards-setting) and Sprint (the U.S. telecommunication services provider), Rutkowski knows whereof he speaks.

> Thirty years of experience in this field in about a dozen different corners of it — many of them strategic planning — have taught me that relying on cable and telephone companies is off the mark. In fact, if the last 30 years of history have taught us anything, it's that the telcos and catv people will not produce much that's very innovative or advanced. In fact, almost everything they've touched has failed — video telephone, two-way cable, ISDN (a service providing integrated voice and data on a single network, etc.).

The seven Regional Bell Operating Companies (RBOCs) created after the break-up of AT&T have done business as monopolies in highly regulated regions. They have been more focused on government requirements than on competition. Although some competition is beginning to get their attention, the setup is not an environment that promotes innovation and creativity. Rutkowski addresses this:

> This is largely because in culture and expertise they've remained largely unchanged. Computer technology has literally left them holding little more than the telecom garden hose.
>
> I emphasize I'm not particularly anti-telco or anti-catv. I've worked with them and for them for years. They play a vital role in providing lower-layer "pipes" (basic network services to support superhighway applications) and the more competition among them, the better, to push the prices of the pipes down toward cost. But this isn't where

significant new information infrastructure developments
have emerged or are likely to emerge.

There are not only cultural forces holding back innovation within these industries. The regional phone companies and cable television firms continually receive
mixed signals from regulators who are determined to
lower cable prices. Simultaneously, the mercurial reactions of Wall Street investment firms are reflected in their
stock prices. The difficulty is that these industries are
measured solely by their short-term revenue and profit,
ignoring the fact that the superhighway is one of the
world's biggest-ever research and development projects,
with little or no immediate financial payback in sight.

The national long-distance carriers face these same
dilemmas. Currently, they are not extensively involved
in providing local services, so they will have to directly
compete with the RBOCs and cable TV providers to
deliver such access. This will not only mean a dramatic change in stance for the companies' market picture, but would also require adjustment to federal and
state regulations.

So if telecommunications and cable television firms
are not the likely leaders of the information superhighway initiative and if government can lead with
rhetoric but without direct or immediate action, who
will bring this highway about and when?

What about the entertainment and information
industries? High-profile companies such as Time Warner
and Sega, the movie studios, and video vendors have
been making their share of pronouncements about the
superhighway. Are these the likely champions that will
bring the superhighway to your home? Will content lead
the way?

Despite, a recent *USA Today* article proclaiming
"Content is King" after the Paramount Communications acquisition by Viacom, these firms, along with
their consumer electronics counterparts in the television
business, actually have a very limited view of what the
information superhighway is about. They are also just
as driven by Wall Street's quest for short-term payback
(and are even more vulnerable to it, since they do not

have a regulated monopoly as a safety net). Their view of a superhighway future consists of unlimited channels, featuring movies-on-demand, interactive game shows, and video games.

They are not interested in the diversity of services the true superhighway will provide. Their joint ventures are aimed at entertainment — at a greater expense with greater choice, but still basically just advanced television and in-home movie/game experiences supported by a network. Some banking and shopping services have also been incorporated into the experiments of these companies. But the results have been below their expectations.

The main problem with this approach is that these companies are trying to induce cultural shifts — from passive to active entertainment, for example — without changing the delivery medium enough to signal the shift to most consumers. Television remains a passive, mass-market medium. It can be enhanced somewhat with greater functionality, but it is limited in its ability to introduce two-way communication. The introduction of interactive capability on existing technology does not adequately prepare the consumer for the profound changes the technology brings. Identification with the "old" medium will hurt the functions themselves as well as the likelihood of their usage.

Likewise, without some kind of dramatic change in the "television culture," people just aren't ready to talk back to Peter Jennings or Dan Rather. These people on television symbolize, to many, truth and intelligence. The average person is not ready to put themselves up against such cultural icons.

The medium that features "America's Funniest Home Videos" isn't up to speed for handling downloads of information from research databases or conversations with network users in Japan. It's just too different.

So what is the right medium? Both Rutkowski and Gilder agree that the computer industry has the potential to run away with the show. But this isn't a surprising view from a top executive of the Internet's 20-million-strong personal computer population; nor is it unexpected from a technology guru who has long written about the increased capabilities of computers (Microcosm) and networks (Telecosm). Neither is it any wonder that leading personal-computer visionaries such as Intel's Andy Grove and Microsoft's Bill Gates think that personal computers will out-class televisions in the home in the next five to 10 years.

Gates has been quoted as saying that the good investments aren't clear yet and that there will be a winnowing out of players as the superhighway is developed. But both he and Grove, among other computer industry leaders (such as Oracle's Larry Ellison), are investing heavily in research and development projects aimed at enhancing PC hardware (Intel makes the chips that run most personal computers) and software (Microsoft makes the operating systems and many of the applications that run on most personal computers).

Unlike telecommunications companies, computer firms are born, live, and die in the crucible of competition. Even Intel and Microsoft, which have near-monopolies in their fields, are constantly challenged to stay ahead of the pack. They must constantly perform the dangerous balancing act between innovation, product delivery, and price competition.

Unlike entertainment and consumer electronic firms, the computer companies are not worried about making their products saleable. The industry is continuing to grow at a phenomenal rate in the personal computer, software, and networking arenas, unlike saturated television and consumer electronics sales.

Intel and Microsoft, in particular, are well-positioned to invest in research, on the one hand, while turning out current products to defend their leadership positions, on the other. They also both have the marketing prowess to pull off a major cultural shift to a new medium — the teleputer of the information superhighway.

There are three parallel developments that will determine how the information superhighway is experienced by the average consumer at any given time. These developments amount to an evolution of computers, electronics, and networks that will create the future. The superhighway will not spring into our living rooms one day, fully formed and functional, like Athena sprang, full-grown and armored, from the head of Zeus. Rather, we will experience its evolution as an incremental advancement of our ability to access, experience, and interact with information and entertainment vehicles.

The first major development along the way will be the adaptation of old technologies and industries to the new frontiers of the information superhighway. Efforts in this regard include telephone companies replacing their current copper twisted-pair voice-oriented cables with equipment that will enable them to carry full-motion video. Another area is the creation of set-top consoles that connect to the television in the same way as cable television converter boxes do now to offer additional control of programming and interactive services to the consumer.

The evolution of computers, electronics, and networks will determine how the average consumer will experience the information superhighway.

Late in April 1994, the Interactive Multimedia Association staged what was called the Inter-Industry Set-Top Summit, where two dozen speakers from different quarters of the industry debated the steps necessary to get cable-like set-top television boxes onto the market. Noticeably absent from these discussions, however, were representatives of cable television and local telephone companies.

Many of the speakers, including AT&T's David Robinson, director of video cable TV, said that the industries should quickly devise standards for these systems or the government would do it for them.

For its part, the government has invited industry participation. Thomas Kalil, technology director for the White House National Economic Council, suggested that companies propose that they be included in the Administration's interactive media tests as part of what the government calls the National Information Infrastructure Testbed, a cooperative arrangement involving government sponsorship and industry attempts to design and try out superhighway applications. Despite the summit, unresolved set-top issues remain:

- Companies such as General Instrument want proprietary set-top systems owned by cable companies so that they can control security and access. Essentially, the providers of the service would also provide the systems, just as cable TV firms do now.

- Computer companies that pursue an *open systems strategy*, where each person's computer is able to connect to and exchange programs with everyone else's computer, want the set-top box to be equally open and not controlled by a single company, just as PCs and workstations run a variety of systems today. These companies include Unix operating system heavy-hitters such as Hewlett-Packard and Sun Microsystems, and personal computer and software competitors Apple, Digital Equipment Corp. (DEC), and Oracle.

- Another issue, which may be put before the Federal Communications Commission by Congress, is whether the multimedia capability should reside in the set-top box or be built into the television set. Companies in consumer electronics and cable are divided on this issue.

- Privacy through encryption or coding to protect banking, purchasing, and healthcare transactions over a set-top-based network is also unresolved. Other than the Clinton Administration initiative (nicknamed the Clipper Chip) to migrate government encryption technology to these new devices, no industry proposal or standard has emerged for this vital need. Many people are disturbed by the Clinton initiative because it allows the government to retain the "keys" or code-breaking information to unlock the encryption, but doesn't give this access to anyone else. The government justifies this position by its assertion that as more commerce takes place over the superhighway, the more likely the scenario where it will need to use the superhighway to gather evidence of criminal activity, much as telephone wiretapping is used today.

As I stated earlier, the set-top systems proposed by telephone, cable, and entertainment companies are far less powerful than the true superhighway applications and technology that can be provided through the adaptation of personal computers. Nevertheless, advertising, business strategies, and financial resources are already being dedicated to the revitalization of telecommunications, television, and traditional entertainment because of the huge existing investment in these arenas. For the next five years at least, many people will see this as the information superhighway. It will be important to keep in mind that, despite claims to the contrary, this still represents only a dirt road that will not be able to bring about the revolutionary applications promised by the year 2000.

Five years, it turns out, is a good timeframe to expect the personal computer to come up to speed as a teleputer. During that time as well, telecommunications companies will be busily enhancing the underlying *pipes* — their basic network — to support the high capacity that teleputers will need. The investment in both the network and the computers are present and ongoing. According to *Businessweek*, users spent $22 billion from 1989 to 1993. The magazine also forecasts that the RBOCs are expected to spend between $25 and 50 billion on the information superhighway between now and 1998. These investments are a good start on the path to the $200 billion, 10-year forecast of the amount required to create the superhighway.

The majority of the telecommunications investments will be in fiber-optic cables, advanced network software, and switches. The mass-media image of fiber optics is still fuzzy, though. Probably the best depiction of its benefits is the Sprint commercial where the listener can hear a pin drop at the other end of a phone line. This speaks to the increase in clarity provided by fiber-optic cable.

The other, less-publicized, value of fiber is its increased capacity. Imagine it this way — if current copper phone cables are garden hoses, then a single fiber-optic strand is a fire hose. You can send that much more information — whether it's voice, data, or full-motion video — across the network with this increased bandwidth (capacity) and with high-speed transmission equipment. And fiber is installed in cables containing thousands of these strands, upgrading capacity to an almost unimaginable degree.

No doubt the first to use these superior networks will be entertainment firms, who will offer various ways to select or enhance current programs. Basic services like banking and home shopping will also be available. But multimedia and truly rich information sharing will have to wait for the teleputer because of the limited capability of the television.

Prototypes of the teleputer already exist. Apple's Macintosh Quadra 840AV can display, store, transmit, and edit video. Imagine a system that lets you capture TV programming on your home screen, save it for later viewing, send it to someone else, or change it at will. These are all the functions that average computers do today with data files — the only difference is that instead of words, numbers, and still pictures, the Quadra can manipulate video programs.

You can also use the Quadra as a telephone, stereo, and speech-recognition system. What more could you ask for? Just imagine if it were connected to a powerful network that delivers and provides access to sophisticated programming and a complete world of information and interaction. Its price is also still an issue for many consumers — in the thousands of dollars, rather than the hundreds that TV buyers are used to.

The Quadra system requires software called Quicktime, which manages video programs. Apple also now sells a Macintosh TV, which receives signals from a cable line directly into the Macintosh computer that has an add-on stereo CD drive. It can connect to a VCR or camcorder, laserdisc, or video game player, and costs about $2,000.

Nice technology. But Apple's ability to continue its breakthrough research and development is hampered by difficulty in maintaining its present share of the personal computer business. Having lost its visionaries — Steve Jobs and John Sculley — Apple is trying to break out of its maverick mold. The company's initial success rested on offering computers that were easier to use than the IBM PC, through a smart marketing campaign aimed at individuality. The advent of easier-to-use PCs running Microsoft's Windows, and the multiplicity of vendors matching the original IBM/Intel-based standard has severely limited Apple's growth. The call of the industry today is compatibility and interchangeability. Apple's products have only gradually become open enough to match other systems, though they offer computers that can read both Macintosh and PC disks. They have collected many loyal customers by not allowing the Macintosh to be copied. Joint efforts between Apple and IBM are producing PowerPC systems, which will bridge the gap between Apple's proprietary approach and the rest of the computing world.

Apple reported weak sales early in 1994 (earnings dropped to $17.4 million from 1993's total of $110 million for the second quarter), despite the fact that PC sales in general were growing. Personal computer competitors Compaq and IBM both reported strong earnings for the same period.

One of Apple's best hopes right now is a partnership with IBM and Motorola to create a personal computer and operating system that is more powerful, but less costly, than Intel's, and software with richer functions than Microsoft's.

IBM now finds itself in the same boat as Apple. Having made a strategic decision to shun the original IBM PC design in favor of a proprietary line — still based on Intel but using IBM's own operating system — the largest computer company in the world is now struggling for its life in the personal computer world. Although IBM has multimedia projects and voice-recognition computers, it has often been distracted from moving toward the future by its present-day battles and business problems across its large systems line. The PC business has also had a rough ride because IBM's original premium pricing caused many buyers to acquire mail-order clone systems.

Intel and Microsoft are also working on multimedia technology, though quietly when compared to their grand marketing campaigns for the current Intel Pentium — the latest, fastest processor — and Microsoft's future Windows systems and applications. Microsoft is exploring new software alternatives through a spin-off called Continuum Productions. The company is also hedging its bets by working with TCI, a leading cable-TV provider, on interactive programming in limited test markets.

Intel also has a number of short- and long-term initiatives in place. Most recently, the company announced a deal with Cable News Network (CNN) to begin interactive broadcasts over local area networks (LANs) at selected companies in San Francisco. While aimed at a limited business application, this is an attempt to make live TV broadcasts available on personal computers without any special translation equipment. Additional programming may include interactive tutoring sessions or education about medical services.

The key to the test is Intel's Indeo video technology. In an announcement in April 1994, Intel promised to increase Indeo's capabilities for real-time video integrated with Microsoft's Windows software. Further enhancements are expected in 1995.

Back at the lab, Intel is collaborating with Microsoft to define standards to allow personal computers to serve as programmable telephones. Future Intel-based computers will be able to arrange telephone conference calls and serve as the microphone and speaker, as well.

What do companies have to accomplish to make teleputers a reality? According to Apple multimedia researcher Eric Hoffert, the following technical hurdles remain:

> *Intel is collaborating with Microsoft to produce computers that will be able to arrange telephone conference calls, acting as both the microphone and speaker.*

- A connection from the personal computer to the state-of-the-art telecommunications networking technology — asynchronous transfer mode (ATM), which would allow quick and flexible access to fiber-optic networks in place and being built by the phone companies.

- Fast, real-time translation of information called *compression* — squeezing all the computer data necessary to present interactive video into the memory of a personal computer in an efficient manner — and *decompression* — pulling the information back out of its compressed state.

- An operating system that can schedule events as they happen to facilitate video and multimedia presentations.
- Faster PC processing capability. This is measured in bits, and the current standard is 32 bits. A 64-bit microprocessor would be ideal for what we can envision in the near future.
- Internal secondary processors to handle unique tasks such as high-definition video information. The speed of operation for these secondary processors needs to be measured in gigabytes per second.
- Standardized software for managing multimedia applications running across a network.
- Improved methods that allow users to access and manipulate multimedia images and information stored in databases on the network.
- Large storage capacity for the average personal computer, again measured in gigabytes.
- Privacy and security safeguards provided through encryption or coding software.
- Metering software that allows the providers of programs to track usage and send users a bill for the services rendered.

This technology is available today in very expensive, high-powered workstations and in some corporate computer installations. Some of these services are even accessible over the Internet. But they have a long way to go before they are packaged and priced at a level easy for the average consumer to obtain and use.

Five years may seem like a quick development cycle, but it is an eternity in the computer industry. Storage capacity and processor speed are rising exponentially every couple of years and the gigabyte and 64-bit barriers may fall for mass-market systems well before the year 2000.

Intel CEO Andy Grove has been quoted as saying, "The personal computer is emerging as a sort of electronic Swiss Army knife that can be used as a mass-market personal productivity, communications, and entertainment appliance."

In 1993, American consumers bought nearly six million personal computers, worth $7 billion. One out of three households now has a personal computer. Nearly three-quarters of families with incomes of more than $100,000 own personal computers. Only half owned them in 1992.

Personal computers can be purchased at discount stores anywhere, from B.J.'s Wholesale Club to department stores like Lechmere and Sears. You can buy a fully functional system for $1,500 that would have cost you $3,500 in 1991.

Systems like IBM's PS/1 come fully loaded with software. All you have to do is plug it in. This is true for the communications systems, as well as common word processing, spreadsheet, and database applications.

Already, nearly half of the personal computers used at home perform job-related functions. More than a third are used for children's schoolwork, home tax records, or financial management.

Compact discs, which are now commonly used for musical entertainment, also support software programs for personal computers equipped with CD-ROM players. Each CD-ROM stores as much information as 400 ordinary floppy disks. This makes it possible for you to use multimedia applications, which require much greater storage capacity than traditional programs.

About 15% of the home computers shipped in 1993 year were equipped with CD players. Some popular CD-based programs that include sound, animation, and video, are:

- Microsoft's "Encarta" — a multimedia encyclopedia. Instead of reading about a topic, you see and hear it demonstrated. ($90)
- Broderbund Software's "The Tortoise and the Hare" — a "living book" in which children using the program can call up the pages, hear them read aloud, and watch the characters act out the stories.

The children can also change events by interacting with screen objects through a mouse. ($40)

- Virgin Games' "The 7th Guest" — a mystery for older children and adults, featuring videos of actors mixed with computer graphics of a haunted house. ($55)

While leading new groups of consumers into the personal computer world, these and other programs are setting the stage for the teleputer. They are sensitizing our minds and our pocketbooks to the wonders and price points of technology that will be our powerful access point on the superhighway.

The difference between these applications and the future is the network. Instead of a few CDs that you can play on your home personal computer, the network that links the system to the outside world will allow you to choose from hundreds, or even thousands, of education, entertainment, or information-related experiences.

Two rudimentary examples of this are defining the limits of old technology. The first is current enhancements to the Internet. The second is the more than 300 experiments of communications, entertainment, and computer companies with interactive multimedia services piped into homes using cable TV systems and related technology.

Unfortunately, industry executives are looking at these examples as the test markets that will let them determine consumer interest in information-highway-like applications and how fast that interest and the technology's capability to fulfill it is likely to grow. Like the Wall Street requirement that communications companies show a profit in the research phase of fiber-optic deployment, this is a shortsighted view.

These trials are an opportunity to make the mistakes necessary to create a multimedia, networked future. They will provide valuable lessons that can be used when new technology is ready to be deployed in the coming five years. If we insist on trying to force them into immediate market success, then they are doomed to be seen as poor investments.

A better approach is to treat these early products as prototyping experiments, where it is understood that half the work will have to be rewritten or discarded as the project gets closer to full-scale implementation that will meet its customers' needs.

Ameritech, the Chicago-based RBOC, has announced plans to spend $4.4 billion to bring a video network to 6 million customers by the year 2000. An extension of the company's Project Looking Glass, the network includes video-on demand, home healthcare, education, interactive games, shopping, entertainment, and information services.

Besides its much publicized failed merger with cable-provider TCI, Bell Atlantic, the Virginia-based RBOC, has plans to provide 1.2 million homes with interactive networks by the end of 1995.

The Hearst Corp. has joined in a consortium with five Canadian companies to develop an interactive, mul-timedia network. The $200 million project is designed to use existing cable systems to offer combined consumer services in Quebec province.

Southwestern Bell, the southern RBOC, is launching a video service for 2,000 homes by 1995. To be deployed in Richardson, Texas, the service will be based on com-bined fiber-optic and traditional coaxial phone cable. Existing cable television programs, pay-per-view, and video-on-demand services are planned, as well as interac-tive games, home shopping, and educational services.

NYNEX, the New England and New York RBOC, plans to connect 2 million homes and businesses by 1996 across an interactive network. Initially, the project will include a 60,000-home system in Warwick, Rhode Island.

Another such test is Time Warner Cable's Full Ser-vice Network project. Designed for launch in Orlando, Florida — ironically, the home of some of the best multi-media/virtual-reality complexes in the world (at Disney World) — the experiment is due to begin by the end of 1994. It will require no less than 11 companies to pro-vide a range of 20–25 interactive services to set-top sys-tems across Time Warner's cable lines.

Silicon Graphics Inc., a Mountain View, California, workstation hardware and software maker, is providing systems integration services, server platforms for the service providers, operating systems software, computer tools to build Time Warner's system, and the crucial set-top system design. SGI will essentially miniaturize the design of its $7,000 Indy graphics workstation to make the set-top design.

The software that runs the system will be key. Silicon Graphics will create the operating system, which will act as the traffic cop for hundreds of users seeking simultaneous access to services provided by at least eight large-scale workstations known as servers. It will also built a graphical, three-dimensional user interface called Navigator that will act as the main menu for the system.

Scientific Atlanta will manufacture the set-top systems, while Qualcomm, AT&T, Hitachi, Toshiba, and Thomson will contribute other key communications and control components. Open Systems Interconnection will provide billing and network-management software. The content will come from Warner Brothers, which is readying 300 movies for digital distribution. Other applications will be provided by Spiegel and the U.S. Postal Service, among others.

Orlando residents will be able to select the movies they want when they want them, participate in home shopping offerings, and take part in interactive games once the system is up and running. Other applications, including wireless telephones and home-office networks, are also in the planning stages.

Pricing plans for these set-top systems call for $1,000 in 1995, to be reduced to $300 by 1996. Already, the electronics industry is arguing about whether this is too costly for the consumer and suggesting that decreased functions — by reducing the sophistication of the set-top system — would lower cost and allow for further reduced prices.

There is no question that this is the wrong direction. Cost and function-cutting moves will only make the set-top systems in Orlando obsolete when more and more services join the network, and when this network is connected to others like it. But a focus on swift success embodied by high demand and high profits will motivate company executives to think in terms of short-term costs rather than long-term capability.

This discussion brings us back to the personal computer industry, where the dynamics are different for leading-edge technology — where high function is the name of the game, and where costs come down when the capability goes up over the long term.

As addressed earlier, ease-of-use still prevents many users from having cozy feelings about personal computers, despite the price/function advantage they have over consumer electronics and telecommunications.

Recent Internet advances on the ease-of-use front, combined with the software work going at places like Apple and Microsoft, could conquer this dilemma. One company making a business out of ease-of-use on the Internet is Netcom On-Line Communications Services, Inc., in San Jose, California.

Netcomm's "NetCruiser" software automatically sets up an account with Internet and puts your personal computer on the network in less than 10 minutes. Once hooked up, you can navigate the complexities of the Internet by using a mouse to click on buttons that control a series of screens. These screens, and the software commands behind them, lead you into the realm of Internet riches — library, university, and government databases all over the world, published materials, and the ability to conduct on-line conversations with other Internet users, either locally or in distant countries.

In another effort to simplify the Internet, O'Reilly and Associates has introduced "Internet in a Box" — an all-in-one Internet connection kit developed with software from Spry Inc. of Seattle.

Perhaps the best known Internet interface for ease-of-use is Mosaic, which is based on hyperlinking text and graphics — the ability to have the program point to additional information based on a word or phrase on the screen and have the system retrieve the related material automatically, no matter where it's located or what form it's in.

> *Ease-of-use still prevents many users from having cozy feelings about personal computers, despite the price/function advantage they have over telecommunications and consumer electronics.*

Mosaic also allows information publishers to create their own home pages with full graphics and sound or video. An estimated 250,000 copies have been distributed (completely free) and many more are in use, since there is no restriction on copying the software (except for sale or profit).

But whether these and other graphical approaches add up to the ultimate in ease-of-use is still a matter of debate. Says the Internet's Rutkowski, "My seven-year-old son can access and cruise the network with the new graphical interfaces. With Windows 4.0 it will be even more integrated."

Yet Daniel Dern, former editor of *Internet World* magazine, wrote,

> The nature of Internet access is another area still beshrouded in mystery. If you've had any chance to use Mosaic on a system with a reasonably high-speed Internet connection, you know what a truly exciting front-end it can be.

> But try to use Mosaic over a 9600/14400kbps modem link and you'll see that graphics and document-intensive items go very slowly — too slow for meaningful interactive use.

This too will change as networks and PCs upgrade with faster, more direct connections.

Flight *of the* Navigator

How will users access and interact with the networks and services that will be available on the information superhighway? There are numerous efforts now underway to create the easiest-to-use, most feature-rich computer access software. It will be inexpensive and it will enable any user to navigate through the information superhighway's content maze.

A professor of art at Harvard University recently created a *vocal installation* as the culmination of his first year in residence at the school. It consists of tape recordings of students and faculty reading their own stories and passages from literature. The speakers are hidden in trees throughout the park area known as Harvard Yard, where commencement is held each year and where students congregate for casual conversations.

As passersby walk through the yard, they hear voices from the trees, describing their raptures and agonies. Men and women speak out from each tree in a mixture of tongues and emotions. Moving to one tree, visitors hear only a single voice. Standing in the center or at certain cross-paths, however, they hear mixtures of two or more speakers and their stories.

This constant stream of information, emotions, and cultural diversity is the audible equivalent of the information superhighway. The superhighway's paths will contain countless experiences from different creators, all available simultaneously. You will be able to focus on a single experience or join numerous simultaneous encounters.

What will make this possible is unique technology that enables you to interact as you wish with the networks and services of the superhighway. This technology is being built into what computer and communications companies call "the navigator."

While there are many technical components needed to make the information superhighway work, the one that will matter most to the average person is the navigator. The navigator is software that runs on the teleputer or enhanced television to guide the user quickly and easily around the program choices and different networks on the information highway. It's the steering wheel of the various vehicles of entertainment, education, and information available on the highway.

It may be obvious that we need a very simple access system with lots of richness (options), but it's difficult to envision what it would be and what it would really need to do, since we have nothing like it now.

> *The paths of the* superhighway will contain countless experiences from different creators, all available simultaneously. You will be able to focus on a single experience or have numerous simultaneous encounters.

"The individual user doesn't need to be aware of the complexity of the network," says Thomas Pardun, CEO and President of U S WEST's Marketing Resources Group, which is working closely with Time Warner and other companies to conduct multi-city trials of multimedia services using cable television networks.

"There will be an intelligent agent that will represent the user in this complex world," Pardun continues, "This navigator will learn over time. It will learn to screen out things that I don't want and prioritize access to things that I do want."

Within the next five years, this navigation software will be widely available on information superhighway access systems. So how does it differ from what's available today?

Television today offers an immediate, intuitive way to view entertainment and to get information and education. You are placed immediately in the context of the program. There is essentially no access system — no steering wheel — because there is an extremely limited choice. You can either change the channel or turn the set off. You cannot choose to watch something that's not also being broadcast to others.

With the addition of a VCR, you have a third and fourth choice. You can choose to record a program and watch it at your convenience or you can rent a program from your local video store or borrow programs from friends, neighbors, and often from your local library. Your VCR gives you a degree of control over the vehicle, since it lets you pause, rewind, or fast-forward the program.

The information superhighway navigator will incorporate these capabilities and more. It will allow program choice, provide the ability to manipulate the program, and will create a system that will let you intuitively access programs without being aware of the steering wheel.

The telephone also provides intuitive access. You dial the number and are connected. Dialing represents a slight increase in the level of difficulty over the television — my two-year-old can control the power and change channels on my television unassisted, but she can't dial specific numbers in a seven-digit sequence. But the result — instant communication with the other party on the line — is more defined and interactive than television viewing, which is passive.

Interactivity will be a mainstay of the navigator and the programs it allows access to. Users will be able to call forth whatever type of program they choose and actively participate in it by talking, typing, or touching the screen.

Today, personal computers provide access to programs that must be loaded from a disk drive or from memory, or that must be acquired through a network. By and large, you need to know a lot about the program you want to run: where the program files are located, what command(s) to use to run them, if there are any special things you have to do to set up the computer to run the program, how much storage space the program requires, and so on. Generally, these programs are interactive, but they are usually not intuitive. They require a "learning curve." You must work with them frequently over time until you learn to use them well. Unlike television, personal computers must run a special program designed for children just to translate access commands into terms they understand.

One of the side effects of this learning curve is that few users ever master their computer programs. Power users — the ones who invest the time and possess the ability to understand all of the capabilities of a program — are a relatively rare breed. Surveys report that 90% of computer users only use about 10% of the features in any given program.

Most of today's popular systems have come a long way, though they are still far from intuitive. Windows, for example, manages the complexities of the personal computer for you. It is the navigator for most home computers (Apple's Macintosh takes care of most of the rest). Its icon-based menus cover most common tasks that most users will ever want to perform. Frequently, though, after you've moved beyond these basics, you still have to fall back on word-based commands. Even though some of them can still be accessed through your mouse or trackball, you still have to learn enough about the commands to know what the computer will do when you use them.

The information superhighway's navigator will, by necessity, be far easier to use than today's personal computer programs.

The navigator that will be designed for the information superhighway must, of necessity, be much easier for the average person to use, while providing even more interactivity and flexibility. As Steve Lang, Director of Public Relations for U S WEST's Multimedia Group describes it:

> The navigator will have ten times the depth and user friendliness of Windows or (Apple Computer's) Macintosh. There will be different navigators for different kinds of users. Some of us might want it to feel like we're driving a helicopter into a futuristic city. Educators might want a text-based system. Kids might want a cartoon navigator they can use.

A number of companies are now working on prototypes of these navigators.

U S WEST is perhaps the most ambitious of the RBOCs. It has partnerships with different companies to try out different kinds of navigators in cable-based multimedia projects in Orlando, Florida and Omaha, Nebraska. U S WEST owns a 25 percent share of Time Warner's cable division, which is running the Orlando project and is relying on Silicon Graphics to design the navigator. The trial will start in the fourth quarter of 1994 and is expected to be available to 4,000 consumers by year's end. The whole project is slated to cost $5 billion over five years. This investment will fund expansion to cover 85 percent of Time Warner's cable subscribers by the end of 1998.

The Omaha project features a partnership with AT&T, Digital Equipment Corp., and Scientific Atlanta. 3DO, a California company founded to develop a multimedia platform for home users, is designing the TV set-top system. New Century Communications will create the navigator Omaha residents will use to view movies

> *The navigator that will be designed for the information superhighway must be much easier for the average person to use, while providing more interactivity and flexibility.*

when they want them, partake of at-home shopping, and enjoy games and other interactive services.

Beginning in the third quarter of 1994, 2,500 homes will be connected. By the end of 1994, 60,000 residents will have access to the system. With an investment of $750 million over two years, this system is expected to include 20 cities within the next five years, including Denver, Colorado; Minneapolis and St. Paul, Minnesota; Portland, Oregon; Boise, Idaho; and Salt Lake City, Utah.

Pacific Bell is struggling to overcome resistance by cable companies and city governments as it attempts to deploy a video network alongside the one cable subscribers now use. The company will offer consumers the option of a wider array of channels with a set-top system that has interactive functions including navigator software developed by the phone company. By the end of 1996, 490,000 homes in Southern California will have access to this system.

Bell Atlantic has a navigator called Star Gazer for its trials of multimedia networks; the other regional phone companies are preparing navigators for their trials, as well.

Computer companies have been less public about their efforts, but Microsoft, the owner of the most popular personal computer desktop navigator, is also reported to be working on multimedia applications and control systems. In May 1994, Microsoft announced that it will produce software (code-named Tiger) to run the computers that feed videos to network users. The servers used, which are made by Compaq, will enable cable TV and telephone companies to offer video-on-demand using lower-cost standard computer systems than those proposed by other manufacturers. Called, "The Frontline Partnership," the deal also involves Intel, which provides the powerful processors within the Compaq computers. The firms plan to run field trials late in 1994.

Microsoft CEO Bill Gates is also hedging his bets as he commonly does. (Who else could have simultaneously partnered with IBM to build a personal computer operating system, but competed against them at the same time?) He has joined with Craig McCaw, CEO of McCaw

Cellular Communications, one of the largest cellular phone providers, to create Teledesic Corp. The $9 billion company promises to develop a global satellite system that allows information, including video and high resolution images, to be transmitted from anywhere to anywhere using McCaw's wireless technology. This alternate information superhighway would provide consumers and businesses with the same level of services, without relying on the traditional telephone or cable companies. It would also open an exclusive field for Microsoft to provide the navigation software worldwide.

The venture is viewed skeptically for many reasons. While wireless technology is available using combinations of satellite and cellular systems, reliability and cost remain problematic. Transmissions that are interrupted frequently and that require a higher-than-normal investment are not likely to win many customers. Also, McCaw is in the midst of a $12.6 billion merger with AT&T, which has its own investments in the network-based superhighway. Nevertheless, the project goal remains to build 840 satellites by the year 2000 and launch them in 2001.

IBM and Apple have formed Kaleida Labs, Inc. to build tools for multimedia applications. The company is currently working on a navigator for a $600 million project in which Ameritech will deliver multimedia services over its phone lines. Scientific-Atlanta is again involved in creating the set-top systems, for which Kaleida is creating the navigator. Called the Consumer Operating System or COS, the project involves 126 workers. Separate units were recently created in Kaleida to handle this work, so that it would not interfere with the company's objective of building a personal computer multimedia-creation tool. Both IBM and Apple also reportedly have interactive multimedia projects underway separately.

With such a powerful mix of competitors from the computer industry, can the phone companies provide a competitive navigator?

"Two smart guys in a garage can design a navigator. That's the easy part," says U S WEST's Pardun, "What's important is the depth of its capability and the quality it provides. Consumers will want variety and flexibility."

Why does a regional telephone company like U S WEST care about navigation software anyway? After all, telephone companies are expected to be in the business of providing networks — essentially the pavement of the highway — while cable, entertainment, and computer companies do the rest.

Current legislation bars the RBOCs from building set-top boxes or personal computers. Despite this barrier, which is subject to change as the federal government devises new ways to encourage competition, U S WEST is pioneering a new concept called "packaging." They plan to not only provide the network, but to also own the navigator and devices used to access it.

"We want to stay the brand provider for the consumer. They've come to us for phone service, now we want to be the people who bring them this complex world of networks. We want to create our own service, which we can combine with Time Warner's programming to give us the whole value chain — the networks, navigator packaging, and content," says Pardun.

This vision places U S WEST as the total service provider. If it's successful, consumers might receive their information superhighway bills in the same envelopes as their phone bills, with itemized hourly charges for programming or network time they've used.

"We serve nine million homes and 25 million human beings. We want to continue to serve them in this new capacity," Pardun adds.

The vision further plays out this way: a number of telephone or other network providers each develop their own sophisticated multimedia service packages in their regions. These networks are then linked to each other, so the consumer can access a nationwide network of interactive multimedia services. Beyond that, the superhighway of networks would have Internet connections, giving users access to a global superhighway from their living rooms.

"We know there's a market out there. We've seen the results of trials in Denver with TCI and AT&T. There is a $16 billion video rental business, which means that people are willing to go to the store and pay two or three dollars to watch what they want and return it to the store. We can make it a lot easier than that," Lang says.

Of course the idea of being identified as the chauffeur who provides the vehicle and secures the road on the information superhighway is attractive to many firms. Long-distance carriers such as AT&T and MCI communications are positioning themselves to dominate the major national thoroughfares through fiber-optic networks and multimedia systems of their own.

Just as Time Warner is positioning itself to take advantage of the superhighway through its cable and Warner Bros. offerings, other entertainment firms are investing in navigators and multimedia tools for the superhighway. These include Blockbuster, the video rental company, which has joint ventures with IBM, and Viacom, which recently took over Paramount Communications. A merger between Viacom and Blockbuster is also in the works.

Who will earn the consumer's allegiance first with the richest, easiest- to-use navigator at the most reasonable price? That is still very much undecided. But the question will be settled within next few years.

Regardless of which firm wins the brand battle, its navigator will be the key. The navigator will define the experience for consumers the way Microsoft Windows, Apple Macintosh, or other computer software systems define what computing is to many home users now.

Consumer will want many things from this experience. To deliver them, the navigator must possess the following qualities:

1. The ability to be customized to suit individual tastes and interests.

2. Transparent connectivity with all network services — from local video services to worldwide databases and software programs.

> *The idea of being the chauffeur who provides the vehicle and secures the road on the information superhighway is attractive to many firms.*

3. Extreme simplicity. A young child should be able to access cartoons, interactive programs, and learning experiences as easily as an adult. And, an adult must be able to — just as easily — restrict access to inappropriate material or programs that require additional fees.

4. It must be at least as reliable as today's TV sets — instantly connecting to the services without interruption or delay.

5. It must provide the means to secure the system against intrusion from harmful software programs, unwanted outside communication or monitoring and unwanted services or programming.

The testing ground for the navigator is, again, the Internet (with Mosaic and similar programs, such as Lynx) and the numerous consumer- and business-oriented on-line services. America Online is known for a well-designed, easy-to-access navigator. Based on the windows-and-icon metaphor, it gives you immediate access to news, educational, technical, or interactive services by first presenting an icon representing the service and then displaying printed directions and information in a window, giving you a deeper look at the subject.

The America Online navigator also has a "Flashbar" that lets you click on more icons to read or create electronic mail, save a file, or access other services ranging from travel information to shopping and stock quotes. You can also quickly access and read *USA Today*, *Time*, or *Omni* magazine on-line.

Other on-line services, such as CompuServe, MCI Mail, GEnie, and Prodigy have accessory software available to help you add browsing capabilities and connection management utilities to the basic system, thereby simplifying and customizing the navigator. Ironically, these systems are all offering gateways to the Internet, but you cannot use them to access the other on-line services.

Another early example of a navigator has been demonstrated by Oracle, which builds software to store large amounts of information in databases that run on a wide range of computers. Massive processors with enormous databases will be necessary to provide extensive video and information services across the telephone and cable networks being designed by Time Warner and U S WEST, among others. Oracle's test navigator asked people turning on an "intelligent" TV to identify themselves by selecting their picture from those of family members shown on the screen by using a single-button remote control. A "video assistant" greeted each person as they selected the picture. The assistant said the person's name, notified them of any new messages, asked if they would like to order food, and then described TV programming available based on their individualized preferences.

This TV-like approach lacks the flexibility of the kinds of information a computer keyboard, mouse, or trackball can relay to the system, but it greatly simplifies overall access.

General Instrument Corp., a major electronics company, has set its sights on developing set-top boxes, and has formed a partnership with Microsoft to use elements of Windows as its navigator. The system will eventually provide program guides that help viewers search through different subjects on the screen to find a program they want to watch.

When we look at all these competing navigator test runs and looming battles between telephone, consumer electronics, cable, and computer firms, it isn't easy to predict which is likely to provide the navigator we'll see in our homes in 1999 and beyond.

The answer lies in two opposing forces: competition and government regulation. The Clinton Administration has made universal access, reliability, security, and protection of property rights the mainstays of its pronouncements on the information superhighway. It has also stated that government must provide an open field of competition to keep prices down and has acknowledged the reality that government funding is scarce.

These tenets of the Clinton plan are enough to give legislators pause when they consider bills to deregulate telecommunications and open up competition between telephone and cable TV firms.

But the result of the administration's efforts could be to establish common interface standards. These standards would determine how the navigation software will look and feel and would limit companies' freedom to add all kinds of design wrinkles to it.

Faced with the prospect of pending standards that might not favor their particular approach, major companies involved in navigator design are moving as fast as they can to create products and get them into the market as quickly as the test sites will allow.

Computer companies, in particular, have learned the lesson that once a product is established in the market, it is more likely to set standards than it is to be influenced by them. Ultimately, government mandates frequently end up incorporating substantial parts of the design of this de facto standard in its final official standard.

The best example of this is Microsoft's Windows personal computer operating system, which is widely recognized as not being the best technology for the task. However, it has become the de facto standard because it is so widely installed. This is the case despite the best efforts of the computer industry and government standards organizations to crown the Unix operating system as the standard.

One result of this turn of events is that Unix has become easier to use — one of Windows' claims to fame — and Windows is increasingly gaining more capability to manage programs and networks — Unix's traditional area of strength. Still, Microsoft is the only company that provides the "true" Windows and, therefore, it remains in a strong position in the industry. There are a number of competing Unix vendors, including IBM, Hewlett-Packard, Sun Microsystems, and Silicon Graphics. These vendors are also vying for position to supply systems for the early superhighway applications.

Worried about Microsoft's dominance and the potential that it could try to control application programs the way it does operating systems, the U.S. Department of Justice launched an anti-trust investigation. This investigation ended in August 1994 with a settlement that has, as yet, had no strong effect on Microsoft's practices.

> *Faced with the prospect of pending standards that might not be their's, major companies involved in navigator design are moving as fast as they can to create products and get them into the market.*

In the context of the information superhighway, both Windows and Unix are playing a significant role in early applications. Many Internet users hook up to the network by having their personal computers running Windows dial in to the server, or work directly with the server in a company network. Some users also possess navigators with Windows capability for non-DOS machines (DOS is the operating system underlying Windows). These other navigators, which have their roots in Unix, include X-Windows, Motif, SunView, and Apple's System 7 for Macintosh.

Unix itself, on the other hand, is the primary navigator for Internet servers, video servers, and other high-powered systems in early superhighway applications. Because of its native TCP/IP capability, wide variety of programs, and portability across multiple versions, many technical specialists prefer it to Windows. Also, Unix is the primary system used by scientists and engineers, the builders and first users of the Internet. Still, it is harder to use than Windows, and has not been widely distributed on more affordable personal computers.

Major vendors, including AT&T, have tried and failed to provide PC users with Unix navigators and operating systems. But DOS was there first in most cases. PC users chose to wait for Windows rather than throw away DOS and replace it with Unix. Also, the PCs at that time were not powerful enough to take advantage of Unix's capabilities. This may change, as PCs have become as powerful as workstations through enhanced microprocessors like the RISC-based PowerPC from IBM and Apple, and the Pentium from Intel. Also, Unix has been modified and made somewhat more PC-friendly.

In addition to computer and communications companies working on navigators, information providers (such as newspapers, magazines, and broadcast media) are also quickly trying to transform their products into information superhighway vehicles. For them and other content providers, regulations are less of an issue, competition with other programs is assured, and national distribution is a strong likelihood.

The difficulty for content providers is that most are used to working in two-dimensional forms like paper and television. They can introduce a sense of three dimensions with clever art and camera angles. But they can't get out of being a one-way service tied to the date their publication is finalized. In the case of print media, they can't really guide you through the pages; words and art devices may get you where you want to go or they may not. None of these products are customized, so you have to accept the best that can be offered for the mass interest of all of their subscriber population, rather than information tailored for your personal taste.

Publishers on the front lines of electronic publications are trying to change all that. The *San Jose Mercury News*, for example, provides daily electronic services to subscribers throughout the country. You can get all the text of all of the articles without ever needing to receive the newspaper. The headlines and text are searchable, and you can customize the interface to see only the stories you want to see.

Time and other publications are also available through on-line services such as America Online.

Compared to the future, this is just a small start. On-line services from IDG and Ziff-Davis, as already mentioned, have interactive links to other services, but they still rely on what is essentially "old news." The content has been published in a weekly or monthly publication and probably needs updating by the time it's online. Often, stories need updating even by the time they're printed in a daily or weekly cycle.

Two models of newspaper navigators are on the drawing board. One — "the daily in a box" — is delivered one or more times a day as information changes or as updates are requested. The navigator accesses the main stories of the day in a multimedia format, and the information is linked to computers at the main office of the newspaper, where information banks, containing the in-depth background of the story, related stories, or a history of the topic as covered by the newspaper, can be accessed by the casual reader.

Advertisements would be delivered along with each story. Similar information banks at the main office or at the advertisers' offices would await requests for more information, and could put readers in touch with a sales representative.

The second model is a newspaper screen divided into multiple windows. Each window can contain a different newspaper, all covering the same topic. Using this navigator you could, for example, look at national coverage of the election or the Super Bowl and compare how the *New York Times*, *USA Today* and the *Washington Post* cover the same issues.

Or, you could look at regional editions, local editions, or even individualized custom editions of your favorite periodical. You could compare these editions in various windows, or could pull related stories into different windows. The windows might also have a "drill down" capability, which would let you access a central information bank to get story background, history, and advertising contacts.

Using all of these models, the journalist becomes a tour guide through the news, rather than a filter for it. You, as the reader/observer, become the news chooser — you get only as much information as you want.

Some magazines are trying out their navigator wings in multimedia CD-ROMs, available off the shelf for multimedia computers today, but ready for networked information highway cruisers in the near future.

One of these is *Newsweek Interactive*, available quarterly for $59 a year. This CD includes three months of the print magazine, plus related stories from its sister publication, the *Washington Post*. Although the initial version is reportedly difficult to install, the CD magazine uses hypertext to enable readers to quickly move to information they want and to access photos, charts, and videos.

Using *Newsweek Interactive*, you pick your own slice of information (particularly with the opinion surveys, which offer different views of the results based on your request) — something two-dimensional magazines just don't allow.

We'll see another new CD-ROM navigator with *A2Z*, which is $9 per issue (or $59 a year). You select the type of media in which you want to receive information — words, images, still pictures, or videos. More than 7,000 Associated Press stories will be available each month in this mixed-media format.

In the end, the navigator may be composed of standard components such as windows, icons, hyperlinks, and other point-and-shoot devices (like the traditional mouse/trackball, laser light beams, or pen-like devices). But we will be in control of rearranging and customizing the way we access information and the choice of media (voice, video, image, still pictures, or words).

Next Generation Internet

Will the Internet evolve as an important aspect of the information superhighway? The government is encouraging upgrades to major Internet connections through contracts with telecommunications companies. But while these upgrades may give the Internet superhighway capabilities, culture clashes between new users and Internet veterans may hinder progress.

T he Internet, that now familiar collective term for more than 44,000 networks, gives computer users worldwide access to a multitude of services — the forerunners of the information superhighway. As I've noted elsewhere in this book, companies and research centers are working on software that will make the Internet and its equivalent superhighway counterparts easier to use, thereby giving access to the rest of us.

But what about the Internet itself? What role will it play in the information superhighway? Will it be abandoned as superior networks with easy-access navigators fueled by video-on-demand services come on-line? Or will it evolve into a more advanced form to match the high-capacity fiber-optic systems being constructed by phone and cable companies?

The evolution of the Internet is well underway. It will evolve into a more advanced form to match the high-capacity fiber-optic systems being constructed by phone and cable companies.

Its evolution is not only likely, but is well underway. The government is currently encouraging upgrades to major Internet connections through contracts with telecommunications companies. But before we get into that, let's review a little history.

Back in the 1960s, the scientists and engineers involved in the creation of the precursors to the Internet weren't interested in marketing or even in payback for their investments of time and energy. They didn't care about entertainment or about ease-of-use. They simply wanted to communicate with each other.

Government technologists and researchers worked with university technical and academic specialists to gain access to distant computers at each other's institutions to interconnect resources and encourage collaboration, as well as to fulfill research goals that required large amounts of computing power. They also wanted to share knowledge — the lifeblood of academia. The U.S. Department of Defense footed the bill for these efforts because it needed an alternative way to communicate throughout the nation and to safeguard key research projects in the event of a disaster.

These early efforts solved the major technical problems of linking remote computers. They developed a standard method by which every computer using a certain protocol, called TCP/IP (Transmission Control Protocol/ Internet Protocol), could act as a fully functional participant in a network, sending and receiving information.

In the course of creating these pathways, those who actually created the technology of the Internet became enamored of their ability to push the envelope of the technology itself. Rather than leave it as it was, they continued to develop its capabilities and reach. This worked well for the evolution of the Internet.

In the early 1980s, there were only about 25 networks making up the Internet, with only a few hundred primary computers linked together. Today, there are more than 44,000 network "domains" and more than 3.2 million linked host computers.

The Internet's first "booster shot" came when the National Science Foundation (NSF) invested in the network as a way to tie together the computer centers located at university research facilities throughout the country. With this funding, embodied in what's known as NSFNET, the National Science Foundation also opened a Pandora's box, allowing the general population to access the Internet.

Because of this, the Internet has evolved from being purely a dedicated research pipeline into a community playground. Those who used it for both purposes were dedicated to relatively free and open access, but the new users were generally less "serious" about the value of the technology and more interested in the benefits it provided.

The researchers and non-technical users developed an Internet community of peaceful coexistence, but one thing remained clear: use of the Net to sell products was strongly discouraged.

Until recently, the NSFNET's acceptable-use policy stated the following:

> NSFNET Backbone services are provided to support open research and education in and among U.S. research and instructional institutions, plus research arms of for-profit firms when engaged in open scholarly communication and research. Use for other purposes is not acceptable.

The Internet has evolved from being purely a dedicated research pipeline into a community playground.

Despite this prohibition, some parts of the Internet quickly opened themselves up for commercial use. In 1991, the Commercial Internet Exchange Association (CIX) was formed by three Internet-connection providers to offer services exclusively for businesses. International service providers also opened their connections to businesses, and companies were soon able to bypass the restrictions on the government-run networks.

Soon, unrestricted commercial access was available throughout the world, except on NSFNET, which still served as a powerful national network pulling together five major computer research centers and allowing a wide-ranging community to join in.

Since then, the NSF has re-evaluated its role as a provider of one of the four major, public, high-capacity networks in the country. To upgrade the network and provide better service, in 1994 NSF began awarding a $50 million contract to communications companies to develop next-generation Internet services. The contract is known as NSFNET II. Sprint's Jim Payne commented:

> The Internet is at an important juncture in its development. NSFNET II is a good example of the higher bandwidth networks of the information superhighway. It's a move away from direct government dollars for the Internet. It's part of a cultural change. The Internet is moving out of product development into a service for a user-friendly society.

In March, Sprint was chosen to operate one of the gateways for NSFNET II. Sprint will provide the New York Network Access Point, one of three primary access points distributed around the country. These network access points will act as traffic cops for commercial traffic, allowing businesses to take advantage of NSFNET II's 155 Mbps (Megabits per second) operating capacity.

The presence of these access points addresses the commercial interest in the Internet, which is growing at 20% per month.

"The Internet is overwhelmingly commercial today," says Internet Society Executive Director Tony

Rutkowski, "We're scaling up to gigabit speeds."
Rutkowski also sees NSFNET II as a example of a useful
interconnection model:

> It certainly is nationally. I'm not sure NSFNET II is a good
> term, though, since it's really NSFNET Zero. The only
> thing NSF is doing is establishing the architecture —
> then the industry and the world will maintain and emulate
> it. It's roughly analogous to what the FCC did with the
> telephone network architecture.

But cultures do not change easily. Controversies over
favoritism in the awarding of the NSFNET II contracts
and concerns that Internet costs will increase once private
companies take over the service are delaying progress.

Sprint is unhappy with NSF's decision to award a
major piece of the contract to its rival MCI. This
involves upgrading the primary NSFNET that connects
supercomputer research centers in Ithaca (NY), Boulder
(CO), Urbana-Champaign (IL), Pittsburgh (PA), San
Diego (CA), and the commercial access points in New
York, Washington (DC), Chicago, and California into a
national very-high-speed Internet. Sprint has filed a
protest with the General Accounting Office protesting
the award because it claims that NSF has close ties with
MCI that interfered with the decision.

Meanwhile, another group, the Taxpayers' Asset Project (TAP), is asking the NSF to create a consumer advisory board to work with the agency and contractors to set
prices and make policy decisions regarding NSFNET II.
The group is concerned that private companies will
include both monthly charges and usage-based fees for
NSFNET II users, increasing their costs significantly.

While upgrades to the Internet will give it enough
capacity to match the superhighway capabilities of the
telephone and cable networks being developed — such
as video-on-demand — and although software developments will improve its ease-of-use, it may take a long
time to bridge cultural differences. The telephone and
cable companies are leading with entertainment applications for the average person, but Internet veterans have a
different vision.

"The average person has trouble using a television set," says Rutkowski, "The National/Global Information Infrastructure is not about bringing more Beavis and Butthead to Joe Sixpack. It's about providing intuitive, powerful network-based capabilities to people for business, research, professional, and governmental kinds of needs — which will become increasingly pervasive through exposure, training, and activities designed to make this happen. Indeed, probably the most significant dimension of NII/GII are the activities in dealing with people to make this happen."

Other technology-savvy observers are concerned that reducing direct government involvement with the Internet and information superhighway is the wrong way to go. For example, Massachusetts Institute of Technology Professor Roger Samuelson says:

> The government funded the computer revolution through research and development money and that funding is needed for the communications infrastructure. There are critical technological issues unresolved, such as broadband communication and ease of use and we're running out of government research funds.

Like Rutkowski, Samuelson sees our best value from the Internet (and similar networks) in providing critical services. "We need to deliver lots of bits to the home to support applications in healthcare and education. We're trying to imagine an easy interface for doctors and we don't even have an easy interface for programmers. Medical applications need 100% security. Right now the density of the Internet hides the lack of privacy that exists," he says.

Yet, Samuelson, too, must pay attention to where the investment is. He and his colleagues are currently working with IBM to create one of the largest video server systems.

The future of the Internet and its relationship to the superhighway will be greatly influenced by government policies. The Clinton Administration's basic position is to limit public funding and encourage applications that benefit society or that enhance the competitiveness of our businesses and industries. Ironically, the contradictions of this position may have a very different effect than the government desires.

Since the government wants private industry to pay for network enhancements, improved service will be dependent on whether businesses can make a profit. This means that if network users are willing to pay more for entertainment and information supported by television-style advertising campaigns than they are for healthcare or educational services, then entertainment and advertising will be what they receive. Fees for accessing these services will foot the bill for building the networks, access systems, and navigators.

Neither the Clinton Administration or Internet veterans would be happy if the information superhighway looked like continual movie marathons, interspersed with virtual reality rides — such as those at Disney World — and interactive advertising. But with limited funding, the administration can only use policy backed by constant speech-making about the noble purposes of the superhighway. Internet users right now have the more effective tool of communal allegiance to the goals of open access, technological advancement, and no advertising or marketing of products in a direct manner.

As I described earlier, open access to the Internet is provided by employers who pay a fee to a regional service provider or through service providers that meet the needs of individual users by charging a low access rate and per-hour payment. The technology to gain access is also relatively low-cost and widely available — a telephone and computer with a modem.

The only barrier to this access is the ability and willingness of the user to learn the technology enough to manage the network access. Services like CompuServe, Prodigy, and America Online — in addition to Windows-based programs — make this even less painful, but for a higher cost.

Technological advancement is guaranteed by the many programmers, scientists, engineers, and academics whose life's work is to tinker and build on the Internet, creating new and more interesting ways to access information and communicate. Much of their programming

Neither the Clinton Administration or Internet veterans would be happy if the information superhighway looked like continual movie marathons, interspersed with virtual reality rides and interactive advertising.

genius is available for free, simply by copying a program they've created into your local system. This freeware (or shareware, as it's sometimes known), allows unsophisticated users to get beneficial tools as easily as they can from computer stores, and at no (or relatively little) cost.

The culture of the Internet is protected by an etiquette (affectionately known as "netiquette") that has grown out of the long-term experience of the user population. How well someone uses the Net's many shorthand symbols and jargon is what often distinguishes veterans from "newbies." While courtesy is the predominant mode of the average Internet user, hostility can quickly come to the fore when basic cultural tenets are violated, such as blatant advertising on the Net.

> *A self-policing culture has enabled the Internet to grow in a steady evolutionary path without losing its basic nature.*

Two forms of punishment are often used to sink anyone trying to advertise over the Internet. The first is called "flaming" — the delivery of rude messages to the violator. Although in extreme cases personal safety has been threatened, by and large the severest messages say they will contact the abuser's system administrator and have the abuser's Internet access terminated. Numbers count as much as the nastiness of the sentiment. With millions of Internet users, the potential to be flamed by thousands of people is quite likely.

Bombing the violator with copies of files that are far too large for most computer systems is the second and more severe punishment, which is usually reserved for repeat offenders. The files quickly fill or overload the capacity of the user or the service provider, slowing or completely stopping network traffic. Service providers often react to this problem by cancelling service for this violator of the Internet's cultural taboos.

This self-policing culture has enabled the Internet to grow in a steady evolutionary path without losing its basic nature. The usage has increased, slowing things down somewhat, but more and more users with more information have joined in. Through it all, the culture and capabilities of the Net have remained constant.

But the twin tides of superhighway creation and increased user interest in the Internet itself threaten to swamp this evolution in a revolutionary wave of change.

Internet Society co-founder (and creator of TCP/IP) Vinton Cerf has said that it is conceivable for the Internet to someday be composed of 600 million networks. He states that, technically, the Internet can handle up to a billion networks. Large-scale routers, which move information from one part of the network to another, and software with enough intelligence to manage all the data the networks could produce are needed to handle such capacity.

Also, TCP/IP and the Internet architecture, which is based on getting information to the right address most of the time, is probably too limited for new applications that include voice, video, and critical business and personal communications.

Internet technologists are being amply challenged to create a more robust set of networks, software, and devices to master these new technologies. The Internet has absorbed and improved itself through every communications upgrade in the last 20 years. How long can it continue to do so?

The answer depends on how quickly it must adapt. If superhighway applications based on new technology and new architectures get far ahead of the Internet's ability to remake itself, then those superhighway applications will become the vehicles of choice and the Internet may revert to its original scientific and research-oriented roots.

The cultural revolution may be the more difficult challenge. The growth of the Internet will add many more new users — who may be more entertainment oriented — and its increasing use by businesses will move it away from technical and community needs to profit-oriented applications.

This change is akin to that faced by rural areas, when targeted for industrial development — norms are well-defined and outsiders are forced to adapt. New businesses may bring much-needed income from taxes, but they also bring with them a host of new residents with different expectations and needs. The original residents find themselves with a decreasing share of the real estate and, eventually, with a minority position in community politics and decision-making.

With more advanced services and systems that must be funded by companies with profit motives and with easier-to-use access that attracts non-technical users, the Internet's future may be very different from its past. It may look more like the superhighway that cable and phone companies are building and less like the research and government networks from which it was born.

Already, those who fear the loss of the Internet's early culture complain about the new inhabitants and commercialization. Some have formed their own, segregated portions of the Net, closing off access to new entrants. These corners of old culture will likely remain closely guarded and out of the mainstream of the future.

Government's role in this transformation will be twofold. It can invest in government networks, thus funding advancement without a commercial price-tag (although its foray into NSFNET II clouds the distinction, since phone companies will operate it). Its second role will be to use the law to safeguard privacy and guarantee open access. The administration is working on both these issues.

It is more than likely that any new government regulations will apply equally to all electronic networks, including the Internet. This can be good news or bad news for Internet veterans. New laws before Congress would require network providers to comply with common standards for network design and access and to remain open to providers of all kinds of content, rather than limit access to certain companies.

But policies (like the Clipper security chip) being discussed by the Administration would place the power to probe network goings-on in government's hands — not in the purview of the average person. This thought alarmed network advocates and conjured up images of George Orwell's novel *1984*, in which "Big Brother" (a pseudonym for the government) watched everyone to enforce conformance to socially appropriate behavior. Because of the uproar over the Clipper Chip proposal, the government is reconsidering its advocacy of the plan, but the issue is still unresolved.

In addition to these initiatives, the government is investing in public networks and publicizing the "noble" vision of the superhighway wherever it can.

For example, there is Federal Telecommunications System (FTS) 2000, the government's own telecommunications network. By contract, it has been upgraded by Sprint and AT&T to prime it for the information superhighway. With work begun in 1988, before the superhighway was even conceived, administrators are measuring current development against the administration's superhighway policy statements.

The FTS 2000 10-year contract ends in 1998, at which time continued upgrades to FTS will be jointly funded by the civilian side of government — represented by the General Services Administration (GSA) — and the Department of Defense (DOD), which will combine the needs of its own Defense Information System Network (DISN) with the FTS requirements. DISN is aimed at servicing two million users, as well as acting as transport for data from military computer centers and worldwide military bases.

According to a Joint GSA/Sprint Applications and Technology Quality Team, FTS 2000 satisfies the Administration's vision of the information superhighway for government services. "As the Federal Government's state-of-the-art voice, video, and data telecommunications network and one of the largest non-military contracts ever awarded, FTS 2000 functions as both a precursor and as a model for the future of the nation's information superhighway," the team reported.

Measured against the goal of promoting private sector investment, FTS 2000 meets the requirement by contracting development to two vendors rather than one, according to the team. Although the Administration is clearly looking for more than two large companies to help build the superhighway, the fact that AT&T and Sprint share responsibility for development has kept costs down, according to the GSA.

In addition, the team reports that hundreds of jobs have been created, some through the use of a number of subcontractors from small and minority businesses.

Sprint alone awarded more than $31 million in contracts to such firms.

The administration's universal service policy was matched to the FTS 2000 contract as well. The team reported that FTS 2000 "provided a broad range of advanced telecommunications services to all agencies, regardless of size, at competitive prices. As a result all agencies equally benefit when service enhancements are provided."

Though the current call for universal service extends to the private citizen rather than federal agencies, FTS 2000's streamlined integrated network replaces a 26-year-old voice-only network, for which multiple providers charged high prices for inconsistent service.

For example, the Bureau of Labor Statistics now uses FTS 2000 to collect and disseminate employment and labor-related information between its regional offices and Washington, D.C.

As a catalyst to promote technological innovation and new applications, FTS 2000 met one of the Administration's information superhighway goals. New technology to provide integrated voice, data, and video was built into the contract, the team reported. In addition, agencies have used the technology to create new ways of providing services to the public.

Efficient, interactive access to the superhighway and its services is also addressed by this initiative. FTS 2000 will meet this requirement through common video-conferencing access for all network users and government-wide electronic mail for 15 agencies, ranging from the White House to the Department of Agriculture.

Within the U.S. Court system, FTS 2000 will allow more than 24,000 court employees to access legal databases, electronic mail, and video-conferencing services, and will give them the ability to transfer images of documents throughout the federal courts. Similar networks are deployed or being developed for the IRS, Small Business Administration, Department of Labor, FBI, and the General Services Administration.

Standard integrated services, however, are easier to accomplish with two contractors than it will be with the hundreds of companies that are expected to create information superhighway services.

Another Administration goal is guaranteeing the security and reliability of the network. The team reported that National Security/Emergency Preparedness measures are in place to prevent security or reliability problems in FTS 2000. To carry out these measures, Sprint maintains an Integrated Network Management Center in Herndon, Virginia.

Each information superhighway provider will have to offer some form of security and reliability guarantee and will need to create safeguards to prevent problems, just as Sprint has done for FTS 2000. Guaranteeing the expectation for security and reliability is a major hurdle yet to be crossed for the superhighway.

The team chose not to address the Administration's information superhighway goals of improving management of the radio frequency spectrum and protecting intellectual property rights. While they may not be directly applicable to FTS 2000, providing more network access and traffic via a broader radio frequency spectrum and safeguarding intellectual property are major challenges for the Administration.

Who should be allowed access to increased radio broadcasting? How are documents sent over the air or over the networks copyrighted and how will these copyrights be protected?

The final two goals — to coordinate access to the superhighway with other levels of government and other nations and to provide access to government information — are satisfied by FTS 2000 in the following ways.

The GSA and IRS, among other agencies, use videoconferencing to communicate with employees at remote locations. In addition, a number of government-wide working groups are studying electronic mail and other technologies to see how they can be used to improve interagency coordination. The team concludes:

The FTS 2000 contract has greatly expanded public and private access to government information, and improved government procurement, while saving taxpayers hundreds of millions of dollars. Today, progressive planning is underway for FTS 2010 encompassing additional services and broader technology capabilities to ensure continued availability of services to the citizens.

Another area where the government is making progress on its superhighway goals is the concept of a national or global digital library.

"Soon, every child in America — whether in a big city, or in my home town of Carthage, Tennessee, will be able to come home from school and instead of playing Nintendo or watching cartoons, they'll be able to plug into the Library of Congress." So spoke Vice President Al Gore to the NII Public Interest Forum in March 1994.

Senator Edward Kennedy provides this view: "Public libraries are a vital information link between the government and the public. Libraries must continue to play a critical role in providing broad access to the public and in guiding citizens of all ages through the world of computer networks. Libraries will make the government less remote and more responsive to the needs of individual citizens."

Clearly, libraries are a "noble" use of the information superhighway. It is also clear that there is little profit in providing access to them, since their materials are available free of charge. This set of circumstances is the perfect combination for government intervention.

It can be argued that a virtual library containing the world's storehouse of knowledge does exist. After all, Internet users can tap into files on any server connected to one of the networks linked to the Net. There are servers at major universities, research centers, and libraries around the world.

Three counterpoints to this argument are:

1. For all that is available today, there remains a vast amount of material that must be placed in digital form before the bulk of human knowledge is

available electronically. At some point, the capacity of the technology will be tested and there will come a time when some potentially valuable information will have to "wait its turn" to be digitized. Who determines what information becomes available when will be determined by whichever forces — commercial, government, or academic — are in control at that time.

2. Ease of use, organization, and network access issues must be addressed to open up the majority of our libraries' information to all users.

3. Copyright issues must be resolved to safeguard works already stored electronically and newly created documents.

In a white paper issued by the government's National Information Infrastructure (NII) task force, the vision of a digital library was laid out as follows:

> Libraries will be sources of free or inexpensive digital information; provide access to an improved flow of electronic government information and worldwide digital resources . . . and provide long term access to the records and expressions of culture and scholarship.

> The evolving information infrastructure is already dramatically changing traditional operations within and among libraries their providers and users. It is also offering new challenges. New forms of unpublished, and often unauthenticated, digitized materials are emerging as millions of people are linked by worldwide networks.

> Digitized information can be easily updated, manipulated, and combined with other materials and displayed in multiple ways. Digital data thus creates enormous new amounts of knowledge that may be accessed and manipulated by computers, existing temporarily and never stored anywhere permanently. Libraries may provide access to these materials without ever physically controlling them, and readers at multiple sites have access to the same material at the same time.

These visions are enough to give a librarian a headache. The once-permanent controllable resource —

the library book, recording, or document — will no longer be physically tangible. It will exist as an electronic file. Borrowers who were governed by the number of books per library card (no more than three on one subject at my local branch) will have limitless access to these files, which they can copy to their own storage areas and use as long and as often as they want. Dozens, hundreds, even thousands of users could access the same file, read it, and save it for themselves simultaneously.

Librarians then will become more like computer-service professionals. "Librarians will increasingly function as facilitators, enablers, and teachers of network users; library systems and consortia will negotiate information access rights on behalf of public users of the digital library. Librarians will become guides to network tools in much the same way they have acted as guides to the use of traditional materials," the task force states.

The definition of a library might change, the white paper speculates. Since anyone with network knowledge and access to files of public interest can perform a library function in the digital age, publishers, researchers, universities, and corporations can also act as "librarians" or "libraries."

These organizations could be also multinational. "Because the infrastructure permits international access to digital information in a way that is impossible in the traditional library model, new international relationships and models can and will emerge."

These capabilities raise both local and international copyright issues. "In a global system, a user in one country will be able to manipulate information resources in another country in ways that may violate that country's copyright laws. Copyright laws are territorial; international copyright conventions and other multilateral agreements allow for significant differences in national laws. Work must begin to harmonize international copyright laws to accommodate a digital world," the task force recommends.

Since the information in the future digital library can contain multiple media (voice, text, images, sound, video) and may not necessarily be located on one computer or

Since anyone with network knowledge and access to files of public interest can perform library functions in the digital age, publishers, researchers, universities, and corporations can also act as librarians or libraries.

network, the information highway will have to provide the following, according to the task force:

1. **Interconnected and interoperable networks** (such as a high-powered Internet).

2. **Decentralized data and processing** — allowing information from one source to be manipulated and sent from that source or another remote source.

3. **Databases** — archives of digital information containing the structure and key aspects of the library's files.

4. **Navigation and retrieval tools** — similar to the navigator for home users, standardized and designed for the unique complexities of library access, storage, and retrieval.

5. **Document delivery** — While the technical issues are not trivial, the key problem for delivery is copyright. How much material can a user copy for personal or commercial use without infringing on the author's copyright, and at what point does a license fee need to be considered?

6. **Presentation** — How do we make sure that computer representations of the material are accurately presented in the library files?

7. **Mass storage** — Massive computer capacity will be needed to store all the files, databases, and copies of materials. The continuing trend of lower prices for greater amounts of computer storage will begin to address this problem. The concept of a network, where every computer's storage capacity contributes to the whole network's ability to store data, will also help.

8. **Human resources** — The task force says, "This component assumes the education of a new generation of librarians as knowledge navigators; training and retraining current librarians; and training of the public in the new technology and the use of electronic information resources."

The goal of the digital library would be to help the information superhighway benefit everyone for free (or nearly free). Far more information would be available far more quickly and easily through the systems and capabilities just described.

Nationally, at 87,000 public and private school libraries, 9,000 public libraries, 4,600 college and university libraries, and hundreds of specialized business, state, and federal libraries, work is beginning on entering the digital world. More than 182,000 librarians are beginning to face retraining and adaptation.

According to the National Commission on Libraries and Information Science, only about 21% of libraries responding to a recent survey are connected to the Internet today. But 84.6% of public libraries serving 500,000 or more people are on the Internet.

A number of federal agencies, from NASA to the National Science Foundation, are researching and developing technology to facilitate the digital library. More than 40 organizations in the federal government have on-line access to their records, some through Fedworld, operated by the National Technical Information Service. Fedworld includes access to digital libraries, more than 130 federal electronic "bulletin boards," and documents from the White House. Internet, CompuServe, and America Online can also access digital documents produced by the government.

Non-government efforts include the Colorado Alliance of Research Libraries (CARL), the On-Line Computer Library Center (OCLC), and the Research Libraries Group (RLG). These organizations are delivering documents right now over networks on the Internet.

Despite these efforts and the clarity of the vision for digital libraries, conflicts must be resolved. The task force states:

> There is a great divergence between current library services, technology, and funding on the one hand, and the vision of the NII for digital libraries on the other. The NII envisions "universal access," yet the infrastructure is incomplete. Work to be done includes everything from fiber optic cabling to installing modems at the local public

library, to the creation of software to make the navigation of diverse platforms easy, and the creation of the standard to make it all work.

The material to be considered for transformation to digital form includes more than 500 years worth of printed material, 150 years of photographs, and 100 years of movies. Clearly, there is a lot of work to do. In addition, the advent of desktop publishing has produced numerous unaccounted-for publications from non-traditional sources. Since these started as computer projects, perhaps they will become accessible over the superhighway more rapidly than traditional works.

But we shouldn't forget that at one time there was no printed material. Thousands of years of handwritten manuscripts had to be converted to print when the Gutenberg press was invented. On a smaller scale, card catalogues used to be made of actual cards. Today, most local libraries have computer-based catalogues. Some are part of networks that provide information about materials at all the libraries in the region.

Again, our society will face the need to choose — what works will become part of the highway first? Which ones may never be considered? Who determines what priorities to set? Numerous works never made it to the early printing presses and their value was lost to us forever because those in charge at the time made a judgment that the works were not worth the expense of printing. We will face the same dilemma.

As with nearly every initiative of the information superhighway, we can almost see, taste, and touch the future — but we're not quite there yet. The hard part will be inching our way through the many baby steps we must take as new technologies and policies are developed and deployed.

Back *to the* *Future*

History repeats itself through the development and application of technology to society's needs. If we look at precursors to the superhighway, such as radio, television, and the personal computer, we will learn some valuable lessons for the future. Only then will we be able to make educated predictions about the impact of the information superhighway on our lives.

The capability and creativity of information technology and its users changes much faster than any other technology ever has, making it impossible to determine outcomes with certainty.

"One thing we have learned from history is that we now know that we don't know how all this will turn out," says Harvard Business School Professor Richard Tedlow. "That is the one thing we have that earlier viewers of technology changes didn't have. They thought they knew what would happen in the future and they were often quite wrong. People watching the development of the automobile and the beginning of the industrial age had no idea that everyone would have their own car or that the landscapes would be rebuilt to accommodate private transportation." He adds, "In 1925, nobody believed that there would be no horses in the city. Horses were the major form of transportation."

When the matter involves computer technology, Tedlow's views are even more on target. The capability and creativity of information technology and its users changes much faster than any other technology ever has, making it impossible to determine outcomes with certainty. "Now we can find out we're wrong faster than ever before. Our predecessors had to wait decades to see things change, now its only a matter of a few years or a few months before new developments create change."

Some of the most successful people in the computer industry were wrong about where it was headed. IBM Chairman Thomas Watson could not see the need for more than a few "large computers" in strategic locations throughout the country. Digital Equipment Corp. founder Ken Olsen discounted the personal computer as a serious business tool.

Despite the knowledge that we can't predict the future, looking back at historical changes in technology can help us identify likely scenarios for where we're going. In addition, it can give us an opportunity to avoid repeating costly mistakes as we prepare for what's ahead.

How far back should we go? There are a couple of ways to approach looking at the information superhighway as an historical event. We can see it as a new phenomenon that will change what we do and how we do it. Or, we can see it as a new tool that we will adapt to meet needs and objectives we are already meeting with other tools. In other words, it will either shape us and our lifestyles or we'll mold it into what we need it to be.

Both views are useful. Computers were historically used to help us to do things faster, like make products, calculate numbers, and write stories. Without computers, worldwide financial markets would have no way to move investments around the globe within seconds. We would still have to stand in long lines at the bank, grocery store, or concert hall without computer-based ways of processing our requests for money, payments for food, and entertainment.

But computers also create new and sometimes unexpected things. Without them, there would not be the concept of video games, we would not have landed on the moon, and the concept of an information superhighway would not even exist.

The idea of using new technology to do the same tasks better is the most predictable aspect of change. But in automating tasks, we often find that the tasks change in unpredictable ways. Before television, for example, people spent their evenings sitting on the front porch listening to the radio or talking with neighbors. Television brought everyone inside to watch "Ed Sullivan," "Jackie Gleason," and "I Love Lucy." Within a decade, front porches were no longer considered desirable for new house construction, since people didn't use them. People also didn't sit outside anymore and wave to their neighbors.

> *The idea of using new technology to do the same tasks better is the most predictable aspect of change. But in automating tasks, we often find that the tasks change in unpredictable ways.*

Television, designed as a medium to simply communicate information to people more quickly and effectively than the audio-only medium of radio, resulted in profound changes in our society's concept of "community" itself. It changed how most of us connect with our larger community, moving it from an extroverted focus — greeting others from the front porch — to an introverted focus — observing the larger world through an impersonal video screen within the safety of our four walls.

"The change was inconceivable to those who grew up before television," says Tedlow.

Looking further back, historians have observed other surprises that started out as just a better way to do the same thing. In ancient Egypt, according to historian Harold Innis, the grain harvest was once reported by writing on stone tablets. These tablets cost a great deal to move from place to place, so they were only created and given to powerful members of society. This key information, which was needed for survival and to thrive economically, was the province of the wealthy few, who could use it to grow wealthier from the knowledge.

Then it was discovered that papyrus was an ideal substance for writing these reports of the grain harvest results. Suddenly, more people had access to the information, breaking down some of the power structure and resulting in a more distributed sharing of the wealth of the society.

The Gutenberg printing press caused similar shifts in society. Before the invention of the printing press, written material was painstakingly copied by hand and distributed only to those with the power or wealth to command the privilege. Suddenly, mass printing allow broad access to information — both scientific and cultural. According to historian Erik Barnouw, King Henry the VIII reacted to this by proclaiming that operation of a printing press required a royal license. Many authors and educators, among them Milton, created the first "underground publications," printing and circulating their works without royal permission.

In addition to the royal concerns about free access to information, religious leaders were none too pleased when they had to give up control over the creation of manuscripts. Prior to the invention of the printing press, most written communications were done by those in religious orders and approved by the Church. The opening of access to works not authorized by the Church changed the nature of civilization at the time.

As Barnouw points out in his book, *Tube of Plenty*, the founding fathers took this lesson to heart when they created a Bill of Rights that included freedom of the press. "They were determined that in the new nation, no one would need government permission to communicate with the public," Barnouw states. "Ironically, when broadcasting began and produced an early spectrum of chaos, a licensing system seemed a technological necessity to make the invention work."

So technology not only influences the things that it makes efficient, but it also causes those things to be viewed or even controlled differently than they were before. Mitch Kapor, the former head of Lotus Development Corp., and co-founder of the Electronic Frontier Foundation, has also reached back to the founding-fathers' idea of democracy to explain his basic view of how the information superhighway might evolve into a very valuable and open resource. His statement, printed in *Wired* magazine in 1993, influenced the Clinton Administration's policies on the National Information Infrastructure.

> In fact, life in cyberspace seems to be shaping up exactly like Thomas Jefferson would have wanted: founded on the primacy of individual liberty and a commitment to pluralism, diversity, and community.

This linkage between the development of technology and the ideals of society is not coincidental. One of the things that we can learn from history is that, in its early stages, technology often develops in a form that matches the structure of its society. As it matures and becomes a force to reckon with, the forces of society attempt to mold it to their aims. Sometimes society is successful, making technology bolster its power. Other times, the existing power structure is overcome by the impact of the technological change.

The same types of characters who broke out of British colonialism and extended the country to cover a significant portion of the continent can be found at the forefront of new technologies like radio, television, and the computer. Internet is the essence of pioneering technology, adapted whenever and wherever people are interested in obtaining and sharing information. At what stage will the Internet (and computer networking in general) shift from the province of pioneers into the control — or the attempt to control — of society's power structures? Are we there already?

> *One of the things we can learn from history is that, in its early stages, technology often develops in a form that matches the structure of its society.*

Once again, looking back might help us navigate the future of technology a bit better. Speaking of developments that led to radio and television, Barnouw states,

> Individually, their histories show striking parallels. All stemmed mainly from the work of individual experimenters — not corporation laboratories — and seem, in this respect, to reflect an age now vanishing. All won attention as toys, hobbies, or fairground curiosities. Yet the patents soon became corporation assets and the subject of violent patent wars and monopoly litigation. More than that, they became stakes in international struggles between military-industrial complexes. Each in turn was felt to have a pervasive and unsettling social impact, not readily defined.

Before looking deeper at the evolutions Barnouw describes, it's important to assess the building blocks of communication that preceded today's developments. The first major change that paved the way for new technology was the Industrial Revolution, which caused the population to move into cities and away from a small-town agricultural lifestyle. The concentration of people in the cities caused the need and market for mass communication.

The notion of developing entertainment and information for the average person, rather than for the upper crust of society who could afford expensive access to both, was first initiated by newspapers. In the 1830s, penny newspapers became available to everyone. Because they depended on a large circulation to pay the bills, the newspapers' content was an ever-broadening, varied, and colloquial mix of gossip, crime stories, features, and sports. Within a decade, these newspapers had millions of readers.

In the early 1900s, vaudeville exposed the average person to further samples of mass entertainment and created a market for performances that was to carry into future technologies. In the following decades, radio and television became ways to continue the vaudeville tradition of mass-market entertainment.

The first incursion of entertainment technology into the home was the phonograph. Phonograph cabinets,

which supported machinery that reproduced live performances and discussions, prepared many homes for the
entry of radio and television. At the same time, motion
pictures were initiating people to pre-recorded, mass-
market visual entertainment and information. Eventually,
talking films created a format the would mirror television
in many ways.

Meanwhile, the telegraph and telephone were
helping people get used to the idea of interactive communication over wires. These technologies also helped
the government learn about balancing regulation and
private investment in new communications industries.
The first telegraph line was installed by the U.S. government in 1844. But Congress feared it would compete
with federal ownership of the U.S. Postal Service, so the
government sold off the telegraph to private investors,
but retained the right to regulate it. Western Union eventually dominated the private business of telegraphy.

Underwater cabling made the telegraph a worldwide phenomenon, allowing Europe and America to
share news and information as it was happening. In
1877, Alexander Graham Bell created the Bell Telephone
Company, which eventually became AT&T — American
Telephone and Telegraph. AT&T initially spread the cost
of constructing nationwide telephone services by developing franchises in various regions. The deal traded the
rights to Bell's patents in exchange for stock ownership
of the regional companies by AT&T. When the patents
expired, the stock ownership remained, giving AT&T
control of the regional franchises.

AT&T also constructed "long-line" networks connecting the regions to each other. Like other mega-
corporations of its time, AT&T set about controlling the
means of production by purchasing Western Electric, the
manufacturer of telephone equipment.

The next development preceding radio was known as
"wireless," which involved early experiments to duplicate
first telegraphic and then voice communication without
costly phone or telegraph equipment. Another pioneer,
Guglielmo Marconi, started experimenting with wireless
in the 1890s. Rejected by his own Italian government,

he brought his invention to England. The British, who badly needed to communicate with their extensive fleets without depending on cables, strongly supported Marconi, giving him the funding and encouragement he needed to develop radio.

Other inventors built on Marconi's ideas until the basic technology to send and receive radio signals became a reality. But before it became pervasive, radio was controlled by large corporations and by wealthy individuals who could afford the price of these new ways to send and receive messages. This control of technology by the wealthy had tragic results in April of 1912. In his speeches, Vice President Gore uses this event, the sinking of the Titanic, to explain why government should influence the development of the information superhighway.

There is a lot of romance surrounding the sinking of the Titanic 91 years ago. But when you strip the romance away, a tragic story emerges that tells us a lot about human beings and telecommunications.

Why did the ship that couldn't be sunk steam full speed into an ice field? For in the last few hours before the Titanic collided, other ships were sending messages like this one from the Mesaba: "Lat42N to 41.25 Long 49W to Long 50.30W. Saw much heavy pack ice and great number large icebergs also field ice."

And why, when the Titanic operators sent distress signal after distress signal did so few ships respond?

The answer is that — as the investigation proved — the wireless business then was just that, a business. Operators had no obligation to remain on duty. They were to do what was profitable. When the day's work was done — often the lucrative transmissions from wealthy passengers — operators shut off their sets and went to sleep. In fact, when the last ice warnings were sent, the Titanic operators were too involved in sending those private messages from wealthy passengers to take them. And when they sent distress signals, operators on other ships were in bed.

Distress signals couldn't be heard, in other words, because the airwaves were chaos — willy-nilly transmissions without regulation.

The Titanic wound up two miles under the surface of the North Atlantic in part because people hadn't realized that radio was not just a curiosity but a way to save lives.

The Titanic episode led to government regulation of broadcasting. This was followed in 1917 by the complete takeover of broadcasting by the U.S. Navy, which perceived civilian broadcasts as a threat to national security during World War I. A subsequent moratorium on patent lawsuits, combined with the military's encouragement to improve the technology, advanced radio's development.

In 1920, the Navy turned radio back over to private enterprise, after first asking Congress to place the technology permanently under government control. The bill failed, but the mixture of private investment and government regulation carried forward into subsequent technology advances.

General Electric, which created the RCA subsidiary in 1919, joined forces with AT&T and Westinghouse to carve up the early rights to radio technology in a gentlemen's cross-licensing agreement. Within three years, the agreement failed to keep a lid on the industry, however, as hundreds of radio stations sprang up throughout the nation.

In this early development of radio, there are several elements that resemble the growth of computer networks today. The Internet began as a government funded and controlled entity, its technology nurtured and safeguarded through government support. Yet within a short period of time, pioneering Internet builders set up their own servers in thousands of locations worldwide, adding a strong private, and increasingly commercial, piece to it.

Today, while Internet pioneers continue to invent new software to enhance the capabilities of the network, the power of computer networking and communications technologies has grown to the point where major corporations are investing in them, seeking controlling positions.

In the 1920s, two power blocks emerged — a group of radio stations supported by Westinghouse, General Electric, and RCA, and a telephone group, supported by

AT&T and Western Electric. At that time, AT&T viewed the radio as an extension of the telephone. Eventually, despite the similar technology involved, AT&T began to see radio as too different from telephone to merit its involvement. In a shake-out in 1926, AT&T sold its radio businesses, but retained the networking components, while RCA became primarily focused on radio manufacture and broadcasting. The broadcasting arm became the National Broadcasting Company (NBC).

Shortly, Columbia Broadcasting Systems (CBS) was formed to offer rival nationwide broadcasting competition to NBC. The CBS-NBC rivalry survives even today and may yet have a role to play in the information superhighway.

In 1934, Congress created the Federal Communications Commission (FCC) as part of President Franklin Roosevelt's New Deal. The FCC's job was to regulate telegraph, telephone, and radio.

Radio was the dominant broadcast technology for more than a decade, through World War II and beyond. Television developed as a national phenomenon in fits and starts, with its biggest breakthrough in 1948. Barnouw describes the circumstances that allowed for the mass proliferation of a new technology:

> In 1945, as peace came, it was possible to discern an explosive set of circumstance. Electronic assembly lines, freed from production of electronic war materiel, were ready to turn out picture tubes and television sets. Consumers, long confronted by wartime shortages and rationing, had accumulated savings and were ready to buy. Manufacturers of many kinds, ready to switch from armaments back to consumer goods, were eager to advertise. The situation awaited a catalyst, a signal. It came with surprising suddenness.

The catalyst turned out to be government regulation that resolved a "freeze" that had been placed on licensing of broadcasting channels. The FCC allocated the dedicated air wave "spectrum" to FM frequency broadcasts, preserved the majority of radio channels, and allowed expansion for television.

"The pace of television activity quickened," Barnouw states, "By July 1946, the FCC had issued 24 new licenses. Returning servicemen with radar experience, whose knowledge was convertible to television, were snapped up by many stations. Advertising agencies were ready; many had already formed television departments and had experimented with television commercials and programming."

Radio was among the first of the technologies previous generations adopted to allow them to enlarge their worlds — to reach out to other countries and regions, across oceans and mountains. Unlike the telephone, it allowed millions to hear the same message at the same time — to share the ideas of a single set of voices, like FDR in his Fireside Chats, Edward R. Morrow in his wartime broadcasts. The technology was used as a tool to connect society. In making the connection, society was changed, opened, and made more aware of itself.

Television was the perfect technology for a hungry society, ready to consume. The strength of post-war victory, the pent-up need to gratify impulses sacrificed to the war effort, and the need to express a changing national culture all found an outlet in the new medium.

Yet both of these waves of change were started by obscure inventors, captured and ridden by corporations and wealthy individuals, and eventually disseminated to the average person. Government watched and monitored it all, trying to control something that had its own evolutionary destiny.

The early life of computer technology began on the same path as radio and television. In 1935, the digital computer had its beginnings in a combination of forces similar to that of previous technologies.

"Someone could have built a working computer long before 1935," states Paul Ceruzzi in his book, *Reckoners*, "The components (relays, vacuum tubes, teletypes, etc.) had all been around for quite a while. But the burst of activity after 1935 shows that only then were social and economic conditions really favorable for the computer's invention. The demands of business, government, and science had built up to a point where it is not surprising that the idea of an automatic computer occurred simultaneously to a number of inventors at that time. The Second World War was the catalyst that brought those demands together, while providing the necessary technical and (at least in America) financial support."

Early computer projects included Professor Howard Aiken's Harvard Mark I in 1944, George Stibitz's projects at Bell Laboratories in the early 1940s, and the famous ENIAC, which used vacuum tubes and operated at light speed in 1945. These established the basic principles of computer engineering with automatic control, internal storage of information, and very high calculation speeds, Ceruzzi states.

These were also government-sponsored or large-company-backed projects aimed at specific missions, such as supporting government military or administrative needs. Univac, the IBM 701, and the IBM 360 followed almost 20 years after those first efforts. The new technology seemed destined to remain in the hands of corporations and government. Computers were just not practical, or even desirable, for anyone else.

Then, successive changes swept over the technology. In the 1970s came the minicomputer, which allowed single departments or subgroups of companies to have their own access to computer systems. Companies like Digital Equipment Corp. and Wang Laboratories led this wave, with a powerful combination of mid-size computers connected by networks. Then, in the 1980s, first in their garage and then in their own start-up company, Steve Jobs and Steve Wozniak built the prototype for the Apple computer — the first information technology systems designed for everyone. IBM followed with its own personal computer in 1981, and suddenly computers were springing up everywhere. At the same time, networks connecting the computers in internal groups and with distant networks of other computers began providing access to the technology to more and more people. The personal computer revolution, followed by the proliferation of networks, took the technology out of the control of the large organizations and placed it at the disposal of the average person. While radio and television are also available to everyone, they do not provide the power and control over information and communications that computer networks enable.

Unlike radio, television, or early computers, advances in personal computer technology and the hardware and software that go with it do not depend on large organizations making investments in the ideas of a handful of experts. Pioneers are everywhere because the technology is affordable and accessible.

Harvard University's Daniel Bell, the sociologist who coined the term "post-industrial society," stated the difference between previous communications technologies and computers in an article called, "The Social Framework of the Information Society," written in 1979.

> Through the nineteenth and up to the mid-twentieth century, communication could be divided roughly into two distinct realms. One was mail, newspapers, magazines, and books, printed on paper and delivered by physical transport or stored in libraries. The other was telegraph, telephone, radio, and television, coded messages, image, or voice sent by radio signals or through cables from person to person. Technology, which once made for separate industries, is now erasing these distinctions, so that a variety of new alternatives are now available to information users, posing, for that very reason, a major set of policy decisions for the lawmakers of the country.
>
> Inevitably, large vested interests are involved. Just as the substitution of oil for coal in energy and the competition of truck, pipeline, and railroad in transportation created vast economic dislocations in corporate power, occupational structures, trade unions, geographical concentrations, and the like, so the huge changes taking place in communication technology will affect the major industries that are involved in the communications arena. Broadly, there are five major problem areas:
>
> 1. The meshing of the telephone and computer systems, of telecommunications and teleprocessing, into a single mode. A corollary problem is whether transmission will be primarily over telephone-controlled wires or whether there will be independent data-transmission systems. Equally, there is the question of the relative use of microwave relay, satellite transmission, and coaxial cables as transmission systems.

"Technology, which once made for separate industries, is erasing these distinctions, so that a variety of new alternatives are now available to information users...," said Bell.

2. The substitution of electronic media for paper processing. This includes electronic banking to eliminate the use of checks; electronic delivery of mail; the delivery of newspapers or magazines by facsimile rather than by physical transport; and long-distance copying of documents.

3. The expansion of television through cable systems, to allow multiple channels and specialized services, and the linkage to home terminals for direct response to the consumer or home from local or central stations. A corollary is the substitution of telecommunication for transportation through videophone, closed-circuit television and the like.

4. The reorganization of information storage and retrieval systems based on the computer to allow for interactive network communication in team research and direct retrieval from data banks to library or home terminals.

5. The expansion of the education system through computer-aided instruction, the use of satellite communications systems in rural areas, especially in the underdeveloped countries, and the use of video discs for both entertainment and instruction in the home.

Technologically, telecommunications and teleprocessing are merging in a mode that Anthony Oettinger called 'compunications.' As computers come increasingly to be used as switching devices in communications networks and electronic communications facilities become intrinsic elements in computer data processing services, the distinction between processing and communication becomes indistinguishable. The major questions are legal and economic. Should the industry be regulated or competitive? Should it be dominated, in effect, by AT&T or by IBM?

Written 15 years ago, these words could easily describe the phenomenon we are experiencing today. Unaware of the personal computer revolution and fiber-optic networks, Bell nevertheless noted changes that can be observed in today banking-machine systems, the Internet, and early applications of the information superhighway such as the NII test bed, video-on-demand, telemedicine, and remote learning.

The description of technological developments can be taken a bit further by looking at Irwin Lebow's 1991 book, *The Digital Connection*. An MIT graduate,

Lebow served as chief scientist for the Defense Communications Agency. Here is his view of the future:

> When asked to make short term predictions, say five years or so, people usually overestimate the change that will take place. They tend to extrapolate the present optimistically into the future, without giving due regard to the practical impediments to change that always crop up. But in the long term the opposite is almost invariably true. Most of us are smart enough to extrapolate, but not predict inventions or breakthroughs of other sorts that can introduce dramatic changes. We therefore have a strong tendency to underestimate changes that will occur over, say, a 20 year span. With this in mind, what can we say about the future?
>
> It is easy to predict that the digitization of the telecommunications networks in the form of ISDN, or more generally, the trend toward the fusion of communications and computing, will continue unabated. This will have significant economic consequences. It will also have philosophical and social consequences. All forms of information will be treated as computer data and transported by what appears to the consumer to be a single computer network. But it could be more than that. This single network will be able to provide us with information in addition to simple connectivity. It does not take too much imagination to note that computers now used in networks to improve service can also serve as information sources. Thus, the digital networks could become true information utilities — another step in the fusion of computers and communications.
>
> How soon will all this happen? In keeping with my warning about overoptimism in the short run, it will probably take longer than the telecommunications carriers are telling us. ISDN is now available on a test basis in a limited number of locations here and abroad. Its availability will surely increase during the next two decades, but I don't believe that anyone can predict with accuracy when it will become universal. Information services are now being furnished on a small scale by several competing companies, but only minimally by the carriers.
>
> Where else will all this lead? As significant as ISDN and the emerging information utility services may be, they are not likely to be the only new directions that we shall

see in the computing/communications fusion. One strong possibility is that ultimately we will see digital television of extraordinary quality distributed to our homes by a fiber optic cable distribution system. But I am confident that more than this will happen. When we are peering a long way into the future, who can say? New products will be marketed, and new industries will be created all directly resulting from the synergy between computers and communications.

While Bell and Lebow both accurately predict the merging of computers and communications, neither could foresee the multiplicity of companies and products beginning to target emerging systems and applications of the information superhighway. Rather than IBM or AT&T dominating the field, companies such as Microsoft, Silicon Graphics, and the RBOCs, along with cable and entertainment firms, are competing for their share of the new business.

These authors also predicted the need to revise government's position on communications regulation. But they could not have guessed the advent of the Clinton Administration and its aggressive information superhighway policies, nor the huge federal deficit that inhibits the government from making huge investments in the new technologies.

The irony of the technology changes we now face is that while information and communications are coming together in a single digital entity that will allow a single access system and network to carry multiple media, the ability for a single corporation, government agency, or segment of society to control the new information and entertainment pipeline will soon be non-existent.

Paul Saffo, of the Institute for the Future, says:

The biggest difference between past broadcast technologies and the information superhighway is that radio and television were scarce resources, while new technology is an abundant resource. Businesses could charge a monopoly rent for use of the prior generation's resources and government could issue licenses to limit access to them. New technologies mean the end of the structures that were set up to manage and profit from this scarcity. Communication is no longer scarce. It's hyper-abundant. There is more broadcast spectrum available than ever before and we are making more effective use of the spectrum.

Both on the ground and in the air, there is more ability and opportunity to communicate than ever before. Fiber-optic networks, based on laser technology, allow far greater volumes of all types of information and media to be broadcast or transmitted from any point to any point. Wireless and satellite technologies allow data, voice, and images to be sent through the air just like radio, television, and telegraph signals. Broadband networks allow the same level of abundance in ground communications, and cable, telecommunications, and networking companies are laying more cable than ever before to cover every accessible area.

The receivers at the end of these communication links are no longer simple telephone handsets, television monitors, or radio sets. They are microprocessor devices that can act on and react to the information they receive. They are customizable and come with independent storage devices that can contain and process all manner of media and information. They come with compression technology that packs the information into a tight, efficient form that can be easily sent over networks and decompressed at the other end. "There is so much in play and there is an over-proliferation of options. It's very hard to predict when and how things will turn out," Saffo says, "The changes won't happen all at once. They are already happening in fits and starts all around us. Interactive communication over the Internet is already possible. Two-way video is rapidly being developed. We'll be further dragged into the digital age one excruciating step at a time."

In researching the popularity of the Internet and other technologies that have started out slowly, it has become clear that only a few will skyrocket in any given time-frame. Saffo has identified three critical ingredients to facilitate this explosion.

1. **Critical mass.** Enough people have to be able to acquire and find value in using the technology to make it widely available and perceived as worth the investment.

2. **Innovation.** "…entrepreneurs with crazy ideas, operating on a shoestring budget, willing to do things that don't make sense right away."

3. **Big players.** Companies and governments that "make big investments for the wrong reasons." They build the necessary baseline components that allow the entrepreneurs to disseminate their crazy ideas.

Saffo goes on to say:

> TV took 20 years plus time out for a war to reach its peak. But it took Ted Turner with the crazy idea of 24-hour news, and MTV with the crazy idea of music videos for teenagers to bring new life and popularity to the medium. Television itself was started with silly shows like "I Love Lucy." There needs to be room for such innovations. There has to be chaos to allow innovation, but enough order to make it all work.

Gates sees the information superhighway as the first exciting opportunity since the invention of the personal computer.

While this formula enabled the formation of early technology changes, perhaps new formulas will emerge as we move further into the digital age. One sign of this, for example, is the trend at Microsoft, where founder Bill Gates is trying to continue entrepreneurial, innovative thinking in an $8 billion company tied to 1980s technology.

"Companies in this business have often lost their way," Gates told *Businessweek* in June 1994, "We will not fall short for not having an expansive view of how technology can be used."

Gates sees the information superhighway as the first exciting opportunity since the invention of the personal computer, the magazine says. "Personal computing was qualitatively a very, very different thing than the computing that came before," Gates told the interviewer, "The advances in communications likewise will create new ways of using communication for learning, education, and commerce that go far beyond anything done to date."

The entrepreneurs and companies that succeed in this new dynamic business will be cut from a different cloth than the monoliths of the 20th century.

The *Showstopper*

The toughest job on the superhighway falls to the FCC, the government regulators who must balance public access and comfort with competition and deregulation. Unfortunately, the FCC was designed to regulate a very different type of communications business. How well they can rise to the occasion and accomplish their tasks will affect how fast the superhighway is deployed and how much it will cost consumers.

In the third week of July 1994, the United States celebrated the 25th anniversary of the 1969 moon walk. Neil Armstrong, the first man to set foot on the moon, accepted the testimonials offered by government leaders at a White House ceremony. He then proceeded to describe the dedication and super-human effort it took for thousands of Americans to meet President John F. Kennedy's challenge of putting an American in outer space.

This occasion stands as a reminder of what the purposeful will of the nation can do, once it puts its mind to it. Driven by competition with the Soviet Union, the space program received top priority in the federal agenda, as manifested by both funding and public support. As a consequence, the major technical problems were solved and the mission was eventually accomplished.

President Clinton has placed a similar challenge before the country in the proposals to create the information superhighway. But unlike the space program, the government will not fund the research needed to surmount the technical obstacles. Nor is this the only challenge on the public agenda. Right now, the Clinton Administration urgently needs far more support for healthcare reform, crime programs, and deficit reduction than for the national information superhighway.

As previously stated, this lack of funding and focus has not prevented the Administration from making sure that government plays a major role in the proceedings. Through rhetoric and regulation — two significant tools of government — the Administration plans to stay out in front of superhighway developments.

Unfortunately, things are best regulated after they are developed, rather than beforehand. The Federal Communications Commission (FCC), for example, was created by President Franklin Roosevelt in 1934 to regulate the already existing telegraph, telephone, and radio markets. The FCC was also the gatekeeper for early television, holding off on granting licenses for television broadcasts until the major companies had a chance to experiment with it and prepare substantial entries into the market.

Rhetoric and regulation are two significant tools of government that the Administration plans to use to stay out in front of superhighway developments. Even though the government will not fund the research needed to surmount the technical obstacles, they are determined to play a major role.

Regulation itself is a powerful tool because it affects the financial picture for businesses. Following Congressional mandates that often leave details to the regulators, federal and state telecommunications regulators can influence how much telephone and cable firms charge consumers for services. They can allow or prevent companies from entering certain markets or providing certain services. And they can either encourage or discourage the growth of new competitors.

Regulators can impact the available money a firm can invest in overcoming technological or logistical hurdles, such as creating new computer or communications software and laying fiber-optic cable. Because the government is not funding the superhighway directly, its influence over the sources of superhighway funding — namely the telecommunications, television, and computer firms — is crucial.

However, organizations like the FCC are hamstrung when it comes to the superhighway. First, there is no market yet to regulate. So the early regulations and Congressional guidelines are hard to define because their outcomes and impacts are uncertain. The second problem is that the FCC was designed to regulate a different kind of communications business.

Since information and communications technology are merging into a single digital entity, it will be nearly impossible to have separate rules for the providers of digital services. Cable, phone, and computer firms will all have the same product in the future, using the same basic technology.

In addition, information and communications resources, which were very limited when the FCC was designed, are becoming abundant. Who, what, and how to regulate it will be increasingly difficult.

Can regulations that were designed to distribute scarce resources among a few discrete, differentiated industry groups effectively operate in a world of unlimited connections and providers? The ultimate answer is: probably not. But the regulatory system itself will not disappear overnight; it will just gradually become less relevant over time.

Currently, though, it is still quite powerful. While it cannot stop the development of the information superhighway, agencies like the FCC can either postpone or accelerate the time when it will come to fruition.

1994, the first year in which information superhighway policy is being drafted and the first time there are industry projects to test it against, may go down in history as the most confusing example of regulating before the fact. Like the early advent of radio and television, the FCC is attempting to address federal policies of communications both on the ground, via phone and cable wired networks, and in the air, via wireless and cellular transmission.

> *Like the early advent of radio and television, the FCC is attempting to address federal policies of communications both on the ground, via phone and cable wired networks, and in the air, via wireless and cellular transmission.*

Congress and the White House and laying out plenty of guidelines that will make the FCC's job even more difficult.

To his credit, Vice President Gore already recognizes the shift away from traditional communications providers. He names four new industry segments that will participate in the superhighway: the owners or builders of the network technology; the owners and builders of the information access technology; the information providers who make programs, information, and services available using the technology; and everyone who uses the services and interacts with the technology.

Gore's vision of the future is this:

> At some point in the next decades we'll think about the information marketplace in terms of these four components. We won't talk about cable or telephones or cellular or wireless because there will be free and open competition between everyone who provides and delivers information.

Unfortunately, the FCC and Congress must deal with the legacy of separate industry groups that may be using the same basic digital and fiber-optic technology, but who have very different proprietary approaches and business models.

When superhighway legislation is ultimately passed, the FCC will then have the enormous job of reconciling principles that might work in Congress's vision of the superhighway with the legislation's mandates that require it to make specific changes to present industry regulations.

How well is this likely to turn out and what does it mean for the capabilities and timing of the information superhighway? To answer the question, we must look at what the FCC has done in the meantime, while the legislation is passing through Congress and while tests are still underway for the first interactive network applications.

The first move came in the middle of early optimism about the information superhighway. In late 1993, the Clinton Administration began its public campaign to promote the superhighway. Phone companies and cable firms were talking about mergers to pool their assets and accelerate capital investments in the fiber-optic network infrastructure. The deregulation bills, mentioned previously, were introduced in Congress. It was a heady time. Even Wall Street was getting excited about communications merger-mania.

The FCC popped the balloon. Faced with events in 1994 that showed promise for the acceleration of future changes, the FCC took action based on 1992 Congressional legislation. Following a 10% cut in cable rates last year, the FCC mandated cable firms to cut rates again by 7%. In addition, the commission issued a set of regulations that outlined a complex scheme for making sure that cable firms having no competition in their local markets reduce rates by 17% compared to their 1992 levels.

FCC Chairman Reed Hundt explained the move in a May interview with *The Boston Globe*.

> The most important thing about the statute is not the reduction in price (for consumers). The most important thing is that it broke the back on unrestrained huge price increases. From 1986 to 1992 they rose at rates of 10 to 20 percent a year. That has stopped now. Consumers have had a tremendous benefit from that.
>
> We announced that the fair price for basic and enhanced-basic services should be, in total, 17 percent less than in 1992. For the average consumer, about two-thirds last year had nearly a 10 percent reduction. This year there will be a little bit more reduction, several percent more,

for the average consumer. As long as we're talking apples to apples comparison between what they were buying between 1992 and fall 1994.

In real terms, the FCC cable regulations are expected to reduce how much cable customers pay for their channels. But the impact on the superhighway, which was at least partly influenced by the FCC's decision, is the reduction of $1 billion and the loss of a year in TCI's efforts to put in place the capital improvements necessary to build the superhighway. In a July 1994 interview with *Wired* magazine, TCI CEO Malone said that the Bell deal would have enabled his company to complete coverage of the country with a broadband network capable of interactive video services by 1995. Now he expects to finish the job in 1996, barring any unforeseen problems.

> *The cable companies see the superhighway as incremental business to the home services they already provide.*

While the cable companies felt the rate cuts were a punitive measure against them, the regional telephone companies also found their stock prices falling, causing them to pull out of cable partnering ventures. In addition to the Bell Atlantic/TCI deal, Southwestern Bell's plan to join forces with Cox, another cable company, fell through.

Since then, with a few exceptions such as phone/cable partnerships between US WEST and Time Warner, and between Southwestern Bell and a Washington, D.C. cable firm, the relationship between cable providers and regional telephone companies has become increasingly adversarial. They each possess different cultures and business plans for moving into ownership positions of the superhighway networks — another challenge for the FCC.

The cable companies see the superhighway as incremental business to the home services they already provide. Within their existing markets, they can expand their networks and prepare to transmit more sophisticated interactive services. They hope to increase their revenue by charging a premium for the service.

Even with the rate cuts, the FCC action left the door open for cable firms to add business by offering more channels and more services to consumers. Premium channels, such as HBO and Showtime, as well as pay-per-view, are not covered by the regulations.

While the government is concerned about cable firms charging too much for their services and having monopolies in certain regions, the firms seem well-placed to first deliver on information superhighway-like services for the average consumer.

The Regional Bell Operating Companies (RBOCs), on the other hand, have a different set of issues to settle. Still largely monopolies in their own regions, the RBOCs have very closely managed business plans because they are regulated as public utilities. They are expected to provide steady dividends to stockholders, which means keeping their earnings growth steady as well. To do that, they need dependable rates and customer bases. They have to keep debt down to maintain a strong investment rating as well. This means that capital investments outside of projects that directly increase short term revenue are difficult to justify.

The RBOCs need to do a lot of capital investing to develop networks capable of information superhighway applications. To their credit, they have made such investments where they could or promised to. BellSouth has developed the North Carolina Information Superhighway. Bell Atlantic is piloting its own interactive TV and video-on-demand services in Alexandria, VA. Pacific Telesis is planning to develop its own cable services through a $16 billion investment in California.

The investing has also taken the form of raids in other RBOC territory where they can make earnings of new revenue bases. Southwestern Bell's cable venture in Washington and U S WEST's teaming with Time Warner in Orlando are examples of this trend.

Regulations and the technical ability to provide telephone services over cable lines are the drivers of much of the activity. Until present regulations are lifted by pending legislation, RBOCs cannot be very adventurous in their own markets, but new entrants in their territories are receiving light regulatory treatment. Cellular phone companies, for example, have moved into local phone company territory to provide some level of competition within monopoly situations.

Southwestern Bell is seeking regulatory approval to offer cable-based phone service through its partners in

Bell Atlantic's territory. Time Warner Cable is doing the same thing in NYNEX territory in Rochester, NY.

The RBOCs are concerned about these infringements on their home turf and face the need to invest heavily in the upgraded networks and find new earnings streams. These are difficult challenges when we take into consideration the need for stability. Are the RBOCs the best candidates to build the information superhighway? Cable companies will get there first with the networks and basic services. But the RBOCs have more financial backing and political clout. They just have to change the way they manage their businesses.

Is it the FCC's role to pick a winner between the two? With a mandate to provide competition in creating the superhighway, the answer is: probably not. Cable and phone providers should be allowed to compete with any other entrants on an even playing field. Unfortunately, initial FCC moves and Congressional legislation targeted specifically at deregulating local phone markets seem biased toward the RBOCs and against cable.

Such problems can be expected when old regulatory formulas are applied to new or converging technologies and industries.

Another can of worms for the FCC is the wireless world. Another way to transmit information by telephone or computer from person to person is by using wireless technologies, such as cellular phones and personal communications services. These digital-based systems take advantage of the same spectrum of electromagnetic frequencies that are used by radio and television broadcasters.

Supervision and licensing access to this spectrum by broadcasters was the original mission of the FCC during its early days. The spectrum is divided as follows:

Low Frequency (LF). Navigation and boating equipment.

Medium Frequency (MF). AM radio broadcasts.

High Frequency (HF). Shortwave radio, ham radio, and CBs (citizen band radio).

Very High Frequency (VHF). "Regular" television (channels 2-13), FM radio, private emergency services.

Ultrahigh Frequency (UHF). UHF television channels (channels 14-80), microwave long-distance telephones, mobile radio pagers, wireless data networks, personal communications service, cellular phones.

Superhigh Frequency (SHF). Radar, microwave telephones, satellite transmissions, and specialized wireless services

Just as in the early days of radio and television, companies are vying for frequencies to use for communications. These include cellular phone companies, computer and communications companies, long-distance telephone carriers, and the RBOCs.

Representing another threat to their local business, cellular and wireless transmissions of phone conversations have the RBOCs worried, and they are moving quickly to build their own wireless services. At the same time, AT&T is trying to acquire McCaw Cellular Communications, one of the largest cellular phone providers, adding that company's financial and political strength to AT&T's business.

The wireless capability to send voice, data, and video — anything that can be digitally rendered and compressed — is another potential path for information superhighway applications. As such, it is also part the Clinton Administration's policy prescription. Services in this medium must be open to competition and available to all.

Some forecasters predict that wireless will become the predominant way to communicate, once it gets around the cost-intensive issue of building broadband networks. But the technology is still lacking in reliability and its use in access devices is only now emerging. Also, it is very expensive, although the more competition there is in the game, the sooner prices will come down.

Each RBOC already has a cellular effort, with Southwestern Bell out in front with more than two million subscribers. Bell Atlantic, BellSouth, and Pacific Telesis each have more than a million and Ameritech, U S WEST, and NYNEX have more than half a million each.

Enter the FCC. Beginning in June 1994, the Commission set about allocating additional spectrum (dividing available frequencies among a larger number of companies) to allow for increased competition in the wireless market. The prediction is that such competition will help the market grow from 17 million to 100 million consumers over the next 10 years.

The wireless world is another battleground for cable and RBOCs, cellular companies, and long distance carriers. The government's plan also calls for reserving special categories of licenses for spectrum frequencies to rural telephone companies, small businesses, and companies owned by women and minorities.

Allocating spectrum again puts the FCC in the center of trying to balance the government's requirements for fairness, open access, and competition with the competitive positions (and financial requirements) of companies already established in the markets. The commission wants to create at least two new competitors to existing cellular companies in each region, which now have at least two major competitors. The goal is to reduce prices for consumers by increasing competition.

The effort to allocate wireless spectrum indicates the unusual solutions the FCC must use to meet all the requirements placed upon it. In the past, cellular phone licenses were given out based on a lottery — a better system than direct allocation to favored service providers. But a 1993 budget act required they be auctioned, with an eye toward receiving market-value revenue for the federal coffers.

Layering the government's desire to collect revenue on top of the competitive and fairness issues already included in the auction plan makes the FCC's mission nearly impossible. Certainly, it is far from the idea of promoting another path for technology innovation and services for its own sake. Predictions about how much the government could raise range from more than $4 billion to more than $7 billion.

Some observers of the FCC's actions in this case are less worried about the auctions themselves than they are about how the government will dictate competition and fairness by setting aside portions of the spectrum for favored "underprivileged groups." Such government requirements alter the economic balance of the competitive landscape. In addition, the auction will mandate which services the spectrum frequency can be used for.

These mandates draw the parameters perhaps a little too tightly in an environment where technology and entrepreneurial energy are developing so rapidly that no one knows what the best services or delivery systems will be.

One alternative would be to auction spectrum licenses with no strings attached and to release as many licenses as possible. In an opinion piece in the June 9, 1994 *Wall Street Journal*, Lawrence Gasman, president of Communications Industry Researchers, Inc., states:

> Frequency coordination would encourage spectrum owners to do private deals and would shift the emphasis from a rigid concentration on who is transmitting at what frequencies in what area to a more flexible attitude in which the transmitter owners can do whatever they please as long as they do not interfere with other transmitters. This would surely do much to encourage innovation and new services on the information skyway.

Despite such suggestions, the FCC is destined to continue to operate in a way that requires the regulators to define the territory, restrict services and licenses, and then "allow" competition of a defined nature. This is the essential model the FCC has operated under since its inception. But that was a period when communications resources and providers were scarce.

Television is another field where outdated regulations keep the market unbalanced. Television network executives argue that they are already meeting the government's criteria of universal access to information and entertainment services, yet the traditional television networks — not the cable providers — are living with regulations from a time when there was no cable, VCR, or cellular communications.

Rupert Murdoch's acquisition of 12 former ABC, CBS, and NBC affiliate stations and the continued growth of the Fox network has television executives up in arms. But they do not want to regulate Fox into less market power — the first avenue the FCC is examining. The original networks want freedom from restrictions that were created when television first came into being. At the time of those regulations, they certainly reaped the benefits of a three-way monopoly of television broadcasting. But now, their monopoly is being invaded by cable and Fox and soon the information superhighway will take a share, especially if it is a cable-driven, network-based highway and not a broadcast one.

Overall, the FCC is stuck with a system that causes it to look at the markets and technologies from a piecemeal perspective — Who are the major players? What are the costs and rate structures? How can government gain and exercise regulatory leverage?

Congressional mandates will continue to flow in a steady stream supporting the FCC's role and process.

This approach works for established markets and mature technologies where adding players to reduce prices and keeping the monopolies from getting out of control are sensible goals. But in markets at the birthing stage, such as the information superhighway, government must stand back and let the labor pains be felt until a sturdy, economically viable model is in place.

Imagine what would have happened if the Internet were built by regulatory guidelines. Each server and every application would have to be carefully examined and controlled. Each opportunity for innovation would have to be studied for its pros and cons against the established order.

Instead, the Internet thrives on disorder. Loose controls allow entrepreneurship, technological innovation, and the freedom to share knowledge and capability. This is a far better model for the early information superhighway than the regulated cable, phone, or television market the FCC has built.

In its beginnings, before it caught the attention of Congress, the cable industry was just such an entrepreneurial and innovative field. At one time, radio had that nature as well.

> *The Internet thrives on disorder. Loose controls allow entrepreneurship, innovation, and the freedom to share knowledge and capability.*

Perhaps we are witnessing an evolutionary process that will eventually make the FCC obsolete. Perhaps communications technology is following the path taken by the computer industry and networks will migrate from the corporate to the consumer environment.

In the 1960s and '70s, the computer market was dominated by a relatively small number of very large companies, each offering proprietary products that met the major needs of the customer. IBM was the leading and best example of this dominance.

Then, in the 1980s, personal computers (and, with them, local networks) emerged. They quickly became popular among consumers. But the big proprietary companies did not embrace them as rapidly as small entrepreneurial ventures. These smaller companies quickly succeeded on the wave of evolutionary changes in information access.

Today, the computer business is struggling with the notion of client/server computing. These are systems that allow the important tasks of the computer program or application to be distributed directly to the personal computer, distributed to different systems on a network, or shared between a central server or large computer and one or more personal computers.

This is a wrenching technology shift for customers and sellers alike. It is paired with another idea — the idea that all systems should be open, that is, that they can all work with any other system regardless of its manufacturer — the antithesis of proprietary computing. The corporate computing environment, after living with closed systems for years, is moving ahead by establishing standards and making investments in Unix-based systems.

The net effect of these changes is that the large proprietary monopolies are struggling to keep up and remake themselves into flexible client/server and open-systems companies.

Even the former entrepreneurs, like Microsoft, enjoy their front-running status only nervously. They, too, must conform to the client/server and open systems thrust of the market. With their own proprietary legacies and sometimes limited technologies, even the strongest computer companies now must keep changing and innovating to stay ahead of the curve.

It could be that the information superhighway — or at least the consumer-based communications and broadcast part of it — will develop in a similar fashion. Suppose the established telecommunications, television, and consumer electronics companies are the proprietary old guard. Protected by regulations, they have held near-monopolies in various aspects of providing services to consumers. But then cable technology became possible and popular, just as personal computers did in the computer industry.

Cable providers are only now growing large enough to challenge the proprietary companies with new interactive technology and with services that will turn the tables on the market. In the time before personal computers, the large companies dictated what the technology and service advances would be. They had control.

Beginning with the Apple Macintosh's power-to-the-people campaign, the personal computer put the technology and the demand for new services into the hands of the buyers instead of the manufacturers. Client/server computing increased this shift, allowing buyers to begin to control how and where applications were delivered. Open systems will clearly be a move into customer control of computers.

Interactive multimedia applications running on a widely accessible network threaten the monopolies and proprietary systems that are based on scarce, tightly regulated resources. Cable television has already altered the level of control consumers have over their viewing habits. Cable-based telephones and wireless telephones will one day also slim down the monopoly local phone companies have on voice communications in their regions.

If the entrepreneurial cable firms can be compared to the early personal computer makers, then the cable firms too will face the challenge of following customer needs with new technology innovations at a rapid pace.

> *Interactive multimedia applications running on a widely accessible network threaten the monopolies and proprietary systems that are based on scarce, tightly regulated resources.*

History has shown that once the control of the market shifts to the consumers, companies are put under a great deal of pressure to stay ahead of customer needs. If they fail to do so, another company will find a way to meet the needs and the business will be lost.

For consumers, these trends look like a good deal. No doubt there will be premiums to pay, especially in the early years of the superhighway. Early users of personal computers, radios, and televisions paid a premium for those services compared with today's standards.

The key point that links the computer industry with communications advancements is abundance. In the days of a small number of proprietary vendors with defined systems approaches or defined telephone and television choices, customers had limited selections from a scarce, tightly managed resource.

Networks, systems to access them, and information to make available on them have proliferated to such an extent that no single industry segment, company monopoly, or government regulating body can control them. This means that strategies based on limited access and low competition are no longer viable.

This is a sea change in the technological life of society, and government's role should be to acknowledge it, step back, and let the birthing process happen. Old regulatory policies designed to help the old leaders stay on top of the game are a losing proposition.

Such activity will not stop the inevitable development of the information superhighway, but it can delay it. Why not read the writing on the wall?

Cyberspace
Versus Reality

The next generation will embrace
the superhighway and the cyberspace
culture easily. They will intuitively
understand it and manipulate its
applications. Discover what life might
be like on the superhighway based on
early experiments with cyberspace,
what types of cultures are emerging,
and what profound effect it will have
on our society.

I n the original "Star Trek" television series, Mr. Spock, an alien of super intelligence, was able to lay his hands on Captain Kirk's temples and travel inside of Kirk's mind. Through the same connection, and in the same instant, Kirk could absorb the contents of Spock's mind. Today, network users can travel alone or with other "minds" as they sit at their computers. Their minds enter cyberspace — a real place in which they can exchange ideas or emotions, but in which no physical presence or face-to-face contact is necessary.

The superhighway is the ultimate platform for cyberspace. It will allow billions of minds to mingle at the touch of a keystroke or button. As such, it is guaranteed to profoundly impact our culture today and the lives of future generations. This impact reaches far beyond the simple availability of information or the presence of conduits to communication. It reaches beyond what we can now imagine.

Every generation faces some type of cultural transition that allows it to define itself and to differentiate itself from previous generations. Often, technology has played a key role in these transitions, and in some cases, technological developments have driven or defined them. Examples of this include the popularization of the mass-produced automobile, the invention of television, and, now, the widespread availability of computers.

The media is already sensitizing us to the term "cyberspace," which grew out of the term "cybernetics," coined by Norbert Wiener of the Massachusetts Institute of Technology, who was designing control systems for World War II anti-aircraft guns. The essence of his systems were computer-like electronic brains that made key connections in directing artillery.

If you listen, you can already hear the term "cyberspace" being bantered about in the popular media. Unfortunately, most journalists today are in the business of presenting extremes and simplifications. The result is that most electronic news is either characterized as the miraculous capability of this new cyberspace thing, or as examples of how truly frightening and potentially disrupting "virtual reality" can be. And, in most cases, neither could be further from the truth.

> *Cyberspace finds its* ultimate platform in the superhighway. It will allow billions of minds to mingle at the touch of a keystroke or button. As such, it is guaranteed to profoundly impact our culture today and the lives of future generations.

One recent television sitcom, for example, used a mixture of virtual reality and television images to create a plot in which a husband and wife were given the chance to decide between an encounter with their real-world partner or a "virtual" romantic encounter with a model, movie star, or "dream" person. This type of exposure may help the public recognize the technology and terminology, but it perpetuates or participates in the creation of stereotypes where cyberculture is a place for illicit acts, and which has dangerous implications for our society.

Previous cultural changes, while not as clearly media events, faced similar challenges. The introduction of automobiles brought negative reactions from the majority of the public. People were no doubt warned about the noise, pollution, and instability that the vehicles would cause — not to mention how road-building would change the landscape. Yet the economic and cultural forces of the change overcame objections to the point where we accept automobiles (and their problems) as commonplace.

We also accepted the profound change the car brought to our society. By making people more mobile, it drew them into metropolitan areas and away from farms and agricultural pursuits. They could live in the outskirts of the city and drive into it for work and recreation. It has also allowed large segments of the population to migrate throughout the state, region, or country, continually joining and leaving communities, disrupting society's stability.

In the end, the automobile was accepted because the majority of the population decided that freedom of mobility and fast access to where they needed to go outweighed the drawbacks associated with their means of transportation.

Another less technology-driven cultural change took place in the 1960s, when an entire generation decided that the restrictions and conformity required by prior generations was too oppressive. They acted out in a counterculture that emphasized individuality and self-expression. It also saw rampant drug use, violence, a loss of moral values, and irresponsibility. Many of the drawbacks are still with us, as are some of the freedoms and sense of self the culture advocated.

Television played a major role in the 1960s cultural shift. It reflected the prevailing 1950s conformity and acted as a forum for reaction, but it also helped document the change and disseminate it at a more rapid pace than would have been possible otherwise.

So technology can act both as a platform for and reflector of cultural change. It is rarely the change itself. As a tool it must yield to the attitudes and needs of the majority of users. It also can, when controlled by a few, help shape the attitudes of the majority in much the way television has influenced our culture.

The tools that are acting as platforms for change in our culture today are the personal computer and network. The information superhighway, which will be constructed using adaptations of these tools, will accelerate and greatly broaden our transformation to a cyberspace culture.

The signs of this new culture are everywhere. Its main attribute is not electronic communication — that's a given. Rather, it is the nature of the interaction that is the signature of cyberspace.

At its simplest form, cyberspace is a storehouse of our symbolic images and information. To a computer, these are just digital signals. To us, though, they are bank-machine transactions, important documents, or mathematical formulas. These are the tamer, more useful sides of the cyberspace culture — transforming our everyday transactions, ideas, and writings into electronic form so that they can be recalled at will.

Substituting electronic signals for paper-based records means that this information will be recorded much more rapidly, shared and recalled more easily, and repeated or reused almost automatically, if we wish. This kind of cyberspace is very productive and can make us more capable, knowledgeable people. Our personal affairs will be better documented and more accessible. We will be able to get instant information and answers, about society's issues, about events, and about other people.

To make this kind of cultural shift successfully requires something that is hard for many of us to do: trust the computer and network the way we trust paper and a postage stamp or the instant satisfaction of the telephone connection. Many companies have connections to worldwide networks — either their own or the Internet — but overnight express mail and package delivery is still the primary method of communicating time-sensitive large documents that could more cheaply and easily be transferred electronically.

It's not just our familiarity and comfort with paper methods that influences these decisions. In the past, computers have often proven themselves to be somewhat untrustworthy — certainly less than 100% reliable. Important information has been lost. Computers make mistakes because their programs contain bugs. People expecting hundreds of dollars from a financial transaction receive thousands instead (or, worse, the opposite!). Relatives continue to receive marketing solicitations for people who are long dead.

It can be argued that computers are only as accurate and reliable as the programmers who write the programs, the technicians who operate the computers, and the users who enter the data. Human error often masquerades as computer error.

Whatever the case, today's relatively low trust level will slow the cultural transition among members of society who have memories of a computer foul-up (or a mistake blamed on a computer). Computers are also seen as the great simplifiers of life. Like any post-industrial machine, they're supposed to make our lives easier. Instead, they have often made it more complex — just remember the last time you waited in line at the grocery store or bank while someone struggled with a computer's unwillingness to compete the transaction.

This issue is exacerbated by the fact that the computer, and now the network/superhighway, are receiving so much attention and being imbued with so many expectations that it is nearly impossible not to be disappointed with the final result. Computers are not magic. Networks are not alive. Neither can really think or correct itself without intervention or pre-programming. The days of true "artificial intelligence" are not yet here.

The next generation, however, will embrace the superhighway and the cyberspace culture as easily as it accepts microwave ovens and cars with air bags. The computer and network will be their aides in learning. People will intuitively understand the superhighway's imperfections, and many will enjoy that they can tinker with programs to change the results.

This trend can already be seen in the subcultures forming on and around today's electronic networks. There are three identifiable aspects:

1. Veteran technologists who have come to understand the internal workings of the systems and are fascinated both by the power computers and networks provide and their ability to manipulate and control outcomes.

2. Younger, avid users of the technology, but not necessarily technologists, many of whom may be followers of the countercultural themes the technology allows. These themes include the cyberpunk notions of independence from and escape from reality or the stretching of its boundaries.

3. The rest of us. Casual users of the technology whose bottom-line question is: how will it enhance my interaction, entertainment, education, or business and how can I get into it easily at an affordable price?

Technologists are found in a variety of places. They work in major corporations making computers and networks meet the requirements of the business the corporation pursues. These company technologists will build the superhighway infrastructure, access devices, and software programs. They will lead the cultural migration among those of the older generation who need to develop trust in the computer.

Many of their companies are already trusted providers of telephone, television, and computer services. The stance that they take toward expanding the cyberspace culture in their organizations and through their products and services will go a long way toward spreading the influence of these trends.

Right now, having seen the effort required to build computer systems for their companies, many of these technologists are skeptical of society's ability to create the superhighway because practical issues like funding and standards are not settled. It would be a prime mission of government and industry leaders to get these computer experts on board the superhighway as quickly as possible.

Slightly ahead of the skeptical crowd are the business technologists who are creating extensions to their companies' networks and linking them to the Internet and on-line services to prepare for business once cyberspace is pervasive. These companies use the network like anyone else — to collect and exchange information. But their willingness to link internal systems to the outside world gives them a head start on bringing their internal cultures up to speed in cyberspace in the years to come.

> *The Internet is the product of many technologists working in collaboration and as "lone wolves."*

The Internet itself is the product of many technologists working in collaboration and as "lone wolves." As Carl Malamud stated in his book, *Exploring the Internet,* these lone wolves have the ability to mobilize human and technical resources and understand technology enough to know its implications. These people have brought whole organizations, regions, and countries into the world of cyberspace.

But they are closer in attitude to the counterculture group of technology users than they are to the corporate technologists. Often, the networks comprising the Internet were built in spite of a bureaucracy that did not understand the requirements or provide funding. In other cases, institutional support was available, but not to a level that would make the job easy for the technologist. Both of these situations led many early Internet contributors and builders to see themselves as working "outside the system."

Like pioneers of the old West, these technologists are individualists. Most have a sense of command and instinctively know the appropriateness of technology development and application. They also have a desire to allow free, unencumbered access — the backbone of the Internet itself. To them, the superhighway is appealing as a universal access platform, but remains distasteful as a commercial vehicle. They are concerned about it becoming a mass-media entertainment vehicle that will allow television-like ads and programming to overpower technical and academic discussions. Many of them are based in research environments where knowledge is the medium of exchange.

This mixture of feelings makes them mixed proponents of the new cyberspace culture provided by the superhighway and also makes them fierce guardians of the cyberspace already defined by the Internet. Like their fellow technologists, they will have a lot of influence over the speed of adoption.

One other group of technologists has already had a negative effect on the dissemination of cyberspace. Though living within its bounds and enjoying its freedoms, computer hackers violate the moral and ethical rules held by the technologists and the prevailing non-cyber culture. Believing that anything stored electronically is fair game, they use their technical talents to invade and manipulate sensitive data.

Gangs of hackers have emerged in the 1990s. Their crimes include using their computer skills to break into other computers over the phone line or networks. Once in, they steal credit information, take cash from Western Union, and grab free phone services from telephone companies. Corporate and government computers and networks are the most common targets.

Hackers have been romanticized in popular culture through books and articles, and are admired for their invasion of the well-guarded turf of large institutions. For instance, in the movie *Sneakers*, Robert Redford turns his past life as a hacker into a successful business of invading other people's security systems — at their request.

The computer community — technologists especially — and other large organizations condemn hackers. The wary superhighway users will want protection against these invasions, as well.

Another threat to security is the computer virus. These are software programs that can be planted on a disk or network and disseminated automatically to all the other computer systems that come in contact with the infected disk or network. At a given time, or in response to a common system command, the virus starts working. Often, it will erase files, broadcast warnings or messages, or just be a nuisance. Viruses are planted by the same destructive, but technically astute, users who want to demonstrate their ability to manipulate technology.

Virus detection software is available, but again, industry and government will have to work hard to safeguard the superhighway against these threats if they want the vast majority of people to feel comfortable using the technology. Two limitations face virus detection today. First, any virus-detection software must know what it's looking for, so the virus must have been previously identified. Second, new viruses are being created every day.

It is important to note that crime exists on the electronic networks. So do arguments, agreements, communication, and negotiation. So does just about every other form of human communication. Everything within our culture will, at some point, be re-created on the network somewhere in cyberspace, since the people creating the network and using it for their communications are the same people who create our society and use its other mediums for communication.

What are some of the less technical aspects of the unique culture of cyberspace?

- **Cyberpunk.** This is a subculture that takes its name from a combination of punk music — basic anti-social rebelliousness — and the term "cyberspace." The essence of cyberpunk is an attitude that combines a love of technology with a disdain for the conventional use of that technology. It's technology with an attitude, according to Stewart Brand, editor of the *Whole Earth Catalog*. Cyberpunk is aimed squarely at disrupting society's comfort level with technology's power and potential.

- **Industrial music.** If you've never heard it, it's best described as a mixture of rhythmic machine clanks, electronic feedback, and radio noise. Used for dancing, this music vibrates at 120–140 beats per minute and is produced by combining computer-generated sounds with synthesized instruments.

- **Raves.** These are all-night dance parties arranged through electronic messages and staged at out-of-the-way locations. Raves are the prime playground for industrial music fans.

- **Virtual communities.** Like-minded people sometimes create their own special-interest groups on the network. Thousands of such groups are on the Internet.

These entertainments are all moving our culture away from traditional behaviors and toward a cyber-space culture. The fact that the cyber culture reflects our society means that we'll see what we really look like in cyberspace — warts and all.

An area of much discussion these days is pornography and sexuality. The Internet, with its free, open style, allows special interest groups, products, and services to be offered without censorship. At its best, virtual relationships can be formed using open social forums. People who otherwise would never meet find each other, converse at length, and decide whether they would like to meet in person.

At its worst, people with less propriety can send inappropriate messages and materials to others. Things not otherwise permitted in our public arenas are allowed to propagate on the network. How do we control it without taking away basic freedoms? This will be the challenge on the superhighway, just as it is in everyday society. It may even be a higher-intensity debate in cyberspace because controls to protect users from unwanted traffic contradict open access and free speech. There is a powerful role available for government and consensus-builders to solve this problem.

All of these are important aspects of the electronic culture we are moving into. But they are only the tip of the iceberg in terms of cultural change. The most intriguing cultural shifts offered by cyberspace will be that anyone will be able to communicate directly with everyone regardless of nationality or location, and the increased sharing of knowledge on a global scale.

It is conceivable that this mixture of capabilities could lead us toward a more homogeneous culture, in which there is a single, worldwide knowledge base — somewhat like that portrayed in the "Star Trek" universe, but on a global, rather than an intergalactic, scale.

Prejudices and long-term conflicts could be resolved through a greater understanding of the differences that have contributed to them. The simple ability to communicate clearly and explain our expectations and motivations to others through a culture-neutral medium can often enable great leaps toward peaceful coexistence.

There is also the potential for profound economic effects from the superhighway, due to the way the financial markets are handled. Today, high-profile investors and traders in the stock market have access to global exchanges connected to worldwide networks. But the majority of investors and private citizens do not.

Since the value of an investment is directly related to how much information the individual or the market has about it, the ability for everyone to have near-perfect access to information will allow more people to take advantage of investment opportunities. It will also prevent others from making disastrous mistakes.

For example, individuals who are not "on-line" may consider investing in a company because they hear that particular industry is a good one. Some of these individuals might stop investigating the potential investment after they receive an annual report showing favorable results. But investors for large institutions or individuals might quickly scan databases for news or research reports on the industry or company, not only in this country but worldwide.

Those institutional investors might find that the company is likely to get socked by a shift in industry trends, placing the economic advantage with foreign companies. They might even invest in the foreign companies instead.

> *The simple ability to communicate clearly and explain our expectations and motivations to others through a culture-neutral medium can often enable great leaps toward peaceful coexistence.*

The individual investor, however, lacking the same information, invests in the original company and loses money.

The superhighway puts both investors on the same footing, because they both have access to global databases offering news and research reports on subjects of interest to them. This doesn't, of course, mean that people will no longer lose money on ill-advised stock investments — just that they will have more, and more reliable, information on which to base their investments, which hopefully will lead them down wiser (and safer) paths.

Diplomacy and economics are only two of the cultural shifts that cyberspace will invite. In its early work, the Clinton Administration's Information Infrastructure Task Force has identified some other places where adaptation will be required:

> In the early days of the development of the telephone, some observers noted that the new invention was so clearly useful that in the future every city would need to have one to bring news quickly to the citizenry. What they did not recognize was that the telephone brought with it a fundamental change in communication. Old, highly centralized systems and institutions developed to handle the post and telegraphy weren't appropriate for the new invention and couldn't use it to the best advantage. The National Information Infrastructure brings with it a fundamental change in how information moves and is handled.

> In the application areas of education and commerce in particular, this change will require new ways of functioning — distinctly different from current practices — to achieve the greatest benefits of the NII.

Both the nature and speed with which the superhighway is developed (both in infrastructure and access methodology) will depend on which industry and government policy has the greatest influence on the issues. Likewise, the nature of the resulting culture will be determined by which group leads the changes. We have before us several alternative futures.

If we look to history, we should look at the automotive industry. Since America was fairly homogeneous during the 1940s and 1950s when automobiles really became popular, it might be better to compare the American approach to that of the Japanese.

First, Americans fell in love with luxury. Everyone wanted traveling living rooms with high-powered engines. Aspects of this vision were made affordable in some of the less-fancy models to appease those who couldn't afford the high-priced versions. Our car culture clearly acted as an extension of the consumer lifestyle — you can have it all — of the post-World War II era.

Japan, on the other hand, was simultaneously dealing with fewer resources, seeking efficiency as it rebuilt its nation. So they created a car culture that exemplified these virtues. Small, low-power, efficient, and even uncomfortable models were the norm in Japan, both because of a lack of physical space and because psychological expansiveness was not the order of the day.

Similarly, different information superhighway cultures are emerging. The true American spirit of expansiveness is probably best embodied by the current Internet culture. Pioneering, seeking kindred spirits, and constantly being innovative, Internet aficionados are willing to bear the hardships of difficult operating systems and network hassles to stake a claim in a brave new world.

Alongside these hardy Internet pathfinders are the radicals. This culture, embodied in some of the movements mentioned previously (such as industrial music and raves), is drawn to the freedom of expression and opportunity to re-create their own culture that is provided by the virtual world of electronic networks.

One good way to gain insight into the breadth of difference between these two very different groups of early electronic fanatics is to check out the magazines of record for the respective cultures. On-line magazines (called *zines* in cyberspace) include: *Internet World*, a conventional publication dealing with issues relating to the Internet at large; *Wired*, an unconventional, and somewhat-radical free-for-all publication; *Crypt Newsletter*, which features hard news, techno-political commentary, and satire; *Coder-Zine*, dealing with computer-related humor; and *Scream Baby*, dedicated to music, literature, art, and weird space-time kinks.

> *Pioneering, seeking kindred spirits, and constantly being innovative, the Internet aficionados are willing to bear the hardships of difficult operating systems and network hassles to stake a claim in a brave new world.*

The most conventional aspect of *Wired* is the advertising. The cover article in the May 1994 issue, for example, features "zippies," members of "a new and virulent cultural virus ripping through the world. The symptoms of those infected include attacks of optimism, strong feelings of community, lowered stress levels, and outbreaks of pronoia (the sneaking feeling that someone is conspiring behind their backs to help them)," writes Jules Marshall.

However, to read this, you have to strain your eyes across four pages of brilliantly colored photography and images of zippies in action, followed by a mountainous landscape. With columns like "Street Cred" and "Net Surf," this zine is a confusion of images and information. It engenders the feeling that you have to be part of the microsecond culture featured to feel comfortable with its imagery and to fully understand its text. This may, indeed, be its intent.

Internet World is also full of images, but its organization is much more conventional and accessible. The casual reader can still be thrown by articles like "FYFNSA (From Your Friendly Neighborhood System Administrator)," but overall the Internauts (as the Internet users are called) who frequent this zine seem like a friendly bunch with a good sense of humor. Editor Daniel Dern adds to this feeling by ending a column issue with the following:

> Most people aren't used to "thinking Internet" yet. That's fair; for most people it's newer than new. Our job is to grimace, be patient, and try to explain. After all, we were all newbies once upon a time, weren't we?

Both aspects of the electronic culture have insider language that would put off those of us who get our network information from reading the local newspaper or the nightly TV news. But the Internauts clearly seem to be more interested in spreading their wealth than those who frequent the *Wired* world.

Granted, the *Internet World* culture looks and feels more like the highly technical computer systems that have been around for years, while *Wired* presents a culture that resembles virtual reality — a strange place where you can do whatever comes to mind. The crucial point is that both worlds form communities and cultures of their own.

Another alternative future is promulgated by the government and industry. The view is a combination of high-minded public service uses of the superhighway and commercial and entertainment events. Government leadership is creating and enhancing the research-oriented and information-based culture of the public high-speed networks that are part of the Internet. The call of the Clinton Administration is to extend this kind of network to distant schools, hospitals, and public institutions so that government services, educational programs, and healthcare innovations can reach everyone. This image of the superhighway as distribution system is yet another cultural alternative.

Of more economic value will be the opportunity to make the superhighway a platform for any entertainment vehicle, home shopping idea, or marketing concept the consumer businesses can invent. This cultural option speaks to the convenience and comfort that our culture has always savored. But, like we eventually realized that large automobiles burn too much gas, we may someday realize that primarily commercial electronic networks waste too much of our energy on entertainment acquisition and trivial pursuits rather than on learning and information sharing.

Last, there is a network culture forming in many companies that have sophisticated systems and business applications. As I've already mentioned, these businesses are joining the Internet to gain access to consumers and other companies. Their culture is concerned with control and efficiency, similar to the Japanese car culture mentioned earlier. This passion for security and high speeds at low cost will drive the providers of information superhighway connections and services to develop methods to guarantee privacy and develop low-cost services that are scalable — based on a menu of service options from no-frills to high level.

In addition, this company-based culture introduces a concept called *workgroup computing,* where employees can use the network to collaborate on projects such as documents, engineering designs, or financial exchanges. This workgroup culture is very different from the consumer services contemplated by the communications and entertainment companies; it is just as different from the free access strongholds of the Internet or cyberspace cultures. But employees can be expected to bring their desire for this kind of team-oriented interaction home with them. In fact, many employees involved in collaborative efforts may be those who work at home.

How will these cultural conflicts be resolved? What will be the nature of the information superhighway?

Experience suggests that the culture will contain a mixture of these styles, just as the early superhighway will allow the coexistence of cable-based interactive video services with the more text-based transmissions of the Internet and the virtual reality of cyberspace. It is likely that each cultural aspect will borrow from the others and that they will, in some ways, grow more alike. Home users will become accustomed to text-based electronic mail and data access through ever-easier Internet-like applications and more video and commercial services will be piped into and through the Internet.

Virtual reality will become available through all of these avenues for educational, medical, and public-service purposes, as well as for entertainment and information exchange.

So how can we really understand this cyberspace culture? The best way is to hear about it directly from an experienced and dedicated Internaut. Steve Roberts, known as the "bike guy," has been immortalized in Internet virtual society. Steve has traveled around the United States living simultaneously on his bicycle and in virtual reality. His bike is designed so that he can rest his back, and contains enough computer equipment to allow him to interact with other Internet users wherever his travels take him.

Earlier this year, Steve wrote an article in *Internet World*. He told the magazine's readers that he lives "in the Internet." His friendships are with other Net users around the world.

> *The workgroup culture is very different from the consumer services contemplated by the communications and entertainment companies; it is just as different from the free access strongholds of the Internet or cyberspace cultures.*

Physical location is meaningless, and that means that a circle of friends is no longer constrained by random influences ... Relationships develop because brains are compatible, not because the parties happen to live in the same town. In addition, relationships on line develop without regard to physical appearance.

The net is a central social resource for me ...When I meet someone new in physical space and realize that we should remain in touch, I quickly warn them that I cannot maintain an effective relationship with anyone who is not on-line.

Steve plays, works, does research, and has "hang outs" on the Internet. "It's a mad bizarre place, rich with variety, and I've never found a loud smoky bar that can even begin to compete with these electronic pubs so rich in information and culture.... If brain stimulation is your pleasure you can find enough to last forever on the net."

The information superhighway culture will reflect all these aspects to some degree. It will be like opening another level in our perceptions. Our world and our sense of time and distance will shift just as it shifted when the phone, automobile, and television made our planet seem smaller.

Our physical boundaries will probably change very little in the coming decade or two. But our internal boundaries will expand beyond the limits of today's technology to the ends of global knowledge and community.

The New Reality

The information superhighway's
ultimate destination may well be a
greater sense of community and
connectedness on a global scale.
It may ultimately challenge and alter
the established order and structure
of organizations and society itself.
However, there are signs that we are
coming closer to letting go of our
present way of life and creating a
new one.

The technology

changes that are taking place are moving our society from the industrial age into the information age. We are moving from a focus on factories and large organizations to a focus on information. But we are also approaching something larger.

"If this is really an information superhighway, then what's the destination? All the talk about building the superhighway is confusing process with content," says Harvard Professor Richard Tedlow.

Tedlow describes the crucial missing link in the way we think about the superhighway. As I mentioned earlier, the superhighway is not an isolated phenomenon or a "big bang" in communications that will blossom full blown into our lives on a given date. Rather, it is a major step in a collection of evolutionary developments in technology, business, and government policy.

"We may be seeing the last decade of the transition from the industrial age to the information age," says Thomas Pardun, CEO and President of U S WEST's Marketing Resources Group. "The national information superhighway and global information highway will be the catalysts of the paradigm shift that will bring us into the information age."

The technology changes that are taking place are moving our society from the industrial age into the information age. The name "information age" also describes how our society expresses itself, and which tools and materials it focuses on. We are moving from a focus on factories and large organizations to a focus on information. But we are also approaching something larger.

As a society, our ultimate purpose in creating technology may be to mirror our collective striving for a connection with a deeper spiritual sense of ourselves and our fellow human beings. The worldwide sense of community that has become possible over the last decade has sharpened people's awareness of their connection to this "greater consciousness" or "collective intelligence."

Spiritually, this goal has manifested itself in a burgeoning interest in meditation and the exploration of Eastern religions. Technologically, the worlds of radio, television, and cyberspace make us aware of limitless realities outside of ourselves. This new awareness contributes to a stronger sense of self — an awareness of individual capabilities within the context of an expansive and abundant universe. All of this adds up to a widespread belief that all we need to do is focus our energy on shaping reality into the way we want it to be and it will happen.

In her 1986 book *Living in the Light*, Shakti Gawain says,

> We are living in a very exciting and powerful time. On the deepest level of consciousness, a radical spiritual transformation is taking place. I believe that, on a worldwide level, we are being challenged to let go of our present way of life and create an entirely new one. We are, in fact, in the process of destroying our world and building a new world in its place.
>
> The old world was based on an external focus — having lost our fundamental spiritual connection, we have believed that the material world was the only reality. Thus, feeling essentially lost, empty, and alone, we have continually attempted to find happiness and fulfillment through external "things" — money, material possessions, relationships, work, fame, good deeds, food, or drugs.
>
> The new world is being built as we open to the higher power of the universe within us and consciously allow that creative energy to move through us. As each of us connects with our inner spiritual awareness, we learn that the creative power of the universe is within us. We also learn that we can create our own reality and take responsibility for doing so.

With the emergence of the information superhighway, there are signs that we are coming closer to matching this heightened sense of individual power and abundant access to limitless realities with our technology.

"Technology is about choice," says futurist Paul Saffo, "Now we are having abundant choices, like the Sorcerer's Apprentice. We have more powerful choices than ever but we have to be careful what we wish for. Our wishes can come true in ways that are different than what we hoped for."

As a society, we have always strived to express ourselves through technology and to create new and different ways to experience life. "Sometimes people say, we are in deep crisis or on the edge of crisis when they are talking about the present," Saffo says,

> But life has gotten better over the long term. Our technology acts out this dual sense of reality. Airplanes were a source of destruction for places like Dresden and Hiroshima, but they are a tool for business and entertainment for the average person. The Internet and cyberspace are feared by some because they threaten to alienate people and because they can become forums for crime and societal conflicts. Yet they also allow creative experiences, bring cultures into new contact with each other and can be helpful in disasters such as the California earthquakes.

> We tend to invest our fondest hopes and deepest fears in the nearest, newest technologies as they come along. The best thing is to be a short term pessimist and a long term optimist.

Optimistically, then, it is easy to imagine the destination of the superhighway. The radio brought average people in closer touch with world events, which they shared with their neighbors in a front porch society. Television caused people to withdraw inside their living rooms as the onslaught of new realities broadcast over television became both the focal point and the fear of modern society.

Each medium was an expression of its culture. Radio was born and promulgated in the aftermath and afterglow of World War I — the war to end all wars — where America showed its ability to operate on the world stage for the first time. It got us through the Depression and gave us our first audio ball games, theatres, and eye-witness news.

Television burst forth amid the turbulence following World War II, when the nation was trying to resettle itself after a preoccupation with Them versus Us. The Cold War and McCarthyism proved that we weren't done with seeking out enemies; our television sets brought us live pictures of "witch hunts" and military preparations for nuclear disaster. No wonder we withdrew inside our homes.

The television culture, with its threats of violence and its get-rich-and-spend commercialism, is part of the "old world" that Gawain speaks of destroying. An internal connection with individual power and abundant reality goes a long way toward supporting a more fulfilling sense of self than watching sitcoms interspersed with news bulletins and commercials.

The individual control and open access to the world afforded by today's Internet and tomorrow's superhighway are a powerful expression of this new spiritual awakening. If you can imagine an individual or family in a sitting room, stretching their consciousness in a joint meditation aimed at connecting to a universal energy, it is not difficult to envision the same setting, aided by technology, providing access to cyberspace, allowing connections with a world of universal knowledge.

To be sure, distant technological developments make these scenes more comparable. Wireless computer devices installed in a media room that can connect, select, and present information and images from anywhere would serve the purpose much better than a single teleputer plugged into the wall. Stay tuned, the future is coming.

Meanwhile, in the present, we are still grasping for ways to describe which aspects of society should be reflected in the superhighway, how we should preserve those we want, and how to prevent those we dislike. We are struggling with the reflection of ourselves we see in the technology mirror, even as the basic foundation is still being laid out.

"Multimedia communication will expand the breadth and depth of our ability to communicate. We will experience a stronger sense of community through added depth (we will be able to explore a subject more intensely) and breadth (we will be able to have access to more subjects and individuals)," says Doug Dunn, AT&T's Vice President for Multimedia.

But what kind of community will it be?

Mitch Kapor, co-founder of the Electronic Frontier Foundation, has been one of the most vocal advocates for a free society different from today's TV or radio culture. "While the on-line pioneers press on, a broad consensus on key business, technological, and political aspects of the National Information Infrastructure is emerging," he states in a 1993 article in *Wired*.

The creation of high-capacity broadband networks by cable and telephone companies seems imminent. Yet even as the necessary agreements between business and government are forged, crucial doubts remain as to whether the re-wiring of America will result in Jeffersonian networks promoting openness, freedom, and diversity that is the true promise of this technology.

In the worst case, we could wind up with networks that have the principal effect of fostering addiction to a new generation of electronic narcotics (glitzy, interactive multimedia successors to Nintendo and MTV): their principal themes revolving around instant gratification through sex, violence, or sexual violence; their uses and content determined by mega-corporations pushing mindless consumption of things we don't need and aren't good for us.

What could prevent such a fate? The purveyors of network services could simply decide that a business strategy that encourages the widest variety of content sources and originators will dramatically increase network usage. A few pennies per transaction will eventually add up to billions of dollars in revenue.

> *The idea that the information superhighway is based on abundant access to communications and computer capabilities lends strength to the view that the superhighway must remain an open path of individual choice.*

The idea that, unlike prior technologies, the information superhighway is based on abundant access to communications and computer capabilities lends strength to the view that the superhighway must remain an open path of individual choice. There will simply be too much activity to allow homogeneous control by networking companies, other commercial entities, or even government.

Nevertheless, Kapor provides a prescription to move the superhighway in the Jeffersonian direction. "The future lies somewhere between the optimist's and the pessimist's views. Optimism, combined with vigilance and a commitment to seek government intervention for redress of private enterprise's failures, is the best prescription for coping with the National Information Infrastructure's uncertain future. Organizations like the Electronic Frontier Foundation are committed to developing detailed public policy recommendations and political strategies necessary to close the gap between optimism and emerging reality."

To guarantee an open superhighway, Kapor recommends:

- Competition to keep firms honest in building and managing the superhighway and its services.
- Government intervention that is available but not heavy-handed to enforce basic principles without leaving behind stifling legislation.
- Open access to allow everyone to connect.
- Content openness to allow users to determine what they use the superhighway for.
- The option to allow individuals to play different roles simultaneously, such as consumers or providers of services. The technology will allow anyone to buy or sell products or services without the expensive overhead required by today's marketing and distribution systems.
- Networks that work easily together and allow competitive innovation from third-party firms.
- Guaranteed protection for free speech and privacy.

While none of these goals is simple to achieve, free speech and privacy are perhaps the most controversial in a society where constant debates rage about moral issues and where people and organizations are hungry for information about each other.

"The new information technology makes it possible to store, retrieve and analyze masses of information — records of phone calls, credit card payments, air travel, and so on in huge databanks. Personal data collected by private corporations, government agencies, and other organizations can now be stored on a vast scale, thanks to cheap computing power. What's more, information stored in one automated dossier can be correlated with information in other databases, and can be transmitted around the country in seconds at relatively low cost. The threat to privacy could not be more obvious," states Tom Forester in his 1987 book, *High Tech Society*.

In the last seven years, the amount of data and our ability to merge and access it has only become greater for organizations and businesses. The superhighway will add more speed, availability, and accessibility to this data, and will create the prospect of individuals finding ways to access personal information as well.

Another layer of the problem is the proliferation of the video camera, which consumers may want to combine with their network systems to send pictures to relatives and friends over the superhighway. According to a research report from Olivetti, "to many people, the presence of a video camera in a room is rather too close to Big Brother for comfort."

But the possibility of abuse should not prevent the use of new technologies for the benefit of individuals and society. The Clinton Administration is trying to address this issue. Pending healthcare legislation requires those seeking medical treatment to carry a health security card. Other bills would make computerized medical records and credit information private. A five-member Privacy Protection Commission would become a watchdog agency, governing access to electronic data and pursuing reports of abuses.

The Clinton Administration (through the National Security Agency) has also proposed the installation of a tamper-proof computer chip, called the Clipper Chip, in telephones and computers. This chip would prevent access to private electronic conversations. Government agencies would be able to obtain access to the conversations by obtaining a court order to wire-tap the line. Such access would only be allowed for law enforcement and require the cooperation of multiple agencies and the court. Critics ranging from the American Civil Liberties Union to conservative organizations have attacked the chip as creating a potential "Big Brother" situation where the government has access but no one else does. The NSA and the White House argue that a standard security method is needed that the government can access if needed to maintain law enforcement capability.

The arguments have caused the Clinton Administration to soften its Clipper position by insisting on the need for standard security but not saying it has to be the Clipper technology that implements it.

It is also a difficult dilemma to guarantee freedom of speech while simultaneously protecting parents and individuals who want protection from pornography and violence sent to them over the superhighway. In an interview in the March 1994 issue of *Boston Computer Currents*, Vice President Al Gore addressed this issue:

> There are electronic keys and new tools of various kinds to enhance the authority of parents to protect their children against material for which they're not, in the judgment of the parents, emotionally prepared. And more generic filters can be installed by those families that wish to make that choice. There are a lot of new tools that can help to solve this problem. In addition, however, one of the central points that my wife (Tipper) has made for many years applies here as well. Responsible companies — which are, after all, groups of human beings who are not just in business to make money, but because that's the way they spend a large part of their lives — have a role to play in exercising ethical judgment about what contribution they want to make to the future of our society. And more and more consumers of information, and consumers of products, are curious about the ethical judgments being made by the businesses they patronize.
>
> And I dare say that these new information tools can also enhance the power of consumers who wish to register their disapproval of this company or that company by exercising their First Amendment rights, even if it is by withholding their patronage. That drives the message home pretty forcefully.

> *Too much regulation harms innovation, freedom, and openness. Too little, and the resulting chaos makes the system do more harm than good.*

In line with the idea that individuals must take responsibility for superhighway content and privacy, a group of companies and technologists have formed the National Computer Ethics & Responsibilities Campaign to bring attention to ethics issues and teach users about proper behavior on computer networks. The sponsors include the Software Publishers Association, CompuServe, the National Security Association, and the Computer Ethics Institute.

As with open access issues, we will have to walk a fine line between self-regulation of the users and providers of services, and regulations to prevent abuses. Too much regulation harms innovation, freedom, and openness. Too little, and the resulting chaos makes the system do more harm than good.

Futurist George Gilder is less concerned than most about these issues, however. In the June 1994 issue of *Upside* magazine, Gilder said,

> Some fear of invasion of privacy is misplaced. What is really an invasion of privacy is a telemarketer who gets you out of bed or the shower. They don't have any idea who you are, no notion of what you want. That's what really offends you. Ignorant intrusions, not intrusions from companies that really do understand your needs and know when you liked to be called and the kinds of things you buy and don't buy. They might even be conscious through your entry into some bulletin board, that you want to purchase a new car or house. They call you and try to solve your problem. That is much less of an invasion than an intrusion by a company that doesn't know anything about you.
>
> So a lot of the so-called invasion of privacy will be a positive experience for most people. Computer communications can be sorted through, and you can keep what you want and kill what you don't want. Increasingly, as your communication is channeled through computers, you will increase your control over it. It's the dumb terminal, the phone, which is the model of the violation. It violates your time and your attention because it's dumb. If you have a really smart terminal that can sort through the communications and identify them, you can reject anything you don't want.

The tension between the complexity of the technology and its capability is an important determinant of the role it will play in society. The telephone, for example, is currently very easy to use, but not very smart. At one time, in fact, a human operator was needed to make phone connections for us.

"We've all become our own phone operators," says Saffo, citing the need to remember an endless stream of numbers, including calling cards, country codes, and provider-access codes. "Telephones are tremendously useful. As a technology has value for us, we are willing to adapt. The more value it has the more work we'll put in to learning how to use it," he says, "Computers are like that. They take a lot of learning now. The more valuable they become as part of the information super-highway, the more we'll adapt to them."

Rather than the predominant view that technology must be made as easy to use a possible, Saffo holds that users adapt to the technology because they want to. They will go through learning curves if there's a payoff.

"Driving a car is not easy. We spend years mastering the skill because we find transportation very valuable," he says, "Devices in the future will become more complex. But we won't notice because we will learn to adapt along with the technology."

A research paper by AT&T Multimedia Chief Strategy Officer Waring Partridge predicts that the operator will come back into the phone system. But this time, operator functions will be performed by computer software rather than a live person.

> The intelligent agent could help bring back the technological equivalent of Mabel, the friendly, helpful operator of yesterday. (Sorry folks, we are bringing back Mabel, not Ma Bell!)

> The task ahead is to make our intelligent agent as helpful without a live person and live voice. This sets up a stiff challenge since a live person using voice has virtually unimpeded, real time, two-way connection with the world's most powerful computer, the human mind.

Like visions of teleputer navigators, telephone agents would place calls, find information, exchange information, and generally facilitate our communications needs. But they can't possibly get any easier to use than what we have today.

Tools like telephone agents will certainly be needed if information becomes as abundant as expected. Think again about the fundamental difference between today's technology developments and those of the past. In the past, scarce broadcast resources were delivered to "dumb" devices, such as the phone, the radio, and the television. These were single-purpose systems that became easy to use because we knew what to expect from them — a voice, a sitcom, or music. They broadened but did not overturn our existing relationship to society.

The information superhighway, just like the spiritual revolution mentioned earlier, provides access to a new abundance. Information will not be scarce. It will not be easily controlled and we will be able to do what we want with it and access it at our convenience. How will this abundance change us and our society?

One early adaptation to this new reality will be ideas and systems that help us make sense of it all. "Not all information is created equal," Saffo says, "Meta information (information that tells you what things mean and where they can be found) will be more important."

In this new world of abundance, context will be scarce. Knowing the value of things and how to use them to best advantage will be the training and adaptation challenge of the next decade.

Just like meditation novices who must slowly learn to relax before they can connect with and channel universal energy, we will all be novices in the world of acquiring and selecting the information that is important to us and turning it into knowledge.

"The highest-quality power, however, comes from the application of knowledge," says Alvin Toffler in his book, *Power Shift*.

In spiritual terms, Shakti Gawain describes it this way:

> Our rational mind is like a computer — it processes the input it receives, and calculates logical conclusions based on this information. But the rational mind is finite; it can only compute with the input it has received directly. In other words, our rational mind can only operate on the basis of the direct experience each of us has had in this lifetime.
>
> The intuitive mind, on the other hand, seems to have access to an infinite supply of information. It appears to be able to tap into a deep storehouse of knowledge and wisdom, the universal mind. It is also able to sort out this information and supply us with exactly what we need, when we need it. Though the messages may come

through a bit at a time, if we learn to follow this supply of information piece by piece, the necessary course of action will unfold. As we learn to rely on this guidance, life takes on a flowing, effortless quality. Our life, feelings, and actions interweave harmoniously with those of others around us."

What Gawain describes is only currently attainable through spiritual contact with our inner, intuitive selves. But the technological revolution is enabling us to create and have access to tools that go beyond the products of simple, rational thinking. The information super-highway and associated systems allow for the creative connection of information and knowledge produced by millions of minds. They will produce new and unex-pected concepts and images that may hold the answers to what we need to know. Humanity is, perhaps, moving closer to using technology to manifest its own spiritual and societal nature.

If the destination of the information superhighway is abundant knowledge and community, then what will it take to get there? Many writers, Gawain and Toffler among them, have said that the path to the future lies through the destruction and rubble of society as we know it, particularly that of the major institutions of society that rely on parceling out resources and with-holding wealth, including knowledge wealth, from the average person. Gawain writes,

For many people, this time may be distressing, because the world situation and/or our personal lives may seem to be going from bad to worse. It's as if many things that used to work are not working anymore. I believe things are falling apart and will continue to do so with even greater intensity, but I do not feel this is negative. It will only be upsetting to the degree that we are emotionally attached to our old way of living and steadfastly follow old patterns, rather than trying to open our eyes to the profound changes that are occurring.

Paradoxical as it may seem, these changes are the most incredible blessing that any of us could imagine. The sim-ple truth is that the old way of life that we have been fol-lowing for centuries does not work. It has never brought us the deep fulfillment, satisfaction, and joy that we have always sought.

In his introduction to *Power Shift*, Toffler writes:

This book is about power at the edge of the 21st century. It deals with violence, wealth, and knowledge and the roles they play in our lives. It is about the new paths to power opened by a world in upheaval…

For this is the dawn of the Powershift Era. We live at a moment when the entire structure of power that held the world together is disintegrating. A radically different structure of power is taking form. And this is happening at every level of human society.

Yet another predictor of the future and observer of the present casts technology at the center of this upheaval. According to Charles Handy in his 1989 book, *The Age of Unreason*,

It is the combination of changing technology and economics, in particular information technology and biotechnology and the economics associated with them, which causes this discontinuity. Between them they will make the world a different place.

Information technology links the processing power of the computer with the microwaves, the satellites, and the fiber-optic cables of telecommunications. It is a technology which is leaping rather than creeping into the future…

Discontinuous change requires discontinuous thinking. If the new way of doing things is going to be different from the old, not just an improvement on it, then we shall need to look at everything in a new way.

If, in fact, the combination of societal and spiritual change is reflected in how we use the new technology that is at our disposal and this leads to the upheaval of traditional structures and beliefs, one researcher who would roundly applaud these changes is Joseph Weizenbaum. An MIT professor of computer science, Weizenbaum developed the SLIP list processing language and the ELIZA natural language processing system. Yet he chose to focus on the impact of computers on society. In 1973, he wrote *Computer Power and Human Reason*, a critical account of how we have

> *Toffler said: "We live at a moment when the entire structure of power that held the world together is disintegrating. A radically different structure of power is taking form. And this is happening at every level of human society."*

taken hold of technology without realizing its consequences. In it, he wrote:

> When the first telegraph line connecting Texas with New
> York was laid, doubts were expressed as to whether the
> people in those places would have anything to say to one
> another. But by the time the first digital computer
> emerged from university laboratories and entered the
> American business, military, and industrial establish-
> ments, there were no doubts about its potential utility. To
> the contrary, American managers and technicians agreed
> that the computer had come along just in time to avert
> catastrophic crises: were it not for the timely introduction
> of computers, it was argued, not enough people could
> have been found to staff the banks, the ever increasingly
> complex communication and logistics problems of the
> American armed forces spread all over the world could
> not have been met, and trading on the stock and commod-
> ity exchanges could not have been maintained. The
> American corporation was faced with a "command and
> control" problem similar to that confronting its military
> counterpart. And like the Pentagon, it too was increasing-
> ly diversified and internationalized. Unprecedentedly
> large and complex computational tasks awaited American
> society at the end of the Second World War, and the com-
> puter, almost miraculously it would seem, arrived just in
> time to handle them.
>
> In fact, huge managerial, technological, and scientific
> problems had been solved without the aid of electronic
> computers in the decades preceding the Second World
> War and especially during the war itself. A dominant frac-
> tion of the industrial plants of the United States was coor-
> dinated to provide tools of war — foodstuffs, clothing,
> etc. — and to supply the required transport to vast armies
> spread all over the globe. The Manhattan Project produced
> the atomic bomb without using electronic computers; yet
> scientific and engineering problem solved under its aus-
> pices required probably more computations than had been
> needed for all astronomical calculations performed up to
> that point. The magnitude of its managerial task surely
> rivaled that of the Apollo Project of the sixties. Most peo-
> ple today probably believe that the Apollo Project could
> not have been managed without computers. The history of
> the Manhattan Project seems to contradict that belief.

There are corresponding beliefs about the need for computers in the management of large corporations and of the military, about the indispensability of computers in modern scientific computations, and indeed, about the impossibility of pursuing modern science and modern commerce at all without the aid of computers.

The belief in the indispensability of the computer is not entirely mistaken. The computer becomes an indispensable component of any structure once it is so thoroughly integrated with the structure, so enmeshed in various substructures, that it can no longer be factored out without fatally impairing the whole structure…

Yes, the computer did arrive "just in time." But in time for what? In time to save — and save nearly intact, indeed, to entrench and stabilize — social and political structures that otherwise might have been either radically renovated or allowed to totter under the demands that were sure to be made on them. The computer, then, was used to conserve America's social and political institutions. It buttressed them and immunized them, at least temporarily, against the enormous pressures for change. Its influence has been substantially the same in other societies that have allowed the computer to make substantial inroads upon their institutions: Japan and Germany immediately come to mind.

If the early forms of computers bolstered established order, even rescued it from impending change, then the information superhighway driven by the personal computer and abundant capacity for information could finally overturn these institutions. The new technology allows everyone to access and manage their own information — large organizations no longer have to do it for them. Complex business and scientific problems can be solved by combining the processing power and intelligence of scientists on multiple networks at dispersed research centers. Computer technology can finally become the tool that it was meant to be, rather than the cement of social order, prohibiting change and preventing us from addressing system problems.

"The structures that were built around the idea that information resources were scarce will be remade," says futurist Saffo.

One such structure, the company model built on hierarchy and the need to have all employees located in a single area to access limited resources, is already beginning to tumble. Some predict it will be replaced by what Charles Handy calls "The Shamrock Organization."

> The first leaf of the shamrock represents the core workers, ...the professional core made up of qualified professionals, technicians, and managers. These are the people who are essential to the organization. Between them, they own the organizational knowledge which distinguishes that organization from its counterparts ... Organizations increasingly bind them to themselves with hoops of gold, with high salaries, fringe benefits, and German cars... Not for these people are 40-hour weeks... few take all their holiday entitlements, few see their houses or their families in daylight.

> If the core is smaller than the original corporation, who then does the work? Increasingly, it is contracted out to the organizations I call the second leaf of the shamrock. It is not sensible, after all, to pay premium rates and give premium conditions to people whose work is not crucial to the organization... All nonessential work, work which could be done by someone else, is therefore sensibly contracted out to people who make a specialty of it and who should, in theory, be able to do it better for less cost.

> The third leaf of the shamrock is the flexible labor force, all those part-time workers and temporary workers who are the fastest growing part of the employment scene... It is cheaper by far, although more trouble, to bring in occasional extra labor part time, to cope with extra hours, or temporary labor, to cope with peak periods.

The Shamrock Organization is sometimes described as the electronic shamrock, which implies the extensive use of telecommuting (working at home via computer and network or phone line). The information superhighway will facilitate more advanced telecommuting capabilities than ever, allowing the core employees to more closely collaborate with and manage each other, contractors, and the flexible workforce no matter where they are located or when they work.

A corresponding shift is the idea of a work portfolio: "There are five main categories of work, for the portfolio," Handy states, "wage work and fee work, which are both forms of paid work; home work; gift work; and study work, which are all free work."

The idea is that because of all the upheaval and organizational change, people will not stay with a single organization or even work full-time at a single job. They will maintain a varied portfolio of different jobs, some part-time, some contract. They will incorporate their family, charity, and educational commitments into an integrated whole as part of their work life.

"The world that our parents knew is not the world we live in today; nor is our world any sure guide to the way our children will live and love and work," Handy says "We live in an age of unreason when we can no longer assume that what worked well once will work well again, when most assumptions can be legitimately challenged."

The one clear aspect of the present and the future is that we have the opportunity to choose. We can and should make choices about our participation in the greater spiritual and technological community. But we should be careful what we wish for. Wishes often come true in ways we don't expect.

Living Room Virtual Reality

The next generation of information superhighway services will allow us to create virtual worlds for entertainment, education, and communication. How do we manage these worlds as a society? How do we make best use of them? What issues will we have to resolve? How long will it take to get there?

High-speed, communal information sharing will be within our grasp within the next 5 to 10 years. It will start in isolated regions with limited applications and blossom into full-blown national and global access to sophisticated entertainment, educational, medical, and commercial systems. It will greatly affect the way we live, bringing with it new ways to view ourselves and the world. But the information superhighway's first phase of multimedia applications is only the tip of a very powerful iceberg.

As we move into the 21st century, the availability of instant access to information of all kinds will become commonplace. To future generations, this technology that is so exciting to us will seem as primitive as Morse Code does today. Having interactive access to a wide variety of multimedia systems throughout the world will seem as archaic as being able to send only dots and dashes across the country instead of communicating by voice.

Computers and communications technology will continue to advance. These advances will support the deployment of a technology that is only now beginning to be known or understood outside of scientific laboratories — virtual reality. Virtual reality can be defined in many ways, but at its highest level it is nothing less than the addition of another layer of reality to our possible experiences. The broad availability of virtual reality systems across a network, accessible within the boundaries of our own homes and offices, will alter our perceptions of time and space and free us from the limitations of distance.

The best way to understand virtual reality is to draw on your own imagination. In the world of our minds, we can create whatever reality we want. We can place ourselves in the past or future, in our present location or a distant one, in a real world we have seen or one we can only imagine in our hearts and minds. There are no limits in our imaginations.

This world of the imagination is a virtual reality. It is not real or tangible, but it does exist for us. Virtual reality technology gives us the means to externally

> *The broad availability* of virtual reality systems across a network, that are accessible within the boundaries of our own homes and offices, will alter our perceptions of time and space and free us from the limitations of distance.

interact with this internal virtual world. It can contain the product of our minds or the minds of others. The power of the network will mean it can be shared across distances by multiple people at the same time.

In his book *The Metaphysics of Virtual Reality*, Michael Heim, a well-known lecturer on virtual reality, identifies seven aspects of the technology:

1. **Simulation.** Simulations include computer graphics and image-reproduction systems. "These dataworlds spring from military flight simulators. Now they are being applied to medicine, entertainment, and education and training," Heim states. Their key attribute is to offer a replica of the real environment or object that fools our senses into perceiving the simulation as real.

2. **Interaction.** "Some people consider virtual reality any electronic representation with which they interact," he writes. Take popular personal computer programs such as Windows or Macintosh. These systems present screens containing icons that are not real. They may represent disposing of files (a trashcan) or starting a program (a picture of a word processor or database table), but they live only in the virtual world of the computer screen. Yet, we interact with them as if they were real entities. Heim states that,

   Defined broadly, virtual reality sometimes stretches over many aspects of electronic life. Beyond computer-generated desktops, it includes the virtual persons we know through telephone or computer networks. It includes the entertainer or politician who appears on television to interact on the phone with callers. It includes virtual universities where students attend class on line, visit virtual classrooms, and socialize in virtual cafeterias.

3. **Artificiality.** The virtual reality object, environment, or experience is not real. Like a number of human-made creations that we consider artificial, VR is artificial but we will take it for granted as part of our reality. Artificial sweeteners in our foods, artificial

sunlight in our homes, and artificial medical devices in our bodies are some good examples.

4. **Immersion.** This is one of the best-known attributes of today's virtual reality systems, although some also consider non-immersive technology such as computer-generated images superimposed on real images, to be a version of virtual reality. Users of immersive systems are surrounded by their environment. Their senses "feel" as if they are in the world of the program designer's creation. Common devices that make this illusion possible are called Head-Mounted Displays (HMD), sometimes known as helmets, and gloves. These devices both eliminate sensory contact from the real environment and provide artificial feedback from hand and other movements while projecting users visually and acoustically into a virtual world. Heim describes one real-world application of this technology in widespread use today:

A prime example of immersion comes from the U.S. Air Force, which developed some of this hardware for flight simulation. The computer generates much of the same sensory input that a jet pilot would experience in an actual cockpit. The pilot responds to the sensations by, for instance, turning a control knob, which in turn feeds into the computer, which again adjusts the sensations. In this way, a pilot can get practice or training without leaving the ground. To date, commercial pilots can upgrade their licenses on certain levels by putting in a certain number of hours on a flight simulator.

Computer feedback may do more than readjust the user's sensations to give a pseudoexperience of flying. The feedback may also connect to an actual aircraft, so that when the pilot turns a knob, a real aircraft motor turns over or a real weapon fires. The pilot in this case feels immersed and fully present in a virtual world, which in turn connects to the real world.

When you are flying low in an F-16 Falcon at supersonic speeds over mountainous terrain, the less you see of the real world, the more control you can have over your aircraft. A virtual cockpit filters the real scene and represents a more readable world. In this sense, virtual reality can preserve the human significance of an overwhelming rush of split-second data.

Other virtual reality simulations that provide a filter for our senses include: molecular biology (where virtual reality allows scientists to "see and touch" individual molecules), airflow simulation, medical training, architecture (where the building changes shape as we require it to), and industrial design.

Boeing plans to provide flight controllers with a virtual reality view of an entire airport by projecting data into data suits that will be worn at the controllers' stations. Satellites and cameras will be used to continuously record a bird's-eye view of the airport and transmit it to computers connected to the data suit.

NASA has created a Virtual Interface Environment Workstation (VIEW), which is used to allow an earthbound operator to manipulate objects on distant planets. The virtual reality environment is fed by data from robots positioned on the moon or Mars.

5. **Telepresence.** By using robots that can operate in distant locations while being controlled by an operator in a virtual environment based on the robots' data feedback, we can project our presence elsewhere, even into environments hostile to human life. Heim describes this attribute:

    Virtual reality shades into telepresence when you are present from a distant location — "present" in the sense that you are aware of what's going on, effective, and able to accomplish tasks by observing, reaching, grabbing, and moving objects with your own hands as though they were close up.

Like explorers of the moon and Mars, doctors are experimenting with using computer-controlled robots to project themselves and their capabilities where they cannot easily be physically present. Tiny robots placed inside a patient could project the doctors inside of the body through a virtual depiction of

> *Like explorers of the moon and Mars, doctors are experimenting with computer-controlled robots as a way to project themselves and their capabilities where they cannot easily be physically present.*

the environment, allowing them to examine and even to perform routine operations without major surgery. Reality is beginning to merge with fantasy as we move toward the common use of such technology. The use of robotics in medicine is very similar to the movie *Fantastic Voyage*, in which doctors are miniaturized to conduct a voyage into a patient's body to cure a terminal illness.

6. **Full-body immersion.** This form of virtual reality lets its users project a virtual (computer-generated) image of themselves into an environment. This is accomplished by the strategic placement of cameras designed to pick up, analyze, and transmit data about body movements. Here's what Heim has to say:

> I see a floating ball projected on a screen. My computer-projected hand reaches out and grabs the ball. The computer constantly updates the interaction of my body and the synthetic world that I see, hear, touch.

7. **Networked communications.** It will one day be possible to share virtual reality environments over the network as we now share imaginary thoughts over our telephone lines. These virtual worlds can be communicated from individual to individual or could be jointly created by one or more people. Ultimately, they may take on their own "reality" as new forms of communication and interaction are developed.

One day it will be possible to share virtual reality environments over the network as we now share imaginary thoughts over phone lines.

Whether virtual reality is indeed another reality equal to what we know today is still being debated. "If for two thousand years Western culture has puzzled over the meaning of reality, we cannot expect ourselves in two minutes, or even two decades, to arrive at the meaning of virtual reality," Heim writes.

One place where virtual reality comes to life for thousands of average people is at Epcot Center, Universal Studios, and MGM Studios theme parks in Florida. While there are many simulations, there are three that move beyond anything else in entertainment: "Body Wars" — a trip through a virtual larger-than-life human body at Epcot; "Star Tours" — MGM's Star Wars ride, involving a trip to another planet; and "Back to the Future : The Ride," — an intense time-traveling encounter. These rides differ from simulations, because they make you believe you are in another reality.

"Star Tours" and "Back to the Future" are best equipped to transport your senses because they involve stepping into a vehicle (a star shuttle and a time machine, respectively). The vehicles perfectly match our expectations of the event — how else would one enter outer space or move through the ages? Neither vehicle actually leaves the room they are in, yet they gyrate, angle up and down, and move sideways in such a way that both body and mind believe there is movement. They feel like virtual roller coasters.

Layered onto these platforms are sound and video presentations perfectly sequenced to the movement of the vehicles. This combination of sensory input allows you to be overwhelmed by the "reality" of the moment. It is only your rational mind that must remember a sense of real time and place.

Another dimension that clinches your disorientation is the sense of danger that is promoted by rapid changes in direction and speed of the virtual vehicle combined with video images of collisions and inescapable disasters. There is no steering wheel. You are the victim of a mani-acal robot and a foolhardy scientist who barely seem to have things under control, and who seem unable to anticipate events.

Robots and videos inside the vehicle that stay con-stant during the "trip" provide some measure of consis-tency and safety, while simultaneously adding to the illusion. Their credibility is strained as they "lead" the vehicle through the wrong paths, causing crashes and mayhem throughout the trip.

Wrong-way flying through the takeoff bay, followed by encounters with asteroids, imperial cruisers, and light-speed miscalculations are all packed into the 10 minutes of "Star Tours."

"Buckle up! Doc Brown is sending you screaming through time!" reads the promotion for "Back to the

Future." "Climbing, diving, blasting you into the past for an Ice-Age encounter with avalanches, dinosaurs, and a molten volcano. Then rocketing you into Hill Valley 2015. It's a 21-million-jigowatt-sensurround adventure that brings the blockbuster to life — and makes other thrill rides seem tame!"

Believe it. These trips are very real, challenging the concept of reality. Unfortunately, as in other simulations at these and other theme parks, the only access is by traveling to the location, waiting in line, and paying a premium for a very brief physical experience.

The information superhighway may one day make it possible for such experiences to become available anytime we wish through a network and virtual reality gear in our own homes and workplaces.

How and when will we get there?

Virtual reality expert Michael Heim addresses the issue this way:

> When and how are difficult questions because we need to take into account several factors, and even then we cannot be sure our predictions are not wishful thinking. But first, let me say that the move — from the net to virtual reality — seems inevitable. It's the whole thrust of evolution at this stage.
>
> We have these incredible visualization tools in mind, and our software tools are getting to be visualization enhancers. We have a loop between desire, ability to visualize, and making the desired appear before us. We see prototypes and usable tools like Virtus Walkthru, and we are visualizing with them in greater detail than ever before.
>
> The virtual reality we think about is going to materialize as surely as we are moving now from a command line interface to graphic interfaces. The evolutionary engine propelling us from ASCII to Windows to multimedia will not stop short of VR, which of course is not an interface at all but an immersion in data.
>
> The Internet, despite its hacker feel and nerdy Unix style, has already given birth to the MUDS or Multi-User-Dimensions, which present something envisioned by

Vernor Vinge's superb story "True Names." In that 1980 story, Vinge describes an information superhighway that looks less like Gibson's cyberpunk and more like the actual Internet today. "True Names" shows us computer users who master the data world by using imagination and metaphor. They take on weird personae and envision a medieval world full of magicians, castles, warlocks, molochs, and beautiful damsels — all the while mastering their computer tools through this imaginative overlay. Vinge's story contrasts the ease and skill of those wizard story builders with the literal-minded law enforcement people who never really comprehend the skillful use of computers and who fail to appreciate those who dwell in the rich world of computer imagination.

Our ability to use inner visualization will become ever more dominant as we evolve computer tools. Vinge is right: Animation is a power of the imagination, and those who treat the data world animistically will inherit that world most usefully. We can truly dwell in a world only insofar as we live in it creatively, as Heidegger pointed out. We "make" ourselves at home. So, Vinge's "True Names" correctly crosses the wires of visualization and computer data, quite precisely envisioning what the MUD dwellers are showing us on the Internet today. The MUD can only suggest what hardware will have to accomplish in the next ten years.

The hardware limps behind, of course, as it always has. Remember, Leibniz envisioned his "possible worlds" and his network of monads 300 years ago. It took that long to apply his symbolic logic to switching circuits and to get the hardware up and running. So when we see the MUDS still using ASCII alphabet and Zork-like movement, well, we have to look beyond the state of current hardware and glimpse the trajectory and not the actual usage.

On the Internet, some people are enthusiastic about Mosaic. It's a graphic navigating page. Right now, most people don't have the connection necessary to run Mosaic, and you need workstation or Pentium power hardware to get Mosaic up to speed. But in time, such graphic tools will tame the Internet and make it more friendly. So, more sensory immersions are on the way, but I believe sooner than we think.

I notice many companies coming up with new interface software for the Internet, and as usage grows so will the demand for speed and facility and bandwidth.

As for other venues, the people at Sarnoff Labs, where we got color TV, are taking personal entrepreneurial risks to jump ship and go develop content for the multimedia TV that will spring from the merger of cable and telephone. It's hard to say just when these mergers will actualize but it would be silly to think ten years from now we will lack the multi-sensory approach of virtual reality in our homes.

Full-fledged virtual reality, with immersion of several senses, will always be restricted to specific uses, and would be distracting in contexts where it is not needed. Sometimes we want to focus on non-sensory ideas or narrow bandwidth communications. As a species, we have learned to cut ourselves off from sensory awareness in order to enhance one or another of the senses, and virtual reality will be no exception. We censor our animalistic full immersion in primary reality, so why should virtual reality be different? Just because we can immerse ourselves in imaginary sensory worlds doesn't mean we will do so every opportunity we get.

As a culture, we breed our youngsters to focus their attention and sublimate their senses. We will do the same with virtual reality. Why create virtual worlds that simply duplicate the primary world? We will have specific reasons for each type of virtual world, and each type of virtual reality will come with a price tag.

Multimedia applications with sensory immersion will make sense only where they are needed, whether we are doing medical examinations or taking a recreational break that teaches us something interesting and enriching about the world we live in.

How we might use the new technology is an open question. One good speculation can be found in the science fiction television series, "Star Trek: The Next Generation." It's called the Holodeck, and Heim discusses it, as well:

Along with its cargo bay of imaginative treasures, the starship Enterprise brought the Holodeck. The Holodeck is familiar in the vocabulary of virtual reality pioneers. For most people, the Holodeck portrays the ideal human-computer interface. It is a virtual room that transforms spoken commands into realistic landscapes populated with walking, talking humanoids and detailed artifacts appearing so lifelike that they are indistinguishable from reality. The Holodeck is used by the crew of the starship Enterprise to visit faraway times and places such as medieval England and 1920s America. Generally, the Holodeck offers the crew rest and recreation, escape and entertainment, on long interstellar voyages.

While not every VR pioneer explicitly agrees on goals, the Holodeck draws the research onward...

Disney World's attractions and Universal Studios' "rides" are virtual Holodecks. The visitor is almost as immersed in a virtual reality — complete with humans that play their parts — as Captain John Luc Picard's crew.

One aspect of these experiences that helps make them more real is the visitor's familiarity with the environment being visited. Most visitors to "Star Tours" and "Back to the Future" have seen the movies, some more than once. They have expectations based on these viewings. This gives the creators of the event something to use to grab their attention and allegiance. Nothing is as reassuring as having our expectations met.

There are many people who walk away from Disney's and Universal's virtual Holodecks awed by the idea of having experienced what they were so familiar with. They feel like they flew in the virtual equivalent of the Millennium Falcon, the main ship of *Star Wars*, complete with the actual robots — C3PO and R2D2 — from the movie. They feel like they've passed through time in the DeLorean — the car/time machine in "Back to the Future" — complete with the video presence of Doc Brown.

These experiences are good examples of what a virtual world might be like. Star Trek's Holodeck also relies on experiences that are familiar to the crew. They visit their home worlds, now or in the past, to find what they expect and then explore it a little further. Picard is fond of going into a detective-novel setting in the 1920s when gangsters were common and tough guys were needed.

The Klingon Worf — a part human, part alien warrior — likes to create combat situations to test his skills. Other crewmen create relaxing landscapes or exotic locations.

Familiar surroundings are so convincing that, in one episode, the crew creates a virtual world so closely resembling a real one that a race whose planet is dying can be transplanted there without their realizing it. This enables the crew of the Enterprise to carry them to a safer world without interrupting the normal progress of their culture by introducing them prematurely to the concept of space flight. Instead, they are guided on a "journey" in the Holodeck, where the entire population walks for days to reach their safer destination. The crew cleverly changes the Holodeck environment along the way to look like the new world they are heading into.

The ethics involved in the situation are interesting. One of the travelers accidentally leaves the Holodeck and finds himself suddenly on a ship traveling through space, surrounded by unimaginable technology. His knowledge of their "reality" also means that he can never return to his people, which leads to a despair that eventually kills him. The message here is a powerful one — playing around with reality can be dangerous, so think carefully about the ethics and implications of what you do.

Virtual reality also promises more extensive Holodeck-like experiences. In another "Star Trek" episode, a shy character — Barkley — creates replicas of the crew, particularly the commanding officers he fears. He casts himself and these virtual crewmen in the period of Alexander Dumas' *Three Musketeers*, but making himself the better swordsman. The virtual musketeers are inadequate, stooge-like imbeciles. To add insult to injury, Barkley adds a virtual duplicate of the ship's counselor, who falls passionately at his feet.

Barkley begins spending more and more time in the Holodeck, and becomes less aware of his real-world duties. The senior officers notice this and catch him during one of his Holodeck programs. They are not pleased with their portrayals in Barkley's fantasy world. The issue we will have to contend with here is that our society, like that of the "Star Trek" crew, will need to find its level of tolerance for bending reality. What amount of bending will be acceptable and what should be discouraged will be a difficult line to draw.

When virtual reality arrives through information superhighway applications, it may provide similar values and issues for society to contend with. What policies will we need to prevent abuses? What limits can we put on the applications? What training or counselling will be required to promote safe use of the new systems?

As virtual reality begins to make its way onto the scene, we are beginning to examine some of these questions, and to determine which applications are most suited for the 1990s version of the technology.

The history of virtual reality began in 1970 when Ivan Southerland created the first head-mounted display, thereby creating a virtual world. NASA's Virtual Interface Environment Workstation (VIEW) was developed in 1985. The movie *Lawnmower Man* brought virtual reality to the public's attention most recently, although it was treated as early as the late 1970s in the Disney movie *Tron*. Today, arcades and theme parks offer virtual reality experiences, both with and without headsets.

The market for virtual reality equipment is estimated today at $250 million worldwide and is expected to rise to $570 million by 1998. Developers, researchers, and government agencies, such as the Department of Defense and NASA, are currently the biggest investors in virtual reality.

> *The market for virtual reality equipment is estimated today at $250 million worldwide and is expected to rise to $570 million by 1998.*

Eventually, as with computer technology, applications and research initially invented and funded for the government and military will move into private sector use. Many companies are readying entertainment applications, but so far there have not been the major market successes that will make the investment in multimedia and networks viable for virtual reality.

"Meanwhile, plenty of businesses are finding today's technology good enough to do the job. You've probably heard about the VR arcades and games that are beginning to appear. But VR is also being used to train doctors and astronauts, and evaluate engineering designs. It is becoming an important marketing tool, and it is envisioned as the technology that may enable people with disabilities to lead more 'mainstream' lives. It may be a while before white-collar professionals don HMDs when they sit down at their desks in the morning, but VR is steadily gaining acceptability," states an August 1994 article by Ben Delaney in *New Media* magazine. Delaney publishes *Cyber Edge Journal*, a leading virtual reality newsletter.

Applications cited by *New Media* include:

Marketing/Retailing. Nike and ad agencies are looking at virtual reality applications for store planning. The makers of Cutty Sark scotch are using a virtual reality experience to interest customers in their products. Using an HMD, customers experience a sea voyage that ends with a welcoming party that toasts the voyager with Cutty Sark. The voyage project is making its way around the country.

Canon Business Products in the United Kingdom is using virtual reality to better explain new fax technology at trade shows. Their system lets the user imagine they are a fax traveling through the network.

Medical. Medical researchers and educators are using virtual reality to create diagnostic applications that combine and visualize computer data from tests. They are also using it to test procedures on "virtual patients" before operating on real ones. Schools are using digital representations of the anatomy to teach students.

Space exploration. NASA used virtual reality to teach the space shuttle astronauts how to make the numerous adjustments and repairs for the Hubble space telescope mission in December 1993. The astronauts simulated the space walks and motions they would need to make the repairs while orbiting with the telescope in space.

Delaney's article concludes: "Clearly, VR technology has a ways to go before we all toss our monitors on the junk heap, but breakthroughs are in sight. The Holy Grail of VR is not more powerful computers or better HMDs, but content. Questions to be answered include how to construct a narrative in which the participant can choose any path (not just the path that gets to the climax), how to represent history in the class-

room and how to best present vast amounts of data.
Although multimedia developers also face many of
these dilemmas, others are unique: How does one take
advantage of the new horizons that open up when users
an turn their heads left and right or look up and down?
How does one present an interface that best exploits a
360-degree view? The answer to these and many more
questions will shape the destiny of VR and computing
for years to come."

Making It Happen Now

The information superhighway has attracted several special interest groups, each promoting their own vision of the superhighway, and each working to solve only those problems they see as obstacles to their goals. Will this lack of consensus simply impede the deployment of the superhighway, or could it detour this project for the foreseeable future.

History will look back on 1994 as the year when the idea of creating an information superhighway first penetrated the public consciousness. Having the idea, though, is a far cry from making it happen. The country realized that a man could walk on the moon in the early 1960s, but it took nearly a decade to make it happen. Likewise, the information superhighway may take 5 to 10 years to becomes real and pervasive.

Future generations may look back on this time in amusement as they read how we wrestled with difficult technical, political, social, and economic problems. What may be most confusing to those generations is the manner in which we went about solving these problems.

Rather than one concerted effort that clearly outlines what must be done and musters the resources to do it, we have at least three different interest groups — each with its own mandates and expected outcomes. All of them are working only on the parts of the problem that stand out as the greatest obstacles to their goals, rather than having a comprehensive view of what must be done.

The three versions of the information superhighway in 1994 are:

1. **Private networks.** The cable/telephone company projects that aim to provide video-on-demand and other interactive applications. These efforts face many technical and economic feasibility obstacles. There are at least seven projects underway now in different cities of the U.S.

2. **Grass roots networks.** The Internet is already global and in use and proving its worth across a wide spectrum of information, research, entertainment, education, and medical applications. The Internet developers must tackle ease-of-use, privacy, and security problems. The Internet must also evolve technically to handle multimedia applications on a broad scale and must evolve culturally to allow widespread consumer and commercial use.

3. **Public networks.** The National Information Infrastructure Test Bed and similar government

> *As they read how* we wrestled with difficult technical, political, social, and economic problems, future generations may look back on this time in amusement. They may also be confused by the lack of concerted vision and effort.

projects aimed at using network interconnections to create applications that benefit the public. These government-sponsored model applications target research, economic, educational, and medical needs. How practical they are for widespread adoption and who will fund them when the government cannot are the key questions faced by these initiatives.

Wireless and satellite systems, even as ill-defined as they are today, also hold promise for information super-highway applications. On the entertainment side, for example, Hughes Communications' DirecTv and Hub-bard Broadcasting's United States Satellite Broadcasting are working with Thomson Consumer Electronics to offer digital programs to TV users through inexpensive satellite receivers. Using larger satellite-dish receivers but for lower cost, Primestar Partners rents satellite access to television programming to 70,000 customers. Both systems bypass the limited choices of cable and broadcast television, having more than 50 channels available, as well as pay-per-view movies.

As the FCC parcels out electromagnetic frequencies, even more wireless projects offering everything from voice and data transmissions to broadband applications will be offered to targeted consumers and businesses. The cost, practicality, security, and reliability issues surrounding these endeavors have only begun to surface. But they represent another area where separate players are working at problems unique to their applications on the road to developing usable information superhighway applications.

Just as we are amused by past generations' views of technologies that we enjoy today, future generations will wonder how we could put so much focus on a single information superhighway application like video-on-demand when the technology could do so much more for us. Consider these views of the past:

Marconi, the inventor of radio (or "wireless" as it was called then), saw the main applications of his new technology as communicating between and with ships at sea and getting information to newspapers as quickly as possible so they could print it for mass dissemination.

Bell, the creator of the telephone, saw it only as an improvement to the telegraph systems that dominated the intercontinental communications of the day.

Watkins, the founder of IBM, predicted that the country would only need 10 or 15 of his company's large computers.

With hindsight, it is easy to see that they were all wrong. Perhaps the time and energy it took to develop the technology and the limited experience society had with it caused these pioneers to mistake their powerful new developments for simple enhancements to things they already knew.

By focusing too intently on video-on-demand applications, we may be making the same mistake. Imagination suggests that there are many more interesting ways to use the information superhighway than watching the same shows we already watch on television.

Nevertheless, millions of dollars are being spent on trying to solve the problems associated with delivering this application. The good news is that these dollars need to be spent anyway to further the technology so that interactive multimedia applications can become widely available on the superhighway.

The problems for the cable/telephone applications are:

- **Storage.** A single feature-length movie requires 4,000 Megabytes (MB) of compressed digital data. Specialized storage devices will clearly be needed to accommodate these huge files. Ten times that amount, at least 40,000MB, will be required to store the hundreds of movies consumers now choose from the video store to be delivered on-line. The storage must also take into account the need to make multiple copies (hundreds or thousands perhaps) available simultaneously to network users.

The technology exists to meet these capacity demands. After all, credit-card companies and airlines process and store thousands of transactions every day. But the price to develop such systems runs into the millions — representing a substantial capital

investment for a service that needs to be priced low
enough to compete with the video store.

- **Software.** While the hardware can be found to store
all the data necessary for video and other interactive
applications, the software to manage access to it in
response to consumer needs is still under development. Microsoft, Silicon Graphics, and Oracle are
all bidding on contracts to provide what is called
server software to run these application systems for
interactive multimedia services.

  In addition to software on servers at central locations
  that will coordinate and deliver the movies and other
  applications, we will need navigation software to
  make the system easy for consumers to use. The software is untested at this point, but may be further
  along soon. Like storage, it will require overcoming
  new technical challenges that are bound to cause
  bumps in the early implementations.

- **Incompatibility.** Different development efforts, sponsored by different cable providers, phone companies,
and computer companies, all of whom are working
independently, means there will be incompatibility
problems. The atmosphere of these early trials is
"who can do it first and best?" rather than "how can
we work together?" The winner of this challenge
hopes to migrate their expertise to other ventures.

These competitive battles are bound to postpone the
ability to interconnect cable/telephone-based applications in different regions. This will create a future
obstacle to the goal of creating a nationwide information superhighway.

Add to these technical hurdles one more: the
cable/telephone services have no proven market yet.
Consumers have never experienced video-on-demand or
interactive TV applications. Those who use personal
computers with CD-ROM and on-line applications may
be more ready for them. But overall the market remains
unproven. Under the circumstances, it is difficult to justify huge capital investments without any sense of how
much or whether consumers will pay for the services.

For this reason, the early trials of cable/telephone-company superhighway applications are being closely watched. If they fail to deliver, a wave of pessimism will hit the information superhighway, dampening business investment and consumer enthusiasm just as the collapse of the mega-mergers between cable and phone companies did early in 1994.

But whether these trials succeed or fail, they are only one narrowly focused version of the information superhighway. The Internet and government efforts will continue to advance the superhighway's objectives into the future.

The $50 million NSFNET II contract will allow communications companies to develop the next generation Internet — a good example of the higher bandwidth networks of the information superhighway.

The Internet infrastructure is based on government, educational, and private networks that are already an interconnected, highly utilized, global information highway. Major components of the Internet, such as the portion owned by the National Science Foundation, one of four major public high-capacity networks in the country, will be upgraded over time. The $50 million NSFNET II contract will allow communications companies to develop the next generation Internet — a good example of the higher bandwidth networks of the information superhighway.

NSFNET II will provide 155Mbps operating capacity through three primary access points distributed around the country. The network access points will act as traffic cops for commercial traffic, allowing businesses to take advantage of NSFNET. Future upgrades will bring the Internet to gigabit speeds.

So, unlike the cable/telephone-driven projects, the Internet is already building capacity and has a proven demand for its services. But it, too, faces major obstacles that must be solved so commercial and personal traffic can comfortably use its growing capabilities. The two key issues are security and usability:

Security. Sending money or personal information, or just keeping network usage private are now not possible on most of the Internet. Security measures such as authentication and encryption must be implemented by network providers or the network users themselves. There is now an open debate about how to provide this security. At least two kinds of security are needed: the ability to protect the information at the sending and receiving points, and keeping it secure during transmission. Besides a lack of security systems at each end, the Internet is vulnerable to wiretaps during transmission as the information is sent from one server or hub to the next until it gets to its address.

Some possible security techniques include:

- **Cryptography** — the ability to code transmissions and have the sender hold the key to decode them, giving the key out selectively. Some network providers build the ability to use cryptography into the access protocols that are used for graphical access systems like Mosaic.

  Coded transmissions can also be arranged between two or more Internet sites, where the sending and receiving computers can be programmed with the appropriate transmission coding and decoding capability.

- **Hardware-only solutions** — the government has proposed including new hardware components containing security features on microchips. The Clipper Chip for voice and the Capstone for data would provide another type of coding to protect transmissions. In its initial proposals, the government planned to hold the decoding capability in its own "secure" interagency program. But the furor over the Orwellian implications of this suggestion has caused the government to soften its position.

  Hardware solutions are less viable than software because, unlike cyptographic programs that can be transmitted and downloaded on the network, chips have to be installed directly within the sending and receiving systems. It would take a substantial amount of time before every one of the millions of Internet users installed such a chip or circuit-board on their system at home or work.

Another security concern is the ability of Internet users to analyze network traffic. A long-standing capability that is harmless in the hands of researchers who want to see how busy a server or information resource is, traffic analysis can be used by companies to spy on each other or to gain knowledge about consumers. Other network users might also seek information about other individuals on the system. It will be up to network providers to come up with ways to protect access to this information without affecting overall services or usage.

The best security is to allow limited access. Many companies have *firewalls* — a computer that acts as a "security guard," allowing only company-authorized access to and from the Internet. Another idea being tried for financial transactions is a clearing gateway. This is essentially an electronic clearinghouse or security gate that accepts encrypted transactions and verifies their authenticity.

The Internet has always worked with an honor system. Using that concept, some observers suggest that it is sufficient to guarantee consumers' rights to just say "no," when asked if a commercial outfit can collect and reuse data they get from a transaction. This concept, of course, requires that companies inform consumers when they are collecting information and that they ethically respect their wishes.

Ultimately, security solutions may be sold to Internet users just like any other service. Government and commercial organizations are working to create standards that would guarantee that these and other security plans would not interfere with the smooth interoperability of the Internet — the ability to send and receive transmissions from anywhere to anywhere.

The bottom line is that security and privacy will become increasingly the responsibility of the network user or organizations. Products and standards will be available on the Internet but those wishing to run risky transmissions over it will have to take security into account themselves.

Usability. Before it can become accessible to consumers, the Internet has to become easier to use. While navigators like Mosaic are helping ease-of-use move forward, the fate of this issue rests with the ultimate role of the personal computer. As the PC becomes friendlier through voice-response technology, touch screens, and other interactive capabilities, it will become more adaptable to use by non-computer-literate individuals.

For the time being, Internet access over cable and the increasing value of services being placed on-line make it likely that the tremendous growth in Internet and on-line service connections will continue.

The government's information superhighway initiatives are strong on content, but weak on how quickly and widely they will be disseminated. With the government depending on private industry to pay the cost of building the information superhighway, which applications become broadly disseminated will depend on whether there is a financial incentive to provide them.

For the short term, it seems that the majority of companies are more interested in entertainment and information supported by television-style advertising campaigns then they are in healthcare or educational services. Fees for accessing these services will foot the bill for building the networks, access systems, and navigators. This may work out fine. The research and capability once provided for high-pay-off services will allow for linkages and platforms for public-benefit applications.

The National Information Infrastructure Testbed is a consortium of government, business and universities. The consortium is building applications that rely on existing computer products in scientific research and healthcare.

In another partnership between government as industry, BellSouth has worked with the State of North Carolina to create the North Carolina Information Superhighway. Connecting 106 locations statewide, this superhighway includes educational applications (distance learning), medical applications (telemedicine) and remote access to government services.

These are the types of applications the Administration believes will keep the United States competitive economically, educationally, and in our healthcare system.

Beyond that, the Administration is attacking the goal of a global infrastructure. Vice President Gore has spoken of "a planetary information network that transmits messages and images with the speed of light from the largest city to the smallest village on every continent." But lack of funding and specifics leave the Internet as the closest version of a global network we have today. So the government's initiatives will help point information superhighway initiatives in the right direction, but the cable/telephone-company research and Internet developments will be the keys to making the information superhighway pervasive.

In the meantime, two government-sponsored groups are trying to continue a dialogue on the issues: the Information Infrastructure Task Force (IITF) and the 27-member Advisory Council. IITF consists of high-level representatives of the federal agencies that play a major role in the development and application of information technologies. Working together with the private sector, the Task Force is coordinating Administration efforts to develop, demonstrate, and promote applications of information technology, formulating Administration positions on key telecommunications issues, and addressing critical information policy issues. Secretary of Commerce Ron Brown is the chairman of the IITF.

The federal Information Infrastructure Task Force (IITF) is teaming up with the Council on Competitiveness in September 1994 to demonstrate the latest information superhighway applications. The Council on Competitiveness is a nonprofit, nonpartisan organization of chief executives from business, higher education, and organized labor who have joined together to pursue a single overriding goal: to improve the ability of American companies and workers to compete in world markets while building a rising standard of living at home. Paul Allaire, Chairman and CEO of Xerox Corporation, is the Council's chairman. The demonstration was geared to:

> ... explore the implementation hurdles that users and application developers are experiencing as they create and deploy new applications in health care, education, manufacturing, electronic information management, and commerce, as well as entertainment/home services.

Vice President Gore has spoken of "a planetary information network that transmits messages and images with the speed of light from the largest city to the smallest village on every continent."

Panels of experts will share the lessons they are learning as they grapple with financing issues, contend with legal, policy, and regulatory issues, probe market demand for new applications and services, and cope with the changes individuals and organizations are facing they attempt to embrace these new applications.

The conference's purpose was to allow observers to "more readily grasp the personal benefits this robust infrastructure will deliver."

Conference speakers included: Ron Brown, Secretary of Commerce; Jim Manzi, Chairman and CEO, Lotus Development Corporation; Michael Metz, Managing Director, Oppenheimer & Co.; Arati Prabhakar, Chair, Committee on Applications and Technology and Director, National Institute of Standards and Technology; and Charles Vest, President, Massachusetts Institute of Technology.

Speakers on Healthcare: Michael Wood, M.D., Mayo Foundation; Stanley Fowler, Ph.D., University of South Carolina Medical School; David Gustafson, M.D., University of Wisconsin; Julian Rosenman, M.D., University of North Carolina School of Medicine; Helen Smits, M.D., US Department of Health and Human Services.

Speakers on Electronic Information Management and Commerce: Daniel Schutzer, Vice President and Director for Advanced Technology, Citibank; Carol Christian, Professor of Astrophysics, University of California at Berkeley and the National Information Infrastructure Testbed; Alan Kerry, President and CEO, Image Works; Jim Mulvaney, Senior Consultant, Electric Power Research Institute; Randy Rehn, Information Express Manager, Nordstrom.

Speakers on Manufacturing Applications: Al Narath, President, Sandia National Laboratories; Dale Hougardy, Vice President, Operations, Boeing; Henry Morneau, Director of the Scientific Computing Division, DuPont; Thomas Patterson, Director, Information Security, Microelectronics and Computer Technology Corporation (MCC); William Ranson, Southeast Manufacturing Technology Center, University of South Carolina.

Speakers on Education: Linda Roberts , Special Advisor on Education; Lionel Baldwin, President, National Technical University; Thomas Highton, Superintendent of Schools, Union City, NJ; Jacqueline Shrago Director, Office of Technology Transfer, Vanderbilt University; Connie Stout, Director, Texas Education Network; Leona Williams, President and CEO, Educational and Corporate Technologies, Inc.

Speakers on Entertainment and Home Services Applications: John Cooke, President, The Disney Channel; Gene Quinn, General Manager, Chicago Online; Michael Sherlock, Executive Vice President, Technology, NBC; Stephen Tomlin, Vice President and General Manager, Interactive Technology, QVC.

Twenty-five interactive hands-on demonstrations were selected to reflect how the National Information Infrastructure will influence everyday life. They included:

Advance. The advanced driver and vehicle navigation concept. The application allowed participants to take a simulated ride in an intelligent vehicle that delivers real-time traffic information to drivers. This project is a public/private partnership to evaluate in-vehicle route guidance.

Telemedicine. Pine Ridge Indian Reservation Telemedicine Project. Participants witnessed physicians at the conference performing a remote evaluation of a patient with heart disease in Pine Ridge, South Dakota. A real-time connection was provided by the NASA ACTS satellite. Physicians demonstrated the remote use of ultrasound, and an electrocardiogram. Participants were also able to converse with the patient.

Bill Nye, The Science Guy. An interactive educational program. Through this demonstration, the conference attendees viewed a future interactive children's TV program on science education. Conference attendees were "at-home" participants in on-line experiments, quizzes, games, and various other activities.

On-Line Services. The presentation took the audience through many information, shopping, and interactive on-line services available, including the text of a daily newspaper, event-ticket purchasing, and electronic mail capabilities. Attendees were given an opportunity to individually experiment with the system.

Dynamic Radiation Therapy Planning. A physician led participants through a real-time demonstration of radiation treatment planning for cancerous tumors. The audience saw a computer rendering of the anatomy in real time.

Manufacturing in the Information Age. Through a real-time connection, conference participants were able to remotely control certain elements of the manufacturing process at a fully automated General Motors automobile assembly plant located in Wilmington, Delaware.

Interpractice. This application highlighted for conference participants an electronic environment (paperless system) for practicing physicians and clinical staff. This system allows medical personnel to capture, store, and communicate patient medical information in real time. It also includes on-line order placement (lab, pharmacy, and so on), referral prompts, clinical reminders, and allergy or medical alerts. This demonstration also allowed attendees to explore the next-generation voice activated, intelligent InterPractice System.

Global Schoolhouse. Conference participants were able to participate in an interactive/video conferencing link between several K–12 schools. Global Schoolhouse showed how these students used these advanced video tools to work and learn together with students, teachers, and scientists in other locations.

National Catastrophic Oil Spill Management. This demonstration allowed conference participants to view a state-of-the-art emergency management response tool that is used in the event of an oil spill. This system integrates multiple facets of an oil-spill response effort: initial response decisions, damage mitigation actions, environmental, social, and economic threat assessments, and equipment procurement efforts.

Healthnet. This demonstration showed conference participants a prototype interactive television application that provides healthcare information. Conference participants were able to select informational segments on such topics as breast cancer treatment options, the long-term effects of divorce on children, fitness for women, nutrition for men, and coping with depression.

Eduport. Conference participants were able to explore the use of a digital multimedia library designed to enhance K–12 education. They were able to access video, audio, image, and text information from various sources including the Discovery Museum, NASA, FDR Library, and the Smithsonian.

Law Enforcement. Wireless imagery communications system for crime information. This demonstration illustrated to participants a highly visual and interactive system that provides law enforcement officials on patrol the ability to accurately identify a wanted, missing, or unidentified person within seconds. This device is used to transmit images of fingerprints, mug-shots, stolen objects, contraband, and personal property between state, local, and federal public service and emergency management agencies.

Mathline. Participants were able to see the power of public television's telecommunications highway as it delivered professional development services to teachers throughout the nation in support of Goals 2000. The demonstration featured on-line dialogue among teachers in an electronic learning community who are helping each other to meet Professional Teaching Standards.

Electric Utility Information Network. This demonstration led participants through a comprehensive information system that is used by the entire electric power industry to provide high-value internal information services. At a workstation, participants were able to see how collaborative research is being done as information is traded and received over the network.

Variations in Music. A digital music library enabled conference participants to select audio and visual recordings for review directly from workstations and provided them with the ability to quickly select specific passages for listening or viewing. This tool has been developed to augment the music curriculum at Indiana University.

Picture Exchange. Conference participants were able to witness a new method that many advertising agencies and graphic designers are using to obtain wider access to a variety of work done by photographers. Pictures are stored in an on-line library and are ready for rapid brokerage between photographer and agency.

Chess. The comprehensive health enhancement support system. A home-based workstation demonstration showcased how some hospitals have opted to provide healthcare consumers with the information, referrals, decision support, and social support specific to certain illnesses such as cancer and AIDS. This system is being successfully used to assist patients in the management of their own disease and health care.

Co-Vis. This demonstration showcased three students, located at the conference, as they studied environmental and atmospheric science using collaborative work benches that provide interactive desk-top video-conferencing capabilities. These capabilities will allow them to work with other students located in Indiana, professors at Northwestern University, and researchers at the Center for Atmospheric Studies in San Diego.

These demonstrations are the beginnings of the information superhighway. Another version of the superhighway is permeating the public consciousness through TV commercials.

AT&T has a series of commercials featuring images of future superhighway applications. In one segment, there is a classroom full of small, elegant computers. The camera zooms in on a student asking a boy in another country if he has a bike. The boy from the other country appears as live video on the student's computer screen. The announcer asks: "Have you ever asked a question of a friend who lived in another part of the world?"

Another piece shows a French motorcycle maker conversing with a customer, using video and text on the screen that instantly translates the customer's words into French. The shop owner speaks French in reply, which is translated into the customer's language. The announcer: "Have you ever taken an order from a customer in a language you didn't understand?"

> *In a few years, we will have primitive interactivity on our televisions and computer desktops. In 10 years, multimedia information and entertainment applications and video telephones will be common appliances.*

The third segment shows a husband and wife resting on a train. The wife has a palm-sized computer with a schematic of her house on it. She presses a button and the house's lights come on. "Have you ever checked on your house when you were far from home?" the announcer asks. "You will," he says, "and it'll be brought to you by AT&T."

The information superhighway holds the promise of these applications and hundreds more. They will be produced by all kinds of companies — from giant communications and cable firms to small entrepreneurs.

All the technical, political, and social problems of the information superhighway will be solved — in time. We are now at the cutting edge of the communications revolution the superhighway will foster.

In a few years, we will have primitive interactivity on our televisions and computer desktops. A few years after that, on-line interactive applications will be pervasive. Within 10 years, multimedia information and entertainment applications and video telephones will be common appliances.

After that, we will see the dawn of virtual-reality applications and intelligent agents that, on the one hand, bring us new worlds from our imaginations and, on the other, give us greater control over our real world.

We are at the point where we can imagine many things, but make only a few of them real. Soon, we will be at the point where the things we can make real are beyond what we can imagine today.

Have you seen the future yet?

You will.

Glossary

A

acceptable use policy
The National Science Foundation's policy for the allowable uses of NSFNET, a major national network and part of the Internet in the United States linking research and government locations.

application
Computer systems that are designed to meet a particular need or function, such as word processing, or provide a service, such as allowing financial transactions or access to research databases.

access software
Computer software that allows the use of functions and features of a computer or a network of computers, such as the Internet or information superhighway.

access system
The combination of computer hardware and software that allows access to computer systems and networks.

active memory
The core information storage aspect of a computer system that is immediately available during its operation.

adult education
All manner of continuing education for adults. This is available remotely in the context of the information superhighway.

advanced network software
Computer software that allows faster transmission of information over a network, such as switching or routing systems.

analog cable television
Television signals provided directly to the viewing location via wires rather than airwaves and based on analog signals.

application development tools
Computers software used to build other computer software systems designed for specific functions or services.

Archie
An Internet navigation tool used to locate servers and information on different interconnected networks.

architectures
The underlying structure and plan for computer software and hardware systems, how they work together and support different functions and services.

artificial intelligence
Computer systems that are designed to imitate human decision making and feedback capabilities. Essentially, coding human knowledge into computers.

ASCII alphabet
Standard computer text format used by most systems as simple form of text storage to allow the exchange of information between systems. Stands for American Standard Code for Information Interchange.

AskERIC
An Internet assistance and referral service for educators in elementary, junior high, and high school environments. Stands for Educational Resource Information Center.

ATM (asynchronous transfer mode)
A network protocol capable of carrying voice, data, and video faster than any of the other major transmission methods.

automatic teller machines (ATMs)
Banking transaction machines that allow customers to interact with a computer system by inserting a magnetically coded card to obtain cash, make deposits, and check and manipulate account information.

B

backbone
A large network that interconnects other networks allowing information to be passed between them.

bandwidth
A measure of network capacity. Technically it is the difference between the highest and lowest frequency of a band, which is a range of transmission frequencies.

bits
A binary computer digit (either 0 or 1) which represents data or information to a computer system.

bits per second (bps)
The speed with which bits of computer data move through a network in one second.

brand provider
The company that provides service to the customer. In the context of the superhighway, the idea that a single company, such as a phone or cable firm, could provide the complete services required by the consumer to meet his needs.

broadband networks
Facilities for providing high frequency data transmission.

bulletin boards
Information access servers where a user can "post" information or retrieve files. Generally bulletin boards are based on dial-in remote service requiring the use of a modem.

C

Cable News Network (CNN)
Leading provider of cable television news programming.

cable television services
Companies that provide programming via cables attached directly to the home.

CD
High density storage media based on optical disc.

CD-ROM drive
Stands for Compact-Disc/Read Only Memory. Computer system's access point to read and execute programs stored on a compact disc.

cellular phone
Portable telephone based on cellular technology which receives voice and data transmitted through the airwaves rather than over telephone lines on the ground.

chat rooms
Areas of Internet and on-line services where users can post and exchange messages in an interactive on-line conversation.

circuit boards
Circuits which direct the flow electrical current, attached to a board that can be inserted in a computer system to determine its capabilities.

Clipper chip
The Clinton Administration's attempt to come up with a standard security chip to be inserted in computer and telephone systems to safeguard conversation and data transmissions. It has been controversial because only the government would have access to the codebreaking information.

closed standard
A widely adopted architecture or technology implementation that is standard because it is widely used, but limited in its ability to support other systems of a different nature.

coaxial cable
Conventional copper wire used for voice communication.

collaborative design
Multiple designers at different locations working together on a common project by using a computer network to communicate.

color monitor
Color computer terminal for display only. It contains no processing power.

commands
Key words or signals that communicate to the computer what it should do in response to the user.

Commercial Internet Exchange Association (CIX)
An group of organizations that support access to the Internet by businesses via the Commercial Internet Exchange.

compression
Reducing the size of a transmission or file through computer programming. This allows more information to fit into a smaller space. Compressed programs must be decompressed at the receiving end of the exchange.

computer-based instruction
Teaching based on interaction with a computer program that guides the user through the lesson.

consent decree
The ruling that broke up Ma Bell into AT&T and the Regional Bell Operating Companies (RBOCs).

convergence
The coming together of multiple media — telephone, television, and computers based on the underlying use of digital technology by all three forms.

cryptographic software
Software used to encode or disguise computer programs or communications.

cyberculture
The emerging style and manner of interacting using computer networks rather than face-to-face contact.

cyberpunk
An exaggerated style of dress and behavior popularized by teenagers accustomed to cyberculture.

cyberspace
The on-line world of computer and communications networks, where people interact without physical presence.

 D

data
Anything that is processed by the computer — numbers, text, voice, or video. The term is based on the fact that computers reduce everything to numeric bits.

data suits
Suits developed by virtual reality experts that are equipped with sensors to track the user's movements

so that a virtual reality environment can be projected.

de facto standard
A product that has become so widely accepted and used that it is the standard even though it has not been officially acknowledged as such.

decentralized data and processing
Using multiple processors rather than a single large system to accomplish a computing task.

decision support
Systems designed to provide information to assist decision-making activities.

decision trees
A technique of mapping out alternative choices for analysis in order to predict the outcome of the decision.

decompression
The use of computer systems to process compressed files and make them readable to the user.

deregulation
A government policy to reduce the amount of regulation in a particular area such as telecommunications. The belief is that this will foster competition.

diagnosis-related groups
Medical diagnosis payment system designed by the government to reduce healthcare costs.

dial-up services
On-line services accessed via telephone lines connected to a computer with a modem.

digital
Information represented as digits rather than as variable physical quantities (analog).

disk drives
Storage and access drives on a computer system that provide access to applications and computer memory.

distance learning
The concept of having the teachers and students work together via multimedia applications, even if the they are in different locations.

DOS
Disk Operating System, the oldest and most successful personal-computer-based system that runs all the programs in a computer.

E

electronic address
The computer-based code that identifies an individual user on a network.

electronic mail
Sending and receiving text-based messages over a computer network.

electronic pubs
Publications designed to appear on computer screens and accessed via computer networks.

ENIAC
Electronic Numerical Integrator and Calculator. One of the first electronic digital computers, built in 1946.

equal access
The concept that anyone, anywhere should have access to the information superhighway regardless of social or economic status.

F

FAQ
Frequently Asked Questions. Questions and answers most commonly addressed on the Internet. New users would be wise to look them up before putting general inquiries out into cyberspace.

fax
Facsimile. The transmission of images and documents using a computer and telephone network.

Federal Telecommunications System (FTS)
A U.S. government multivendor contract to upgrade the telecommunications and computer systems of federal agencies.

fiber-optic networks
High-speed networks that use glass fibers and laser technology to transmit information at the speed of light.

file transfer
Moving a file of information from one computer system to another via a network and using file transfer software.

flaming
A frank inflammatory statement sent in an electronic mail message. Internet users conduct Flame Wars when they wish to express a particularly strong view or disagreement.

freeware
Software available for anyone's use without a fee in computer networks and bulletin boards. Users can download the software files to their own computers.

full-body immersion
A virtual reality setup that places the user in an environment where computers read and react to the person's movements and change the environment appropriately.

full-motion video
Video images such as those shown on television and in the movies.

G

gateways
Systems that interconnect different networks with each other so that users can treat them as a single network.

GATT
General Agreement on Trade and Technology. The pact signed between the United States, Mexico, and Canada, breaking down barriers to commerce on the North American continent.

gentlemen's cross-licensing agreement
A deal struck in the early days of broadcasting.

gigabit
One billion bits of computer information.

global information infrastructure
The concept of a worldwide network of computer and communications systems allowing information exchange and global services.

Gopher
One of the most common Internet navigation tools used to locate servers and information on different interconnected networks.

H

hackers
Computer users whose interest is in breaking into other people's computers by means of cracking computer code.

hard disk drive
The main storage drive on a personal computer.

hardware
The physical components of computer systems.

head-mounted display (HMD)
A device worn on the head that immerses the user's senses in a virtual reality experience.

health maintenance organization (HMO)
An alternative health insurance provider, frequently non-profit and geared more toward prevention than treatment of illness.

high resolution images
Images that require a large amount of computer memory and power because they contain a large amount of data.

High-Performance Computing and Communications Initiative
A U.S. government program to encourage the development and use of advanced computer technology.

holodeck
A fictional world from "Star Trek: The Next Generation" television series where the user can create a complete virtual world by using a computer program.

hyperlinks
Connections between software components developed through coding that relate different data and information located in different parts of the computer network to one another.

hypertext
Multiple layers of linked computer data that allows the user easy and instant access to related information.

I

icon
A symbol representing a computer program, system, or data structure, especially in the Apple Macintosh and Microsoft Windows environments.

icon-based menu
A menu system based on icons — a key feature of popular graphical user interfaces.

images
The duplication of text, data, or pictures in a computerized form that can be transmitted as a single form or presentation.

immersion
Submersion in a virtual reality system to the point where the virtual system seems real.

Industrial Revolution
The period in history where factory work overtook rural occupations as the majority employer because of the advent of mass production technology.

information age
The period in history when computer-based information became of significant value and the use and dissemination of information became the primary concern of the vast majority of workers.

Information Infrastructure Task Force (IITF)
A U.S. government body charged with identifying the major issues in the deployment of the National Information Infrastructure and working out possible courses of action to address them.

information service providers
Companies that provide access to information services, such as commercial on-line networks and bulletin boards, that allow access to and exchange of information.

information superhighway
A network of communications-based services that span the globe based on the interconnection of commercial and public computer systems and networks. Services it will provide include commerce, education, entertainment, information exchange, healthcare, and research.

information technologies
Technologies that allow the creation and transmission of information and information services. Includes computers of all sizes, hardware and software, and communications systems.

infotainment
Information-based entertainment experiences where computer and related technologies are used to create a unique experience.

intelligent agent
Computer-based software components containing artificial intelligence so that they are able to "learn" and respond to complex cues from users to provide them with the information they need.

interactive
The ability of computer systems to respond to the user's commands and prompt the user to choose from alternative actions.

Internauts
Internet aficionados with a great deal of experience navigating the interconnected networks and retrieving information from the collection of networks that make up the global Internet.

Internet
An interconnected system of networks with components throughout the world.

Internet Activities Board
The policy-setting group for the Internet concerned with promulgating standards and planning for the future.

interoperability standards
Standard systems designed to work interchangeably with other systems that conform to the same standards.

ISDN
Integrated Services Digital Network. Combines voice and data network transmission technology.

J

joysticks
Hand-controlled video game input devices that enable the user to manipulate characters and objects.

K

keypad
The keyboard or keyset used to interact with the computer for writing, issuing commands, or writing programs.

keyword searching
The ability to call up any document or references from multiple files in varied locations containing a set of words selected by the user.

knowledge workers
Workers whose primary product is information, which they derive

through applying knowledge and experiences.

L

LANs
Local Area Networks. Computer networks of relatively small numbers of users in a single facility.

laptop computers
Computers designed to fit in a person's lap or briefcase.

Lifelong Learning Society
A society that is continuously improving itself through education for all ages of citizens.

M

Macintosh
Apple Computer Corp.'s signature computer which introduced the first graphical-icon based operating system, making it one of the first easy-to-use systems.

memory chip
The part of the computer that retains and processes data and information.

menu
Part of the computer operating system or application that provides program choices for the user.

message boards
Bulletin boards accessed by the computer with information for general or specific users of a particular system or information network.

meta information
Information about information — where it is, what it is, and why it's important.

microchip
The basic building block of computer and electronic systems that is able to rapidly convert numeric symbols into data and information.

microcircuits
Microchips on a circuit board designed for a particular function or capability within the computer or electronic system.

multiple user (or multi-user) dimensions (MUDs)
A virtual reality world available to Internet users based on fantastic characters and scenarios.

N

National Information Infrastructure (NII)
The Clinton Administration's version of the concept of a national interconnected network that will provide commercial, health, education, and public service applications.

National Information Infrastructure Advisory Council
A council of non-government advisors to the Clinton Administration to foster a public discussion of infrastructure issues.

National Information Infrastructure Testbed
The government's initiative to partner with research, educational, and commercial organizations to try out potential technologies and applications for the National Information Infrastructure.

netiquette
The appropriate mannerisms and styles of behavior for users of computer networks, especially the Internet.

network
An interconnection of one or more computers via hardware and software.

newbies
Internet term for new users.

newsgroups
Information about particular news or information which network users can join and receive access to as well as have the option to add or comment on items of interest.

North American Free Trade Agreement (NAFTA)
Agreement to encourage commerce between Mexico, the United States, and Canada. The deal breaks down trade barriers between the countries, especially the U.S. and Mexico.

O

on-line services
Services such as news and electronic mail or discussion groups accessed via computer systems on a interconnected network.

open access
The concept of allowing equal, uninhibited access to network services.

open systems strategy
Similar to standards-based systems, open systems provide interoperability on multiple levels among computers and networks conforming to a common open systems approach.

operating system software
The software that serves as a platform for computer services, allocates storage and interacts with hardware and user input.

P

pay-per-view
Fee-based services where the user pays each time he or she uses the service, such as watching a movie.

Pentium
The latest, fastest microprocessor for IBM-compatible personal computers from Intel Corp.

posting
Placing information in a location on a computer network where others can access it and respond to it.

power users
Users who have mastered the computer technology necessary to use certain systems to their full extent.

R

random access memory (RAM)
Memory that a personal computer uses during operation.

real-time communication
Instant two-way, simultaneous communication.

Regional Bell Operating Companies (RBOCs)
The name for the seven regional telephone companies formed after the breakup of AT&T.

S

scalable
Being able to increase in size in terms of processing power or information services.

servers
Computer systems at key junctions in a network that act as platforms for communications systems, databases, and other services accessed by multiple computers or networks which can receive transmissions from them.

set-top boxes
Computer-enabled systems that would be placed on top of a conventional television set to provide enhanced network services.

speech-recognition system
Computer systems that can process and react to human speech.

stereo sound card
Hardware circuit board that is inserted into a personal computer to allow the playing of sound in a multimedia system.

systems integration services
Organizations that will install and develop computer systems for other firms or organizations.

T

TCP/IP (Transmission Control Protocol/Internet Protocol)
The primary protocol that is a de facto standard enabling different computers on the Internet to communicate with one another.

Telecommunications and Information Infrastructure Assistance Program (TIIAP)
U.S. government grant program providing assistance to foster organizations to develop services and components for the National Information Infrastructure.

telecommuting
Employees using a computer and network to communicate with computers and other employees from a distant location.

telemedicine
Healthcare applications or services on the information superhighway that would allow doctors and patients to interact from remote locations for exchanging information, examinations, and treatment.

telepresence
The ability to be present via computer projections of personality rather than physical presence.

teleputer
Computer-based multimedia system that connects users to the information superhighway's full range of services.

touch screens
Computer screens that are sensitized to a touch of a certain portion of the screen to execute a command.

U

universal access
The concept that everyone can and should have access to the information superhighway and its services.

Unix
The operating system most widely used on the Internet because of its native networking capabilities.

user access fee
Amounts charged by network providers to allow people to use the network services.

V

videoconferencing
Conferences or meetings where participants in remote locations can view each other via real-time video images sent over a computer network.

virtual reality
A second reality created by computer-generated images that seem real to the user's senses.

virus detection software
Software installed on computer systems to destroy programs that attack and damage computer software.

W

Windows
The most common graphical format to access personal computer systems. It allows more than one computer application to used simultaneously and has a common access method.

wireless
The term for radio transmissions in the past, as well as the current concept for transmitting voice, data, and computerized information via broadcasting through the air rather than over wires.

wiretapping
Using electronic equipment to eavesdrop on telephone conversations.

word processors
Computer application software designed to create documents.

workgroup computing
Multiple users working in a computer network collaborating on one or more projects simultaneously.

workstations
Systems designed to run scientific or engineering applications because they have more processing power than traditional personal computers.

worldwide knowledge base
The concept that the information superhighway will allow access to global information.

Z

zines
Magazines containing news and entertainment designed for display and access via the Internet.

BIBLIOGRAPHY

Barnouw, Erik. *Tube of Plenty: The Evolution of American Television*, New York, NY: Oxford University Press, 1975.

Brittan, David. "Being There: The Promise of Multimedia Communications," *MIT Technology Review*, May/June, 1992.

Ceruzzi, Paul E. *Reckoners: The Prehistory of the Digital Computer, from Relays to the Stored Program Concept, 1935-1945*, Westport, CT.: Greenwood Press, 1983.

Cetron, Marvin, et al. *Schools of the Future: How American Business Can Cooperate to Save Our Schools*, New York, NY: McGraw-Hill, 1985.

Cronin, Mary J. *Doing Business on the Internet: How the Electronic Highway is Transforming American Companies*, New York, NY: Van Nostrand Reinhold, 1994.

Dertouzos, Michael L., and Joel Moses. *The Computer Age: A Twenty-Year View*, Cambridge, Mass.: MIT Press, 1979.

Forester, Tom. *High-Tech Society: The Story of the Information Technology Revolution*, Cambridge, MA: The MIT Press, 1987.

Gawain, Shakti. *Living in the Light: A Guide to Personal and Planetary Transformation*, San Rafael, CA: Whatever Publishing, Inc., 1986.

Gilder, George. *Life After Television: The Coming Transformation of Media and American Life*, New York, NY: W. W. Norton & Co., 1992.

Grossman, Jerome. "Plugged-in-Medicine," *MIT Technology Review*, January, 1994.

Handy, Charles. *The Age of Unreason*, Harvard Business School Press, 1989.

Head, Sidney, and Christopher Sterling. *Broadcasting in America: A Survey of Electronic Media*, Boston, MA: Houghton Mifflin Co., 1991.

Heim, Michael. *The Metaphysics of Virtual Reality*, New York, NY: Oxford University Press, 1993.

Lebow, Irwin. *The Digital Connection: A Layman's Guide to the Information Age*, New York, NY: Computer Sciences Press, 1991.

Malamud, Carl. *Exploring The Internet: A Technical Travelogue*, Englewood Cliffs, NJ: Prentice Hall, 1993.

Toffler, Alvin. *Power Shift: Knowledge, Wealth, and Violence at the Edge of the 21st Century*, New York, NY: Bantam Books, November, 1990.

Weizenbaum, Joseph. *Computer Power and Human Reason*, San Francisco, CA: W.H. Freeman & Co., 1976.

Index

CREDITS

Vice President and Publisher
Christopher J. Williams

Editorial Director
Trudy Neuhaus

Brand Manager
Amorette Pedersen

Project Editor
Elizabeth Rogalin

Manuscript Editor
Karen Goeller

Production
Beth A. Roberts
Ronnie K. Bucci

Proofreader
Deborah Kaufmann

Indexer
Seth Maislin

Book and Cover Design
Scally Design

International Data Group's Publications

ARGENTINA'S Computerworld Argentina, Infoworld Argentina;
AUSTRALIA'S Computerworld Australia, Australian PC World, Australian Macworld, Network World, Mobile Business Australia, Reseller, IDG Sources;
AUSTRIA'S Computerwelt Oesterreich, PC Test;
BRAZIL'S Computerworld, Gamepro, Game Power, Mundo IBM, Mundo Unix, PC World, Super Game;
BELGIUM'S Data News (CW);
BULGARIA'S Computerworld Bulgaria, Ediworld, PC & Mac World Bulgaria, Network World Bulgaria;
CANADA'S CIO Canada, Computerworld Canada, Graduate Computerworld, InfoCanada, Network World Canada;
CHILE'S Computerworld Chile, Informatica;
COLOMBIA'S Computerworld Colombia, PC World;
CZECH REPUBLIC'S Computerworld, Elektronika, PC World;
DENMARK'S Communications World, Computerworld Danmark, Macintosh Produktkatalog, Macworld Danmark, PC World Danmark, PC World Produktguide, Tech World, Windows World;
ECUADOR'S PC World Ecuador;
EGYPT'S Computerworld (CW) Middle East, PC World Middle East;
FINLAND'S MikroPC, Tietoviikko, Tietoverkko;
FRANCE'S Distributique, GOLDEN MAC, InfoPC, Languages & Systems, Le Guide du Monde Informatique, Le Monde Informatique, Telecoms & Reseaux;
GERMANY'S Computerwoche, Computerwoche Focus, Computerwoche Extra, Computerwoche Karriere, Information Management, Macwelt, Netzwelt, PC Welt, PC Woche, Publish, Unit;
GREECE'S Infoworld, PC Games;
HUNGARY'S Computerworld SZT, PC World;
HONG KONG'S Computerworld Hong Kong, PC World Hong Kong;
INDIA'S Computers & Communications; IRELAND'S ComputerScope;
ISRAEL'S Computerworld Israel, PC World Israel;
ITALY'S Computerworld Italia, Lotus Magazine, Macworld Italia, Networking Italia, PC Shopping, PC World Italia;
JAPAN'S Computerworld Today, Information Systems World, Macworld Japan, Nikkei Personal Computing, SunWorld Japan, Windows World;
KENYA'S East African Computer News;
KOREA'S Computerworld Korea, Macworld Korea, PC World Korea;
MEXICO'S Compu Edicion, Compu Manufactura, Computacion/Punto de Venta, Computerworld Mexico, MacWorld, Mundo Unix, PC World, Windows;
THE NETHERLANDS' Computer! Totaal, Computable (CW), LAN Magazine, MacWorld, Totaal "Windows";
NEW ZEALAND'S Computer Listings, Computerworld New Zealand, New Zealand PC World, Network World;
NIGERIA'S PC World Africa;
NORWAY'S Computerworld Norge, C/World, Lotusworld Norge, Macworld Norge, Networld, PC World Ekspress, PC World Norge, PC World's Produktguide, Publish& Multimedia World, Student Data, Unix World, Windowsworld; IDG Direct Response;
PAKISTAN'S PC World Pakistan;
PANAMA'S PC World Panama;
PERU'S Computerworld Peru, PC World;
PEOPLE'S REPUBLIC OF CHINA'S China Computerworld, China Infoworld, Electronics Today/Multimedia World, Electronics International, Electronic Product World, China Network World, PC and Communications Magazine, PC World China, Software World Magazine, Telecom Product World; IDG HIGH TECH BEIJING'S New Product World; IDG SHENZHEN'S Computer News Digest;
PHILIPPINES' Computerworld Philippines, PC Digest (PCW);
POLAND'S Computerworld Poland, PC World/Komputer;
PORTUGAL'S Cerebro/PC World, Correio Informatico/Computerworld, Informatica & Comunicacoes Catalogo, MacIn, Nacional de Produtos;
ROMANIA'S Computerworld, PC World;
RUSSIA'S Computerworld-Moscow, Mir - PC, Sety;
SINGAPORE'S Computerworld Southeast Asia, PC World Singapore;
SLOVENIA'S Monitor Magazine;
SOUTH AFRICA'S Computer Mail (CIO),Computing S.A.,Network World S.A., Software World;
SPAIN'S Advanced Systems, Amiga World, Computerworld Espana, Communicaciones World, Macworld Espana, NeXTWORLD, Super Juegos Magazine (GamePro), PC World Espana, Publish;
SWEDEN'S Attack, ComputerSweden, Corporate Computing, Natverk & Kommunikation, Macworld, Mikrodatorn, PC World, Publishing & Design (CAP), Datalngenjoren, Maxi Data,Windows World;
SWITZERLAND'S Computerworld Schweiz, Macworld Schweiz, PC Tip;
TAIWAN'S Computerworld Taiwan, PC World Taiwan;
THAILAND'S Thai Computerworld;
TURKEY'S Computerworld Monitor, Macworld Turkiye, PC World Turkiye; UKRAINE'S Computerworld;
UNITED KINGDOM'S Computing /Computerworld, Connexion/Network World, Lotus Magazine, Macworld, Open Computing/Sunworld;
UNITED STATES' Advanced Systems, AmigaWorld, Cable in the Classroom, CD Review, CIO, Computerworld, Digital Video, DOS Resource Guide, Electronic Entertainment Magazine, Federal Computer Week, Federal Integrator, GamePro, IDG Books, Infoworld, Infoworld Direct, Laser Event, Macworld, Multimedia World, Network World, PC Letter, PC World, PlayRight, Power PC World, Publish, SWATPro, Video Event;
VENEZUELA'S Computerworld Venezuela, PC World;
VIETNAM'S PC World Vietnam.

For More Information...

For general information on IDG Books in the U.S., including information on discounts and premiums, contact IDG Books at 800-434-3422 or 415-312-0650.

For information on where to purchase IDG's books outside the U.S., contact Christina Turner at 415-312-0633.

For information on translations, contact Marc Jeffrey Mikulich, Director, Rights and Licensing, at IDG Books Worldwide; fax number: 415-286-2747.

For sales inquires and special prices for bulk quantities, contact Tony Real at 800-434-3422 or 415-312-0644.

For information on using IDG books in the classroom and ordering examination copies, contact Jim Kelley at 1-800-434-2086.

Detour: The Truth About the Information Superhighway is distributed in the United States by IDG Books Worldwide, Inc. It is distributed in Canada by Macmillan of Canada, a Division of Canada Publishing Corporation; by Computer and Technical Books in Miami, Florida, for South America and the Caribbean; by Longman Singapore in Singapore, Malaysia, Thailand, and Korea; by Toppan Co. Ltd. in Japan; by Asia Computerworld in Hong Kong; by Woodslane Pty. Ltd. in Australia and New Zealand; and by Transword Publishers Ltd. in the U.K. and Europe.

IDG Books Worldwide, Inc. is a subsidiary of International Data Group. The officers are Patrick J. McGovern, Founder and Board Chairman; Walter Boyd, President.

❏ YES!

Please keep me informed about IDG's World of Computer Knowledge. Send me the latest IDG Books catalog.